EVERYTHING SCATTERED WILL BE GATHERED

*Emergence from
Patriarchal Fundamentalism*

Petra Rose

Copyright © 2015 by Petra Sundheim

All rights reserved. No part of this book may be reproduced, scanned, or distributed in any printed or electronic form without permission.

First Edition: August 2015

Printed in the United States of America

ISBN: 978-1-939237-37-8

Published by Suncoast Digital Press, Inc.
Sarasota, Florida, USA

FRONT COVER

The chalice is a classical feminine symbol. The embedded glass fragments in many colors represent the many experiences of our lives, when processed with forgiveness, becoming a chalice of the Christ. In the center of the goblet side is a heart energy symbol with a Chi Rho, the Christ. The words "I Am" are on the pedestal. Symbols of male and female alternate on rim of chalice. Around the base are a few loose pieces of colored glass, experiences that became irrelevant.

The Divine Feminine is the energy of the Chalice, which receives the Divine Masculine, the seed energy of creation. The coming together of the Divine Feminine heart energy with the Divine Masculine seed energy creates an elixir of love to birth a new humanity.

The chalice represents the Divine Feminine energy of receptivity into which the sacred Masculine energies come to rest. The feminine heart can be tuned into judgment or compassion; where there is compassion, there is no judgment. When the violent blade of the non-sacred masculine passes by, if judgment is present, a sting is felt. Where masculine energy promoting action is balanced by the feminine energy of Being, unity is possible.

The chalice implies inclusivity. The gathering of the experiences of our lives through forgiveness forms our unique chalice of many colors. Both our masculine and feminine energies, in balance, complete our chalice.

Thus we become the Christ, the face of God on earth. Jeshua's Four Keys to the Queendom within can bring the scattered pieces of our lives together into a harmonious whole.

DEDICATION

This book is dedicated to my son, Kirk Jonathan Akre, who left his body December 16th, 2011, at age 51. Though addicted to alcohol since adolescence, his loving nature was evident in his recovery process and efforts to stay in touch, plus his commitment to care for his older partner despite his own illness. His words on Memorial Sunday, the day his ashes were buried, *There is no death… Don't waste your life,* provided an unforgettable legacy and triumph of spirit.

This writing is particularly relevant to those who question the patriarchal version of Jesus, and to those who value their faith and want a more intimate connection with the divine. It is also for those who are wounded by the devaluation and rape of the feminine. Anyone desiring spiritual tools for releasing baggage and managing daily life will benefit.

Everything Scattered Will Be Gathered is relevant to anyone open to change, including leaders in the Christian church who are willing to question the assumptions and accuracy of the core teachings. It is for those willing to allow experience of the Beloved Presence to replace stagnant beliefs. It is for those seeking oneness with all life.

It is dedicated to the new children, who are here to lead us into the New Earth. They have come in without blindfolds and many have their 12 core DNA fully activated. They also are free of a vested interest in the old way of doing things.

ACKNOWLEDGMENTS

I am most grateful to my non-physical writing team that comes together whenever I prepare to write. Conscious of their presence, I ask if something is correctly stated. Kinesiology (muscle testing) has been especially useful in discerning their corrections. My team consists of Jeshua, Mary Magdalene, my mother Rose, my brother Luke, and Pam, a past-life mother and author/friend in this life before her transition. Athena, twin soul of Ashtar, has joined the group. I am grateful for my father Peter's priceless transmission letter to my childhood sister friend, "Rene."

Jeshua's very personal and *in the moment* guidance through intuition and transmission is far beyond the doctrinal interpretation of him gleaned from my many years in the church. Awareness of his personal presence is a profound blessing. The italicized messages herein are transmissions from Jeshua and other non-physical beings, whose presence I felt. Trance Channelings are messages usually from the 9th dimension.

There is much gratitude to all the channelers of Jeshua's message which has shaped my life and this book. *A Course in Miracles*, and *The Way of Mastery*, by Jon Mark Hammer, first studied in groups, were foundational. I am especially grateful for Pamela Kribbe's *The Jeshua Channelings*, for bringing in Jeshua's humanity and his directives to lightworkers. If you are drawn to this book you probably are a lightworker, one who desires to shift into the new era of Peace, Love and Joy. The "Anna" books, *Anna, Grandmother of Jesus* by Claire Heartsong, and *Anna, Voice of the Magdalenes*, by Heartsong in co-creation with Catherine Ann Clemett, were most revealing of Jesus as a man, a father, and husband. Contrary to the church's teachings, he was taught by women, especially Mary Magdalene and his mother, Mary. Amazingly, grandmother Anna, who mastered agelessness and lived 800 years, is barely mentioned in history or the Bible. (She understood and practiced sex as a life force far beyond anything taught today.)

My major healing began with Marge Robert's Inner Healing work with the imagery of Jesus' presence. This healing of my birth experience was quickly followed by my healings in Anne Wilson Schaef's Deep Process Intensives. Their work is foundational to my transformation and release of fundamentalism, and I owe each much gratitude.

The following spiritual groups have sustained and fed me: The Way of the Heart family, especially Peggy Watson, an experienced channel for Jeshua's messages, who has attracted several who have become aware of their lifetime with Jesus. The focus on the Jeshua channelings has established this group as my primary spiritual family.

Ariana's channeling group provided the opportunity to connect with my biological father in spirit, to heal, and learn to channel. My mother, Rose, and my brother, Luke, have duplicated themselves and are always with me as guides since I connected with them through Ariana. As part of her Cloverleaf Rescue Circle, I have witnessed the release of souls from the Astral plane.

Gratitude to my friends, Miriam and Suzanne, who went to India for Deeksha training with Sri Bhagavan and Amma to do the Oneness Blessing; they inspired me to take the training on Kauai. This brought me into the Deeksha group both as giver and receiver of the Oneness Blessing.

My appreciation to Lisa—friend, writer, therapist and a holocaust survivor—who lives simply and carefronts when focusing fails me.

Gratitude overflows for Kauai, Hawaii, and the abundance of healing opportunities, connection with nature, and karmic completion of past lives, which have accelerated my ascension journey.

To "Patrik", my grandson, I honor for his act of courage, who at age 14 left his family and friends and came to Kauai to live a few months with me, at my invitation. His coming opened up a whole new life experience for both of us.

To Aniana, a dear friend for proofreading and editing, I am especially grateful for her wisdom and insight.

To Pamela Kribbe, for her blessing and permission to quote extensively from *The Jeshua Channelings*. This book has been a focus of our Way of the Heart group studies.

To Wendy MacIntosh, for assistance with the cover design.

To Laura Angelart, a professional artist, for her rendition and completion of the front cover.

To Barbara Dee, editor and publishing associate with Suncoast Digital Press, Inc.

CONTENTS

Dedication v
Acknowledgments vii
Preface xv
Foreword xix

PART I - EVERYTHING SCATTERED. 1
   1. Birth Experiences Unveiled 3
   2. Clergy Family. 7
   3. The Core Belief In Separation. 13
   4. Launching: First Love, First Vocation 17
   5. Death In The Pulpit. 21
   6. Marriage, Adoption, Teen Challenge 25
   7. Self-Healing: Deep Process Work 31
   8. Ann Arbor 35
   9. Divorce, My First Transformation. 39
  10. Return To Minnesota Alone, Spiritual Outreach . .45
  11. Scattered, Indeed 49
  12. Seven Years In Minnesota Northwoods 55
  13. Professional Upgrades, Romance, Moving On . . .61
  14. The Call To Kauai, Therapist To Coach 65

PART II -WILL BE GATHERED 69
  15. September 1998 Move To Kauai 71

16. Introduction To Past Lives 75
17. Jeshua. 79
18. The Way Of The Heart 83
19. Introduction To Channeling 89
20. Healing Words Of Love Across The Veil 93
21. A Transmission From My Father 101
22. Brother Luke 109
23. Mother Rose 113
24. Receiving the TaBIA Process 121
25. The Tap and Breathe I Am (TaBIA) Process 129
26. The Intuitive Inquiry Process 135
27. Personal Transmission From Rose 139
28. Deeksha. 143
29. Guilt, Chuck's Transition 147
30. Kirk's Transition, December 2011 153
31. Past Life Encounters 157
32. Martha, My Past Life With Jesus 169
33. The Magdalenes. 177
34. Jeshua And Martha Speak To Me 185
35. Jeshua Connects Me To Judas. 191
36. Family (Dis)Connections 199
37. Kirk's Memorial, A Karmic Experience 207
38. Journey Back 211
39. Soul Speak 217
40. Ho'oponopono 223
41. 2013: Aloha Patrik; The New Children 227
42. Transition From Patriarchy To Ascension 237

PART III - ASCENSION AWARENESS 243

43. What Is Ascension? 245
44. Small Group Support 251
45. Effects Of Patriarchy 255
46. The Patriarchal Wound 261
47. Healing Our Wounding. 271
48. True Masculinity And True Femininity 287
49. The Restoration Of The Feminine 301
50. Relationships 311
51. Bridges 319
52. Calibration Of Energy Vibrations. 327
53. The Controllers—The Dark Forces 333
54. Oneness. 341
55. Heaven On Earth, A New Humanity 349
56. Finding Your Purpose 363
57. Embodiment 371
58. The Way Of Mastery 375
59. The World Will End In Laughter 381
Heart Awakening Circles 385
Additional Transmissions From Ascension Master Jeshua 389

Bibliography 403
About The Author 409

PREFACE

Reviewing our lives, past and present, can help us uncover the script we chose, and our life's purpose. *Know thyself* is a theme that empowers us beyond our automatic defense responses to life events. Rooting out fears and their primary causes in the context of a loving observer Self rewards one with a sense of peace, gratitude and completion. Trusting this divine Self to orchestrate the process of life helps us to look for the lessons instead of wallowing in fear, guilt, and regret. When we embrace Life as a school of learning, solutions appear.

This book, *Everything Scattered will be Gathered*, is a memoir of my journey out of patriarchal fundamentalism. It echoes the ascension in consciousness now occurring. It is an assignment from Jeshua Ben Joseph, master of the Ascension process, along with Mary Magdalene, his twin soul. Major transformational shifts delayed the writing until 2012. The call for every human on earth to awaken and accept our divine essence, our core Oneness, became mine. To live as the new humanity on the New Earth will require radical change.

My first Intention was to gather the pieces of my own life as a journey of awakening to the truth of who I am through the Purification process and practice given to me by Jeshua. My second Intention is to reveal the Jeshua, I have come to know, beyond the Jesus of the Patriarchy.

After years of loyalty to Christian fundamentalism, the process of transformative life experiences has melted the rigidity of the beliefs I held. Through awareness of Jeshua's Presence and Surrender to his voice within, I have allowed my old beliefs to be replaced by my experiences through connections of the heart, a journey from the head to the heart.

Patriarchy's dying gasp is seen in the increase in the number of power grabs by corporations; their influence on governments, war, pollution and vigorous denials of global warming. We are permeated with the *belief in separation* from Source, ourselves, each other, and from nature. Mother Earth has consciousness and her vibration is rising. Her tolerance for abuse has ended. Humanity is at risk of extinction unless we wake up and shift our relationship to nature from exploitation to cooperation.

Restoring male-female balance through valuing the wisdom of the heart and letting it master the mind, releases the control of the fear-based ego. The heart is female energy in contrast to the mind based male energy. According to Jesus/Jeshua, Heart Math, Drunvalo Melchizidek and many other spiritual leaders and researchers, our seat of power and wisdom is the spiritual heart. Intuition needs to be primary in the conduct of our life.

Being first born, and the only girl in a clergy family of seven males, set the stage for undoing the patriarchy within as well as without. My programming was fear-based, male-dominated fundamentalism that emphasized separation. The tapestry of re-weaving my life and its relevance for Ascension is my motivation for writing this book.

The message, *Everything Scattered will be Gathered*, came to me as I awakened in a state of bliss in 1980. The significance of these words unfolded over the next 32 years and served as a promise when I faced multiple losses and changes.

The flood of new information, new technologies, increased stimuli, and acceleration of energy can leave us feeling scattered. Few can ignore the time crunch we are feeling. The last statistic I read was that our previous 24 hours is now only 12 hours. We are moving into the timeless, the meaning of coming to the end of the Mayan calendar. Ending the old world allows us to embrace a new world in sync with our Spirit identity. It is a birthing of living from the heart instead of the head, and trusting the process.

The vibrations of the earth are rising and we are feeling this shift in energy. Symptoms such as unusual fatigue, dizziness, sleep changes, and headaches may be due to these vibrational shifts. These shifts in frequency can be measured, as described in *Power vs. Force* by Dr. David Hawkins. Building on his work, I have developed a simplified Feeling Frequency Guide, included in Part III, Ascension Awareness. The Guide was first printed in my 2010 book, *A Journey of P's and Cues to Inner Peace and Power*. As we learn to live vibrationally, we will shift the thoughts and feelings produced by fear causing illness, suffering, and war. We can choose to live from the higher frequencies of Love in the heart, accessed through forgiveness.

Details of human suffering all over the world enter our living room via TV and the internet, and pull our attention in many directions. It is more than we can absorb and integrate, and our power is diluted and scattered. It is time for everything to come into the light and for truth to prevail. Following inner guidance, we choose what is our focus in the context of our lives. We are discovering that the old ways don't work anymore. Co-operation is replacing competition. Channeling and awareness of the nonphysical world is increasing. Intuition and meditation are replacing "figuring it out."

My expectations of Ascension to be a primary topic in churches at this time have been disappointing. In church media, church attendance and conversations with pastors and members of churches, I have heard nothing about Ascension. Bible literalists are speaking of Jesus coming in the clouds to gather his own and take them up to heaven, plus "end of the world" warnings—their version of Ascension. Awareness of the challenges and work of Ascension seem to be coming (for the most part) from sources outside the church—through channeling, quantum physics, and many prophetic voices. Consciously shifting from 3rd dimensional thinking to the 4th dimension involves thinking from the heart. Ascension is a shift in consciousness and the vibration of the heart to embrace the Oneness of the fifth dimension.

May gathering the scattered pieces of my life in my Self-Healing journey help others make sense of their lives. The ultimate goal of gathering what is scattered is to become One; one with Source (God within), one with each other, one with nature, and one with our true Self, ending the belief in separation. This Oneness of the fifth dimension or heaven on earth is a state of consciousness now possible on our ascending Mother earth.

I have presented the truth as I have come to know it. Truth from the heart is only knowable from the heart, and does not need to satisfy 3rd dimensional thinking. Shifting out of this thinking is a conscious shift to thinking with the heart, our work in the 4th dimension of Heart Awakening.

Fictional names are used where anonymity may be desired. I am grateful to each of the players in the play of my life—in my heart we are joined beyond our scripts.

FOREWORD

A "fore" word for you to consider before you delve into the information channeled through Petra Rose: It will expand your consciousness while making you consider the truth of a reality which may startle as well as confirm for you that which you already know to be true.

Let it then guide you gently for we know we are at end times and remarkable new beginnings. We allow that this book is a mirror of many of the changes that will occur—mostly a fresh look at the old stories, which have shackled us with beliefs. Petra invites you to look at the parts of the old stories your hearts have memorized as we courageously face new aspects of the New Earth, release the old expectations, and live life with joy.

In the Love of our journey together,

Peggy Watson, Channel for Sananada Magdalene; i.e., "In That Vibration of the Christing" and "Holding the Resonance for the New Earth"

PART I

EVERYTHING SCATTERED

CHAPTER 1

BIRTH EXPERIENCES UNVEILED

"The unforgivable sin of being born female." These words from Anne Wilson Schaef rang true. Near fifty years old, I was in one of Anne Wilson Schaef's nine-day Intensives doing "deep process" work to clear the past. In constant emotional pain, feeling separate from just about everyone, I felt like a victim most of the time. I was willing, even desperate, to have a breakthrough.

With my rusty BA earned in 1953 from a five-year nursing program, I had gone back to work in a nursing home after not working for ten years while we were adopting our four children. When Kari, my youngest, was 10, my husband and I both felt I needed to start contributing financially to our clergy family.

We celebrated our 25th wedding anniversary in Dearborn, Michigan, where my minister husband was serving a parish. I felt uncomfortable with myself and was searching for inner peace. Attending "Bill G's" charismatic healing classes, I voiced my interest in working at his clinic. Would my background as a psychiatric nurse be sufficient? He said he would pray about it. Soon I was working at his Life Skills clinic as an apprentice. In my first week, he observed that I was "scattered." I didn't know what that meant, but I knew I felt very anxious about this new job. I prayed for strength.

Later that week, I awakened in an unusual state of bliss. Powerful words floated through my mind, **Everything scattered will be gathered.** I pondered the meaning of these words from spirit. This was 1980. In 2012, 32 years later, I was finally ready to receive and understand the meaning, and that this was not only about my life, but applicable to planet earth. The time we are in is unraveling. The old systems don't work anymore. Power and control forces are becoming more obvious. Change is accelerating and scattered lives experience many losses. The gathering of these scattered pieces is our global Ascension process.

My first position as a therapist was in a Christian clinic. As an apprentice, I attended classes for clients in addiction and co-dependency, taught by two senior therapists. My client load included individuals, couples, and groups. I remember one individual who I felt was ministering to me. I became more aware of my neediness and vulnerability. After four years of working at Life Skills, the director had compromised himself with a client and had to close down the clinic. My exit interview with the director was very uncomfortable and my body registered the incongruity of his words in the form of back pain, which later went away after I processed my feelings. My experience at Life Skills prompted me to seek my Master's degree in Social Work at the University of Michigan. My husband had received a call to a 5000-member congregation in Ann Arbor, Michigan, as an assistant pastor.

Inner Healing

The work of Marge Roberts, called *Inner Healing through Imagery Prayer,* attracted me.

I attended her public meetings at a church connected to a Catholic order. She had people pair up and share a personal, traumatic experience. One partner would ask the other to recall a painful experience from childhood. The receiver was asked to image the presence of Jesus. The process proved quite effective in allowing a traumatic memory to surface, then one could feel and express the feelings while re-living the experience in a safe place.

Core Trauma Uncovered

I had issues around feeling safe and wanted someone with experience to work with me. I picked "Lois," a nun. What followed was a pivotal experience exposing the source of my inner pain. She first anointed me with oil as was her custom. I immediately felt a tingling go through my body.

Lois asked me to relate a traumatic childhood memory. I was unable to recall anything specific. My childhood was shame-based, and I simply said, "It was negative." She asked me to image the presence of Jesus offering hands of comfort. This was to create a sense of safety for the recall of a key experience. I couldn't image Jesus. Instead, I saw hands in front of me, menacing hands which grew bigger and bigger. "I must be an infant," I said. "Those are my father's hands! He used to spank babies for crying!" Deep, primordial sobs came up.

Lois became frightened and asked Marge, the director, to come over. Marge asked me about my relationship with my mother. I said it was okay. She said, "Ask her to pick you up and hold you."

I saw my mother, frightened in her attempt to do so, and I said, "Mother, you may pick me up and hold me."

Marge said, "You don't have to give her permission." But I did, as I found out later.

They asked me again to picture Jesus in the situation. This time I saw Jesus sitting and asking the little children to come to him. I saw myself as a two-year-old toddler in a black dress, running and climbing into his lap. The session ended when I was in a place of safety, enjoying the attention of Jesus.

Afterwards, I saw the black dress as a symbol of a low-grade depression that began with the birth of my brother Paul, who was the apple of my father's eye. I was only 14 months old. My young eyes noticed all the attention and affection being lavished on this new baby boy. This contributed to my feeling **defective** throughout my life. Though I had many healings through increased awareness, it would be much later that I would receive a self-healing process to delete the deep-seated program of feeling defective from my bodymind computer.

The block to joy I felt throughout my life fit the description of a depressed personality type. My fundamentalist programming further inhibited joy. I was less inclined to laugh at jokes than others around me, and saw the negatives more easily than the positives in any situation.

I signed up for Marge's program for professionals, a small group project she developed for her doctorate requirements. Psychological testing was part of the program. I tested as "severely introverted" on the Meyers Briggs, an INFP—Intuitive iNtroverted Feeling Perceptual type of personality. This was particularly triggered when I felt shame. However, in some situations I appeared extroverted—my yet-to-be-discovered Attention Deficit Disorder (with its impulsive features) seemed to give that impression, and I was often inappropriately self-disclosing.

Decades later, I asked my mother, in her eighties, if something happened in my infancy. "Yes," she said. "I have been carrying guilt all these years. You seldom cried as an infant. When you did cry and I went to pick you up, your father said, 'She is just a girl! Let her be.' I let you just cry and cry one night, and in the morning I discovered you had an ear infection." This would have been especially painful to my mother who was a nurse.

The healing for both of us was profound. I had uncovered the source of feeling so uncomfortable in my own skin. There was something "wrong" with me I could not fix: "the unforgivable sin of being born female," according to Anne Wilson Schaef. In feeling defective, I had felt the shame of committing the "original sin of being born female" in my father's eyes. My self-consciousness was intense in growing up. I didn't want to be visible and was uncomfortable with anyone looking at me. Finally, I understood. I wish I could say there was an automatic shift in my thoughts and feelings; the change was more gradual as I pursued my *Know Thyself* agenda.

CHAPTER 2

CLERGY FAMILY

Displaced

My brother Paul arrived 14 months after my birth. Witnessing my father's doting attention on him, I grew up resenting Paul. Aware that he could do no wrong in his father's eyes, he took the dominating role of oldest child. Peers would refer to him as "conceited."

A preacher's kid, I felt my parents' stress with the poverty-level income typical of rural ministers and chose the "good girl" and "assistant mother" roles to ease their suffering, and to garner at least a small share of approval.

Seven children in 10 years, plus four miscarriages, was traumatic for my mother's body. She was a dutiful pastor's wife—baking, teaching, visiting the infirmed, and hosting groups and meetings in the parsonage, our home. Her endurance, mental and emotional stability, and her spiritual faith were an inspiration for me and I became like a sister, her confidante. She protected me in some areas of work such as lifting, so as "to save your back for child bearing." She would know!

Our Family Roles: Typical of Alcoholic Families

We had all the scripts of a dysfunctional alcoholic family, without the alcohol. When I started going to Al-Anon meetings and learning about addiction, I discovered my father was actually what is called a "dry drunk." He was very much against drinking, and we never had alcohol in the house. My mother confided in me that my father, Peter, had told her that he was unusually fond of alcohol before his conversion to Christianity as a young man. He feared becoming an alcoholic. With his conversion, he became totally abstinent. He suppressed his fondness for alcohol as "sin," a teaching of fundamentalism.

Fundamentalism can be a lot like alcoholism. When feelings are not acknowledged, they collect and turn into a vessel of anger which frequently boils over. I saw this in my father, particularly towards us children. His own childhood in a large family with a depressed, angry mother did not give him gentle parenting skills. *Spare the rod, spoil the child*, was a frequent Biblical reminder. The denial of cravings and unexpressed, suppressed emotions often erupted like a volcano in his discipline of his children. He experienced tremendous guilt and remorse afterwards—he would hit us in anger and later become angry at himself. Fundamentalism, along with drug addiction and alcoholism, is a dis-ease of the feelings.

My anger began in pre-adolescence. I remember two notable experiences: At age 11, my father lowered my underpants and took me over his knee for a spanking, probably for my smart mouth. I was greatly humiliated as I had become very modest about my body. Another time in adolescence, he seized me and started to hit me. I looked in his eyes and said, "Go ahead and kill me!" Quite startled, he backed off.

My anger remained just below the surface, most of the time, and showed up in photos. Like my father, the anger would turn into depression—anger at self.

My mother, Rose, made a great effort to *obey her husband* as admonished by the Apostle Paul. As I observed her chafing under this rule, withholding her wisdom and counsel, I grew up hating that Bible verse, "Wives obey your husbands!"

In spite of my father's angry outbursts, I did not witness any physical abuse toward my mother. She didn't enjoy sex, mostly because of the fear of pregnancy. Though, in a body that was quite traumatized by frequent birthing, she was a tireless worker and hostess, preparing many goodies I assisted in making. A creative teacher in the church community, she used a flannel graph to illustrate talks and stories.

My father's sermons warned people to repent to avoid hell. Our identity as sinners separated from God was a major teaching I have had to unlearn. I am reminded of a recent pope who, on his deathbed, said the Catholic Church invented hell in order to control the people through fear.

Some people were converted who really liked his fervent preaching of "the truth" and took it to heart. One of them was "Rene," my closest friend, like a sister to me. She grew up to marry a missionary and have eight children. The time came when she chided me for going into worldly things like getting a Master's degree, not appropriate for being subject to one's husband. Then I told her my husband wanted a divorce.

In a phone call to her, after a few minutes of conversation, I heard her husband's voice saying, "Rene, that's enough now." She accepted his control without question, because St. Paul, the Apostle in the New Testament, mandated it.

More about Family Roles

Learning the roles of an alcoholic family while going to Al-Anon after my son, Kirk started drinking, I noted the similarity to my own family. Brother Paul, first born son, was the **hero** child. Second born son, Nels, a colicky nervous child, became the **scapegoat** of my father. Obed, more like myself, was the **lost** child, who quietly avoided trouble. In feeling a connection with Obed, also introverted, I discovered through Inquiry that he is in my soul family. We shared a common interest in taking responsibility for our own health, in pursuing exercise, and use of supplements.

This interest in health was true for some of my other brothers as well. My mother had a keen interest in healthy foods, only to be frustrated by my father who, for example, thought oranges were too expensive to buy—cost determined his food choices rather than health. Mother attributed a developmental issue in Nels to lack of

Vitamin C. It was simply not possible to feed our large family proper, well-balanced meals with our meager means. Much of our food was given to us by parishioner farmers or came from our garden.

David was born with a smile which said to my mother, *I won't cause you any trouble.* He arrived after both parents refused to have mother's "tubes tied" as recommended by the doctor, another effect of fundamentalism always putting its version of righteousness ahead of the individual's well-being. David filled the **clown or mascot** role. Smiling was characteristic of him. A pragmatic kind of guy, he seemed untouched by fundamentalism.

When I was ten, the twins arrived, both boys, a great disappointment to me in want of a sister. Mother asked me, "Which one do you want to take care of?"

"The one I can carry," I replied, referring to Luke Donald, who was two pounds lighter than Luther Daniel. Thus I became a "parentified child," one of the markers of an alcoholic family. Christian fundamentalism was the source of strength to endure painful "not okay" feelings instead of resorting to numbing them with alcohol.

Luther Daniel and Luke Donald were called Dan and Don in their childhood, the sibling's preference. Almost all responsibility for the care and nurturing of Don fell to me. Both in appearance and energetically, the twins were quite different. Dan was placid and heavy-set; Don, or Luke, as he later chose to be called, was a slender, wiry, and more active child. Yet they bonded well and shared the energetic connection so commonly found in twins, even after they were grown up and lived apart. As an adult, Daniel was driving through the Colorado mountains when suddenly and inexplicably, he burst into sobs. One week later, Luke was killed in that very spot. In some healing work after Luke's untimely death, I needed to mourn him as a son as well as a brother.

Chapter 2: Clergy Family

Competing

The *male privilege* enjoyed by my brothers was a source of resentment and competition. (This chip on my shoulder regarding males showed up later in the workplace.)

Racing down a homemade ski jump created by my brothers, I broke my leg at age twelve. I enjoyed being a patient, cared for by my nurse mother, getting special attention with visitors' names written all over my hip-to-ankle cast.

My father bought a farm on the edge of town, in part to put my brothers to work and keep them out of trouble. Occasionally when I would help with the work he would compare, and give me credit for working harder. My climbing on the roof to get a ball when my brothers were too afraid to do so was an example of my attempts to outdo them. Although I excelled in school, they all were more successful later in their vocational careers.

Christian education was a strong value for my parents and my father sacrificed to help us go to Concordia College, his alma mater. Paul and Nels both became ministers and later moved into the field of psychology. Obed dropped out of college and started his own car wash business. David became a psychologist, a college teacher, and playwright.

Luke Donald became an artist and professor of art. Daniel became an electrical engineer. As the "black sheep" in the family, Daniel was a self-proclaimed anarchist; yet, he was a peaceful non-conformist.

In many ways, I didn't mature. A daydreamer in school, I was chided for not listening.

In a boring history class, I read another book placed inside my textbook and received a public scolding from the teacher. I played with dolls until early adolescence.

Before going to sleep, I found refuge in reading the dramas of adventurous lives. Though I was an angry teenager, I did not rebel against my parents, and felt responsible for their peace of mind regarding my brothers. Since the age of ten, I was strongly identified with my parents. Though competitive, I felt separate from my brother's lives. Much later when in my fifties, I realized I never really experienced my adolescence, a normal period of *counter-dependency*. Counter-dependency is the 2nd stage of development between the *dependency* of childhood and the *independency* of adulthood.

My junior year at Augustana Academy, a Christian high school, was a very enjoyable experience. It was another sacrifice by my parents for Christian education, and a relief from my family role. But the tuition cost kept me from graduating from the Academy. Graduating from my small town high school class of 13 as valedictorian, with my best friend Rene as salutatorian, was a satisfying completion of my years at home.

CHAPTER 3

THE CORE BELIEF IN SEPARATION

There are many beliefs stemming from this core belief. There is rebellion against some beliefs without realizing the unconscious effect of other teachings which have seeped into the culture. With liberal churches, or with those who have left the church, I sense at least one of these beliefs exist in almost everyone, to some degree.

<u>Christian fundamentalist teachings/ beliefs:</u>

- God is a male being, and judge, who banished mankind from Eden.
- Eve, first woman, sinned when she first tasted the apple and gave it to Adam;
- Therefore, females are put under the rule of males by the patriarchy.
- Survival depends on hard work, repentance, and worship of a God outside oneself.
- Literal interpretation of the Bible as "inerrant Word of God" with no further revelation.
- Hell, an everlasting fire, is for those who do not turn back to God.
- Our identity is the ego, our true sinful self in a perishable body, ending in death.
- Resurrection of the body would occur when Jesus came again in the body.

- We would then ascend bodily with him into heaven.
- Jesus, the only Son of God, came to save us by dying on a cross for our sins.
- Jesus was celibate, without sin; therefore the priesthood is to be celibate.
- Only unmarried males could serve as priests. Non-Catholic churches allowed marriage, and later females to become ministers.
- Christianity is the only true religion, free from error only in your denomination, one of many interpretations of the male-controlled choice of scriptures, the official Bible.

The 10th belief, *Jesus, the only Son of God came to save us by dying on a cross for our sins,* is the core foundational belief of Christianity that has provided great comfort for many. I am a heretic for including this in the list. Yet it is vital to realize that we are all part of the Sonship as described in *A Course in Miracles* (ACIM), Jesus' words to us correcting the belief in separation.

He is a "savior" in the sense that the gap between us and creator-Source had become greater than we could bridge without his intervention in human history. He is my Master teacher and until we are of one mind, as he suggests, we will tend to regard him as "other."

My journey out of these beliefs was quickened by the many transmissions from Jesus himself where he reveals his true mission and would totally repudiate the church's version of his life. The pain of seeing such a distortion of himself and his message is far greater than the pain of the crucifixion. The slow death that crucifixion intended has been repeated in the distortion of Jesus' message. The time has come to question the Patriarchy and separate the true message of Jesus from the distortions. Many well-intended followers have based their lives on these teachings and have manifested great compassion

Chapter 3: The Core Belief In Separation

and good works despite the teachings because they followed their heart, intuition, and Holy Spirit.

The evils of the crusades (expansive military marches in the Middle Ages which resulted in mass pillaging and murders in the name of Christianity) on one hand, contrast with the dedication of others who listened to their hearts and gave their lives in service to others. This bears witness to Jesus words in the Introduction to ACIM which states, *A Universal theology is impossible, but a universal experience is not only possible but necessary.* Ideas about God in our heads will never be consistent. The knowing that comes from connecting from love in the forgiving heart finds resonance in heart-to-heart connections.

There are many beliefs, even among those who claim Christianity as their religion. Martin Luther broke away from Roman Catholicism and the Lutheran church was established with its many variations, some more liberal than others.

Allowing women to become ordained in the Protestant churches was a big shift. The attitudes coming out of the initial teachings of the church influenced society and women would get less pay for doing the same work. The de-valuing of women in society has religious roots.

Cursing by using words like "Christ," "Jesus," "God," and "holy" has become automatic in our culture. The more illiterate or uneducated the person is, the more likely that these words are spoken in the context of swearing. How this originated in the psyche, other than the manifestation of fear calling for help, I do not know.

Metaphysics, not in my Webster dictionaries, means "above matter." Unity, Religious Science, and Universalists are referred to as New Thought religions. Amazingly, spiritual truth comes forth which resonates with the heart, the Queendom within, the feminine way. Inner work causes a change of heart, resulting in outer shifts in attitude and behavior.

The same Bible is used in the metaphysical approach, even though we now realize how much closer to Jesus' teachings are the Gnostic teachings and the omitted gospels of Thomas, Mary Magdalene,

Everything Scattered Will Be Gathered

Philip and others. *The Book of Love*, by Jesus (much sought after by the Vatican in order to destroy it), lies hidden. I hold the vision that all secrets will come to light as we purify ourselves and the planet for a new humanity. Suppression of truth can no longer be possible in the higher vibrations of earth's ascension.

CHAPTER 4

LAUNCHING: FIRST LOVE, FIRST VOCATION

Concordia College

Scholarships helped me attend Concordia, a Christian college in Moorhead, Minnesota. When I started attending my father's alma mater, I decided on the five-year nursing program, simply because my mother was a nurse. It was a safe vocational choice. I fully enjoyed being a student, and worked part-time in the cafeteria alongside "Jay," my first major love.

Heartbreak

My job in the cafeteria provided both social and financial benefits. Jay was a popular sophomore and becoming his girlfriend was not only exciting but also a real boost to my self-esteem. We had a lot of fun doing things together when not at work or in class; we canoed down the river, attended special events, and played tennis. My parent's injunction to stay pure was at the forefront of my relationship. Guilt around any action where I perceived their possible disapproval was an effective deterrent to my allowing him to even kiss me, although my hormones were raging.

Jay and I traveled together to a Michigan Ashram by bus after school was out. Here he became attracted to the female lifeguard and his time with me became obligatory and awkward. We went home separately, leaving me devastated and depressed. Seeing him at school in the fall was especially painful as there was no acknowledgment of our previous relationship. Although I dated others, he was always "the one who got away."

Unforgettable Apology

Many years later, after my divorce and move to my cabin in Northern Minnesota, I received a call from Jay. He wanted to meet me briefly in Bemidji, where I had a counseling office. In the empty waiting room, he said he wanted to do something I hadn't permitted while we were dating—he kissed me and apologized for abandoning me at the Ashram 44 years ago! And then he left. It was the most amazing experience. There was no further contact.

My Inquiry Process of spirit indicates that Jay and I are soul mates and had a past life as friends. There is a special place for him in my heart. He was also a follower of Jesus in Jesus' lifetime on earth and I knew Jay then as a woman.

Nursing

The two years of my five-year nursing program spent in a hospital setting were challenging, due to my scatteredness and difficulty in focusing. I foraged for food in the break room to relieve my anxiety—behavior I later recognized as an eating disorder.

I did enjoy my work in the delivery room and caring for infants. Later, I worked nights on the maternity ward, enjoying more quiet with less distraction. I considered becoming a midwife. *I now realize I am a midwife in birthing this book and birthing my Christ Self.* This thought came from Athena, a spirit guide who is the feminine partner to Ashtar, a non-physical master who assists Ariana Sheran in her channelings. Athena continued: **Midwife** *is an appropriate term for the feminine energy coming into power on the planet. This shift into a new age calls for many midwives who will claim their role in birthing a new humanity. I will speak to you in greater detail in Part III Ascension Awareness under the heading of 'Birthing a New Humanity.'*

One night, when a doctor known for not liking to be called too early didn't get there in time, I ended up delivering a baby. It was one of many delivery room events that colored my maternity ward experiences, providing a full range of feelings and opportunities to perform under pressure.

Chapter 4: Launching: First Love, First Vocation

The value of practiced relaxation

Even though many of the mothers I attended had previous experience with childbirth, most complained, loudly, and seemed anxious and distraught—and certainly not present to the miracle they were in the midst of. One night when the labor rooms were full, I was busy tending to complaining mothers who had previous deliveries. A quiet patient in her first pregnancy, who had followed the Lamaze system of relaxation, called me to check her. She was crowning, meaning the infant's head was beginning to appear. When I told her that, she smiled. Her calm impressed me with the importance of practiced relaxation and conscious breathing. She demonstrated that dedicated practice in calm times will then be available when under stress or challenge. It is one of the values of meditation and the TaBIA release process.

My desire for a similar birthing experience and the preparation she had was not fulfilled as my husband was unable to impregnate me due to mumps in his adolescence. A later discovery of the abnormal location of my right kidney next to my uterus (since birth) would see this as good fortune.

CHAPTER 5

DEATH IN THE PULPIT

New Year's Day, 1953

It was a snowy New Year's Day in South Dakota. Still single, I was home from a Minneapolis nursing job and my brother Paul was home for the holidays from Luther seminary. The whole family was there. My father had two church services scheduled, one in town in the morning where the family attended; mother, myself, Paul, Nels, Obed, David and the 12-year-old twins, Luke Donald and Luther Daniel. We all had a large meal together at noon before my father left alone to do a 2 p.m. service in a country church.

An hour later, several men from the church arrived carrying in the body of my father. They told us that in the midst of his sermon, he fell backwards. They couldn't revive him. My mother was sobbing and praying, asking him to come back to life. She repeatedly berated herself for the heavy meal she had fed him before he left that afternoon.

As I edited this and was told to rename "a dramatic ending" to *a transition to life,* I felt a jolt of energy that took my breath away, along with other overpowering sensations. Then Peter, my father, gave me these words:

A Transition to Life

Indeed it is the one who played the role of a fundamentalist minister/ father who rejected the feminine in myself, as well as in your embodiment. I provided part of the script you received to address the patriarchal errors in

Christianity. Your six brothers and your role as assistant mother provided even more experience of male privilege and dominance.

As you developed and grew, I came to appreciate you and realized your value. My own programming was so embedded in the theology I received, I saw myself as liberal, compared to my peer minister brothers!

Entering Spirit, I was grateful for the rapid transition. The role I played didn't really fit the desires of my heart to connect with Nature and her role on earth. So when I could choose what my heart desired, I have found great joy in my present work in Spirit, where I partner with Mother Earth. I work with her weather systems. Though the resistance of those on earth trying to control the weather is strong, Nature has the last word. It is not a pleasant time for those on earth while Mother Earth goes through her purification process, which pollution and abuse of resources has made necessary.

When humankind chooses to partner with Nature as at Findhorn, there will be enough for everyone and no reason for war when cooperation rather than competition for resources becomes the prevailing attitude. It requires heart-awakening and the embodiment of Oneness.

This is your path and I am grateful for the choices I see you making. I am here to empower you, especially when you choose to work with nature. Mahalo for this opportunity.

Emotional States

Even though my two oldest brothers, Nels and Paul, became ministers, they didn't seem to be the fundamentalists that our father and I were. My childhood compulsion to please my father and earn his love persisted. Though I was angry throughout childhood and adolescence, I stayed loyal to his religious teachings into my adult years. I had discovered a loving Jesus on an inner personal level, in contrast to the creeds that emphasized our separation from God. I didn't like to make choices between the shoulds of my father's teachings and the desires of my heart.

Chapter 5: Death In The Pulpit

My unresolved anger and depression persisted with the feeling that there was something wrong with me I could not fix. Like my father, the anger was at myself. His anger triggered my anger at his mode of discipline and belief in "Spare the rod and spoil the child!"

I was also angry at my brothers and saw them as arrogant. Paul, not only adored by my father, attracted adoration from other adults as well. My piano teacher observed that he was the one with the musical talent. A magnet for praise, his self-confidence was unshakable in sharp contrast to mine.

My self-concept was revealed in family photos. Smiling was difficult for me, in part because of my self-consciousness about my crooked teeth. We were too poor to afford the braces recommended by the dentist. I was very uncomfortable in my own skin, and envied the ease of my peers who seemed so much more self-accepting. When I did get compliments, I dismissed them because they didn't fit the core beliefs of who I was.

Along with the feeling of inferiority, I fought my feelings of superiority. This seesaw of extremes was characteristic of the Patriarchal dualism of good or bad. It fed an emotional rollercoaster upon which it was hard to achieve balance. Relief came when I could shift from "either/or" to "both/and." My persistent self-doubt didn't let me fully embrace this. My father provided a dramatic exclamation to the years of programming I sat under by his death in the pulpit.

Death in the pulpit is a catalyst for comment on the vibrational energy of fundamentalism. The denial of feelings with the shoulds of fundamentalism has a way of deadening the soul. Denying our identity as eternal spirit, an expression of God, fosters the belief in separation from Source. Espousing fear of hell as our prime motivator, instead of the power of love, empowers the ego and denies the truth of who we are.

A Model of Courage to Move On

My father's death necessitated mother's move out of the parsonage. I was not there to help her. She took patients into her home after she moved to a house in Moorhead with my four brothers. The later stories of managing my adolescent brothers by herself were painful to hear. Going with mother to visit Daniel in jail for some infraction of the law is a memory that prompts me to ask myself, *how much acting out by my teen brothers was unprocessed grief?* One story my mother told was of trying to break up a fight between them and being the recipient of a scissors stab. If I had been there, I would not have been able to contain my anger.

CHAPTER 6

MARRIAGE, ADOPTION, TEEN CHALLENGE

In the spring following my father's death, I met Chuck. My roommate's boyfriend brought him over to our apartment. The men were first-year seminary students. It wasn't love at first sight—yet, he felt right for me. He was kind, outgoing, and easy to be with, and felt *opposite* of my father, a major consideration. (I had learned that we tend to be attracted to someone like our opposite-sex parent.)

Chuck's family, who lived in a small bustling Minnesota town, accepted me. I was working nights in a Minneapolis hospital. With the help of his family, we were married September 1st in his home town. Local donations of flowers for the wedding and food for the reception afterwards made it a community affair. I borrowed my friend, Rene's wedding dress, and curtailed my eating to fit into it, as I had no extra funds for a dress of my own and my newly widowed mother was in no position to help.

During Chuck's internship assignment, I found work in a local hospital. In his senior year at the seminary, I worked as a nurse in the child psych department of the University of Minnesota. There, I cuddled a black four-year-old boy who was being ignored by the all-white staff. I determined to parent a black child if ever I had the chance.

After Chuck's ordination, he accepted a call to a town in southern Minnesota. Settling into the role of pastor's wife, I enjoyed having a large amount of leisure time and friendships with other minister couples.

Adoption, our Option

We were ready to start a family but we soon learned that Chuck didn't have enough sperm to get me pregnant. While we explored adoption, we decided to take in foster children. I became attached to Larry, our first foster child. When his adopting parents picked him up, at least we knew that a baby girl, six weeks old, was waiting for us at Lutheran Social Service. It made the parting with Larry easier.

Kimberly Joy

Our daughter, Kimberly Joy, was a delight to nurture and care for. The adoption policy made it clear that I couldn't work and I was fine with that. I delighted in the care of infants and toddlers. (That would change.)

Kimberly became an energetic more-than-a-handful when she turned two. I began comparing her explorative behaviors to Dennis the Menace. Unfortunately, my germ fears and cleanliness standards were more important than conveying love and acceptance to my very lively toddler. In church, she would crawl under the pews, yell in defiance, and threaten "my authority" as mother. My approach to discipline was definitely not working. Even though I read about the importance of being a nurturing and loving parent, I reacted like my father when my buttons were pushed. Though some young mothers are permissive to a fault, I admire their patience and wisdom in handling young children.

I wasn't prepared for the normal counter-dependency stage of adolescence (before independence can be achieved) in my daughter, because I hadn't experienced it. Taking on my father's belief system to gain his favor, I had remained the *good girl*, and couldn't understand Kimberly's antagonism towards me. Even though I was an angry teenager, I had acted respectfully toward my parents.

Kirk Jonathan

Two years after Kim arrived, we adopted Kirk Jonathan, nine weeks old. A quiet, less independent child. Kirk was passive and more dependent on me and was a welcome contrast to Kimberly. An easy child to care for, he didn't demand or get the attention the others got. Only now I realize I neglected him then. Programmed as I was to respond to negative behavior, he finally got my attention when he became a teenager.

Jeffrey Charles

During the 1960's racial awareness movement, Lutheran Social Service encouraged the adoption of black children. My desire to mother a black child was fulfilled three years after Kirk's arrival by eight-month-old Jeffrey Charles. Chuck accepted the decision to adopt inter-racial children, only after consulting one of his seminary teachers.

When we brought Jeff home, Chuck's aunt looked at him and said, "But you did say he was half Norwegian, didn't you?" We attended meetings for parents of interracial children and felt support from another minister couple, who had also decided to adopt black children.

The song, "Brown Baby," sung by Mahalia Jackson, would constantly go through my head as I admired my brown Gerber baby look-alike. Jeff had a dimpled smile that melted your heart.

Chuck's relationship with Jeff, however, was strained. I adored this beautiful boy and tended to excuse his non-conforming behaviors. In his struggle to learn, he had a charm which attracted help from others.

When Jeff was 2½, I took my three children shopping in the mall. Jeff disappeared. We left the department store and went into the main mall to search for him. He came out of a variety store, running towards us. A nearby couple said they saw this toddler by himself who seemed to know exactly what he was doing—he had gone back into that store to look at toys that he had remembered seeing.

In school he was classified as "learning disabled" and was given tutoring. The tutor noted he was distracted by sounds in the next room. He was very sensitive to his surroundings.

Highly intuitive, he learned differently. In adolescence he became interested in cars and then began to read ads for car repair. After a garage repair service owner took him under his wing, Jeff was able to get a mechanic certification through oral testing and was very proud of his accomplishment in completing a college-level course. Because he couldn't spell or express himself in writing, someone else wrote up the bills. Yet, much later Jeff became a manager.

Kari Jean

To balance gender and race, we adopted Kari Jean three years later. She was ten years younger than her sister Kim, and lighter in skin color than Jeff. Kari, one-fourth each Afro-American, Finish, Irish, and German, could pass for Hispanic. I tended to favor this last baby. All our children got along well together.

Minneapolis Suburban Living

The rural town parish of Waseca, Minnesota, where we spent six years and adopted Kimberly and Kirk, had been a good place to start a family.

Chuck's next call was to serve a young church in a northern suburb of Minneapolis.

The parsonage was in a new development, a friendly neighborhood with frequent coffee parties and families with children the same age as ours. Two families across the street had also adopted their children. Though it was generally a very positive social climate, it was here our son Kirk, at age 11, was introduced to alcohol in the home of a childhood friend.

Kimberly found her niche as piano accompanist for musical plays as well as in acting parts in the local high school. Our insistence on piano lessons, which she had resisted, paid off. Graduating from high school just before our move to Riverview (a suburb of Detroit, Michigan), she chose to stay behind and work.

Most of my parenting mistakes were made with Kimberly. Yet, she was the only one of our children to connect to church, which was our primary life setting and focus. Later, as an adult, she became a minister of music in a suburban church.

Minnesota to a Suburb of Detroit, Michigan

Kirk, now 15, insisted on living in the unfinished basement of the three-story parsonage we moved into. He did not want to share with Jeff the spacious bedroom next to ours on the top floor. Soon, his rationale and intention became clear.

Kirk began having friends come into his basement bedroom to party after we had gone to bed. I would smell marijuana through the vent of our 2nd story bedroom and go down to kick out his friends, asking them to use their homes instead of the church parsonage. They looked at me in horror at my suggestion. My husband's denial was so strong, I was unable to physically awaken him. I hit a wall in my many attempts to discuss it with him. Kirk was past 18 when, in another confrontation, he voiced an unforgettable statement of truth: "Dad will never kick me out!"

Chuck had chosen to be a pal rather than a parent to our children. My "nice guy" husband was personable and well-liked, and placated me however he could. On one occasion, in the presence of my offending son, my husband winked at my son when I brought up his behavior.

I couldn't comprehend this collusion with our teens and felt confused and helpless.

The Family Witch

I consistently felt like the witch in the family. Everyone else was just fine, but I felt crazy. Our family was dysfunctional in many ways, and the danger signs were more and more obvious. Kirk's wedding got him out of the house at age 21. Though married in a church to a daughter of a church family, he insisted on having the reception at a place where his friends could drink. His continued drinking ended his marriage in about two years. Reports came back to me that he drank until he passed out—people had to climb over his body to get out the door at parties he frequented or held.

Kari, at 13, was very enamored with Kirk and his lifestyle. My relationship with her had reversed and she was no longer the empathic child I knew before. There were complaints from school about her refusal to participate in physical education.

Jeff, at 17, was targeted by police for test-driving a car without a working muffler and was detained in jail overnight without our knowledge of his whereabouts. His display of anger towards the police brought a policeman to the house to speak to us. As the only black in a white neighborhood, he was closely watched.

The Body Communicates

The horrible headaches began when I was nine years old and my mother was pregnant with the twins. Moaning from pain, I hid in darkness. Mother had sinus and migraine headaches, which I seemed to inherit.

Later, the headaches were triggered by my menstrual cycle and continued monthly throughout my marriage. They were usually relieved within five days with Fiorenal, a medication with no side effects.

In my 40's I started passing huge bloodclots, and hemorrhaged while in a store where I was shopping. The doctor found advanced endometriosis with the ovaries partially destroyed. Doctors advised a complete hysterectomy, but were concerned with my low blood count. When I said, "Why don't you schedule my surgery *before* my period?" they did. (A needed reminder to the male medical model.)

A kidney specialist was called in to prevent cutting into the abnormally-located right kidney. Pregnancy would have endangered my life—a husband who could not make me pregnant was a gift. The orchestration of my life was going on, despite my unawareness.

CHAPTER 7

SELF-HEALING: DEEP PROCESS WORK

As I've recounted earlier, Marge Robert's *Inner Healing through Imagery Prayer* uncovered my core trauma at birth through an inclusion of Jesus in the process. It felt more risky to participate in the Anne Schaef *Deep Process Training Intensives*, where 15 to 40 people could witness one's emotional unraveling, but I felt compelled to do so.

More than "talk therapy," Anne's Deep Process Intensives promised permanent relief through sharing one's story and feeling your pain. We learned to "do it yourself" by trusting the process of letting the pain come up, leading us to our core issues. Then we could let it go. Anne stated we had many unfinished processes where we were told *not* to feel how we felt, or simply, "Stop it!" **Living in process** is to allow our unhealed stuff to come up, do the emoting or grief work needed, and feel a sense of completion.

Deep Process Work, a Prelude to Living in Process

While still living in Minnesota, I attended five nine-day intensives with Anne Schaef over a period of several years, held in different parts of the country. In addition, local process groups continued my emersion in deep process work. Encouraged to share one's story with feeling, she would stop us if it became merely reporting and not *feeling* what was being said. She stopped me when I persisted in telling my story, focusing on drama over gut feelings. We were taught that the value of sharing was in feeling the feelings and completing the unfinished processes of the past.

The catharsis would involve one's whole physical as well as "inner" being, and required a willingness to pound the available pillows to release grief and anger. This allowed the full expression of the many "don't cry!" moments of childhood. The experience then became a valued lesson.

Anne spoke of the *male system* as mechanistic and addictive. The male system is pervasive and widespread, and even affects the way therapy is done, and the way the medical system, government, religion, society, and interpersonal relationships are programmed.

According to Anne, we were programmed with three characteristics of the addictive Patriarchal system: **The illusion of control** (even going to war if necessary), **dualistic thinking** (right/wrong, good/bad, black/white, etc.), and **dishonesty of feelings** ("I'm fine," and "Don't feel").

Living in process means to let go of our *need to control* to get our needs met. Rather, we can learn to trust the core of love that is in every spiritual heart and speak from the heart. Feel the resonance. The controller believes s/he is unlovable and cannot get his/her needs met any other way.

Letting go of our dualistic thinking means to give up the automatic judgments of our egoic mind. It is to accept "both/and" and to recognize there is a third possibility, or more—not confined to "either/or." It is to intend and accept a win-win solution, not needing to be better or lesser.

"Honesty with feelings" is the third way we live in process, the way of the heart. This takes practice. This is not about sharing negative feelings (often simply fear-based opinions) regarding others, but to share our own feelings in the moment.

Fear of confrontation or disapproval can compel one to "be nice," no matter what is at stake. Anne called this *impression management*, another form of control. My perception was that my husband, Chuck, was addicted to niceness and would not discuss anything controversial, including important parenting issues. Passivity can be a form of control. Acting consistent with assumed mutual goals, i.e., cooperative parenting, was not possible.

The compulsion to fix others can create blindness. It is another way to try and feel okay about oneself. I felt helpless and unsupported, as well as confused by his behavior and refusal to share feelings.

His behavior was also reinforced by my own fear of being wrong. High tolerance for inappropriate behavior by our children was his way of indirectly getting back at me, when he felt angry with me. Passive-aggressive behavior is part of the addictive system of power and control.

My co-dependency involved behaviors equally dysfunctional as a partner. To numb the pain, I involved myself in distractions, appeasement, and compulsive overeating. My ADD impulsivity, tardiness, scatteredness, and impatience tried his patience—yet he was kind to a fault. I am grateful for the freedom I had to grow and explore personal growth options, probably not possible with another partner.

Living in Process, as taught by Anne Wilson Schaef, is the feminine way, counter to the Patriarchal way. It can be defined as being fully aware in the present and observing without judgment, a function of the observer Self. When we tune into the Spiritual Heart, the I Am Love Presence, living in process feels the same as "pray without ceasing," the biblical advice from Jesus. Anne's several books share in detail her observations and experience of deep process work and living in process.

CHAPTER 8

ANN ARBOR

Return to School

Zion, a 5000 member Lutheran church in Ann Arbor, issued a call to Chuck to serve as one of three ministers. His gift for harmony was welcomed in a congregation with a history of conflict between ministers.

Our son Jeff, 17, was still at home and working as a garage mechanic. Kari was acting secretive and having problems in junior high. Chuck supported my decision to get a Masters in Social Work (MSW), credentials for counseling. My going back to school helped divert my focus. As I completed my MSW studies at the University of Michigan, I felt depressed while others were celebrating. Now I had to deal with my unhappy family life and disconnected, silent husband.

My attempt at a private counseling practice had little success. In trying to go back to nursing at a psychiatric hospital, I couldn't remember drug information and was totally unaware of the new ones. It ruled out my return to nursing.

Kari Acts out the Issues in My Marriage

Kari, 16, was skipping her ballet classes in downtown Ann Arbor and was attracted to a young black man who was out of prison on parole. His offense involved violent behavior. Later, we received and accepted collect calls for her from his fellow prisoners, buddies of his. My husband was offended when I put a stop to these calls.

Kari decorated a birthday cake with a green marijuana leaf likeness. Cigarette butts lay on the ground beneath her window. Other signs of drug and alcohol experimentation occurred. I found a letter in her room from the parolee telling her she drank too much. When I informed Chuck, he reprimanded me for snooping.

I had failed to get our two sons into treatment. Time was running out for Kari, now 17.

When I called the local psychiatric team who evaluated an adolescent's need for drug treatment, I was told, "both parents have to come in." Chuck refused to do so.

I had been attending Al-Anon and Tough Love classes. My husband saw no need. "Helen", the church organist, told me their daughter "Anne," Kari's friend, was in a drug treatment center called *Straight*. Anne told her parents she was concerned about Kari's substance abuse. I had been schooled in Intervention, a strategy which cites the effects of drug and alcohol use on relationships in order to gain the addict's acceptance of treatment. Helen and "Mark" invited my husband and I over for a social evening with the intention of confronting my husband, in order to gain his cooperation.

As Chuck and I sat in Mark and Helen's living room, I sensed this could be the end of my marriage. They shared the experience they were having with *Straight Treatment Center,* notably a strict rehab center which required them to travel 200 miles to attend Friday "family nights." After sharing Anne's disclosure regarding Kari, they said, "If you care about your daughter, you will snoop and check closely on her activities."

My husband was speechless and got very red in his face. He was a man who could not express anger. Then I knew my 31-year marriage was over. Rather than expressing anger directly, he later said "murder or divorce" were his only choices. I had humiliated him. He felt no need to change—a third option which he was unable to fathom.

Chapter 8: Ann Arbor

Denial

Earlier, Chuck had told me he asked Kari about drug use and she had replied, "No!" He took her out to dinner for a little talk. I noted that she then made some effort to show up at ballet practice and was a star in a performance of the Ann Arbor Civic Ballet. But it was a bandaide, a temporary solution which didn't address the problem.

Years later, after our divorce, she became involved with heroin. After she stopped using heroin, it was small comfort to have him tell me he asked her, "If I had listened to your mother, would you have gone down that path?" Her answer was not forthcoming.

Al-Anon has helped me accept her choices, her path of learning her life's lessons. The disconnect I feel is muted by my awareness of addiction. Control was impossible, but I can send love. Now I have learned to do Ho'oponopono to shift the energy. This ancient Hawaiian practice of reconciliation and forgiveness works at the soul level and proves the truth of Jesus' statement in ACIM that all minds are joined. Self-forgiveness, love, and gratitude are felt by the other, as well as in oneself, in this amazing practice.

CHAPTER 9

DIVORCE, MY FIRST TRANSFORMATION

When Chuck told me he had been thinking about ending our marriage for the last ten years, I was shocked and devastated. He was a master at pretense. As one of three ministers of a large parish, he would be the second minister to go through divorce; the senior minister was already doing so.

I asked if we could simply separate and wait until Kari graduated in one more year and enjoy her success in ballet. He said he wanted to be free. I learned later that he intended to marry a woman he was counseling, following her divorce. Our close friends were shocked when I told them of our plans to divorce, as no sign of discord had been apparent to them.

Though a feminist in philosophy, I had found my identity and satisfaction in the role of wife and mother. Entertaining in our large home had given me a lot of pleasure. Memories of the six of us sitting down to dinner gave me familiar, "traditional family" comfort. Our friendships with other clergy couples were a treasured part of my life. All that was gone.

My emotional and physical dependency on Chuck was another matter. When I had sought counseling for my depression, he voiced his feelings, "I am not enough for you!" I finally got it, that his attraction for me was based on my needing fixing, and he saw himself as my fixer.

Now, he said things I had never heard before. He didn't believe the migraine headaches were real. Was his empathy fake as well?

In the divorce settlement, I was given the Garfield lake property in Northern Minnesota. Growing up spending summers at our family lakeside cottage provided the fondest memories of my childhood. Then, my father was relaxed and playful. Ministerial duties and appearances were off his mind. I had a special fondness for our lake retreat, which Chuck did not share.

Sexuality and Feeling Lovable

After my hysterectomy, the migraines diminished, much to my relief. The early menopause did not noticeably affect me, except for tissue changes. The absence of a sexual partner was one of my major concerns with my impending divorce. After a shift in our sexual relationship, I realized I had used sex in the marriage to convince myself that I was lovable.

Due to our religious convictions, both Chuck and I had abstained during courtship. When the moment of first intercourse arrived, it was disappointing! An ongoing challenge, orgasms for me were difficult to achieve, something I could not understand. Though I was uptight in many areas due to my religious programming, Chuck said, I was most free in the sexual area. The marriage gave me permission (finally) to be sexual, and I asked for it frequently.

Looking back, I realize that the fundamentalist programming had affected my body's ability to have an orgasm. "Don't take pleasure in having sex—it could lead you astray," was an imprint in my bodymind computer that I forgot at a conscious level. Pre-occupation of having a sexual encounter with him, even while listening to his sermons, gave me twinges of guilt.

In my psychotherapy training, I realized I had the ingredients for sex addiction in my desire to fill the unlovability hole. Feeling unlovable stayed with me since I first became aware of feelings.

When we were sexual, I would try to experience being one with him. Sometimes, Chuck and I would converse. Sharing a funny story would send ripples of laughter mutually felt in our bodies that left me with delight. Here was the joining. Resonating heart to heart—emotionally feeling fully-accepted—left me feeling loved.

Awareness that loving self is a pre-requisite for feeling lovable and loving others, came much later. Loving yourself was wrong according to fundamentalist teachings. That early program persisted at an unconscious cellular level until much later in life.

Christian romance stories shaped my sexuality. My belief was that if we were "making love" I was being loved, and therefore was lovable. In *A Course in Miracles*, Jesus states, "Bodies cannot join, only minds can."

Separation from My Children; The Disconnect

The sense of separation from my children began when they started using drugs and alcohol. Failure to address this issue together, as parent partners, meant they did not get a clear message that their behavior was unacceptable to us as a unit. Alone, I was powerless to do anything about it. The divorce left them without parental support for treatment.

Kari said she didn't want to choose between us, and went to live with her sister, Kim, in Minneapolis. To be near my daughters, I rented part of a friend's home not far from them. A counseling clinic provided my first job using my MSW degree.

Jeff felt he had caused the divorce. I reassured him that it was our lack of honest communication as parents and partners that was the problem. Our children simply acted out what we were NOT saying.

Kim voiced her pleasure, "I am glad Dad divorced you." As a child, she had insisted on sitting between us. In asking spirit if she had a past life with Chuck, I got a *yes* that she had been a wife to him. Further questioning indicated that he left her for another woman. She has carried that energy of bitterness into this lifetime—with more anger at the other woman than at the husband. In her subconscious mind, I am the other woman.

Kirk did not share his feelings and had just been married. He was partying and drinking heavily, so he was anesthetized during the time of our divorce. His drinking not only ended his marriage, it affected his work. One of his close calls with death occurred when he drove a company truck into the river while drunk and had to be pulled out.

Though estranged by his alcoholism, after his drug treatment we finally re-connected by phone. At the Christian-based drug treatment center, he was highly regarded and sometimes gave sermons—a source of satisfaction for him, and a surprise to me. For me, Al-Anon provided a support I never got from church, my environment since birth. This realization was profound for me.

Imposed Disconnect from My Church Community

Chuck told me to leave quietly and not hurt his ministry. On my last Sunday in this large church with many parishioners unknown to me, I gagged when two older women approached me, raving about what a wonderful man I had for a husband. Then, my former university teacher, a buddy of my husband, turned his back on me when I tried to greet him.

Keeping my pain to myself, I prepared a farewell note to put into the church newsletter which simply stated that due to irreconcilable differences, I was leaving for Minnesota to be near my daughters. Chuck would not put that in the church paper until after I left. There were no goodbyes or recognition of my leaving—another disconnect. I simply disappeared.

Death or Profound Change

Before I left, "Jean," an Ann Arbor friend, did a Tarot reading for me. I knew nothing about Tarot. While growing up, I had learned that anything to do with the occult "was of the devil." However, my work in the Anne Schaef Intensives had opened me to choose for myself. When I turned up the *death* card, Jean said it meant, "Death or profound change."

"I choose the profound change!" I said.

Chapter 9: Divorce, My First Transformation

During this transition period, I attended a guided imagery session with Magaly, a highly intuitive spiritual teacher. I was to visualize a long hall with a number of doors and choose one to open, which would give cues to my future. Opening a red door, I saw only darkness and nothing beyond the doorway except empty space. I was stepping into the unknown. Again, it meant *death or profound change!*

Soon after that when I attended an art show, an art piece near the entry boldly challenged onlookers: "CHANGE OR DIE!"

I had already asked for change after reading a book, *Change Me, Teach Me*, four years earlier. "Change me, teach me" had become my daily mantra. Now it made this unthinkable divorce appear to be a part of a Divine plan I had asked for.

CHAPTER 10

RETURN TO MINNESOTA ALONE, SPIRITUAL OUTREACH

Stepping into the unknown

On my parting day of packing the car, Chuck was present. In our last embrace, we shook with sobs. My drive alone across two states was the first of many solitary drives. With no responsibilities as a pastor's wife or mother, I was now free to focus on myself. What began to call to me was a desire to unravel the pain of my childhood.

The grief I experienced was heaviest around the failure to use my professional understanding and awareness of addiction to help my own children get into treatment. The loss of both husband and children shifted my identity as wife and mother to an aging single woman. After a period of much crying, I got it together.

In a seminar focused on self-knowledge and self-healing, the facilitator noted I lacked an ego. It meant I was so identified with my fundamentalist belief system, I had no sense of an individual self. A normal self-awareness was missing. Left out of a deeper process the others went through, I didn't have a clue. Now I understand that I was co-dependent with my parents from a very early age. Their beliefs were my beliefs. Even college didn't seem to shake those beliefs, and I didn't differentiate from my parents until much later in life.

Professional Life as an MSW

Following my move to Minneapolis, I first worked in The Counseling Clinic. When another therapist pointed out my resentment towards men, I took note. The male counselors were different as a whole—less "male" than I was used to—due to their focus on feelings. My experience with them softened my attitude. I co-led a drug dependency group with a male counselor without conflict. Also, facilitating a battered women's group gave me valuable experience in understanding power and control issues.

After four years, I began work at a Christian counseling center. The center eventually merged with the hospital from which I received my RN in nursing. I also worked part-time in the hospital's Eating Disorder program, where I was first exposed to an awareness of the new children. A client in my Eating Disorder group had been living with a drug pusher. When she became pregnant, she got out of the relationship and stopped her drug use. Instead, she became obsessed with her weight following her son's birth, and became a candidate for the Eating Disorder group. She once told me that when her son was three he said to her, "Mom, I thought you would never get your act together so I could come into the world."

Weekends, when I could drive up to Lake Garfield in beautiful Northern Minnesota and enjoy the lake, were precious. Friendships developed with other pastor's wives who vacationed in their summer homes at a nearby lake, sometimes called Preacher's Lake. They attended the Lutheran church in Laporte, which didn't serve me spiritually, but was a place to connect.

When the Christian clinic was taken over by the hospital, the management changed and many therapists left. I also wanted to leave and try to live at my Shangri La in Northern Minnesota, and asked the clinic director to be laid-off with severance pay. This was granted, allowing the move to my beloved place on Lake Garfield.

A Minneapolis couple had befriended me and invited me to stay with them whenever I needed to return to the cities. My daughters took no interest in my life. When I needed help to move, they declined. It made it easier for me to leave.

Chapter 10: Return To Minnesota Alone, Spiritual Outreach

Square Dancing and Lessons from Men

In Minneapolis, I was introduced to square dancing by a much older man I met playing tennis. After consulting the minister of the liberal Lutheran church I attended, I allowed myself to be sexual with him, He was very attentive to taking care of himself after his wife died, and I appreciated the stability he offered. It was my first venture into the single world and it felt safe with "Bob." My belief in celibacy until married was no longer relevant—my delayed adolescence had begun.

Interest in him faded after I invited him to my Lake Garfield cabin. While we were hiking in the woods, I ran ahead in a joyful embrace of nature. He became surly and said, "A woman should never go ahead of the man, and should walk two steps behind him." I voiced my protest and ended the relationship.

Tennis and square dancing were two activities that occupied most of my recreation and dating opportunities in the single world. I met "Bill," also a square dancer and tennis player.

Handsome and impressive, yes, but he was a worrier and seemed preoccupied with his heart condition and never quite present. I didn't feel a heart connection with either man.

Al-Anon

I had started going to Al-Anon before my divorce, while in the midst of Kirk's rebellion. There, I discovered the powerful twelve-step program (modeled after the Alcoholics Anonymous 12-step program) that began my spiritual journey outside of religious dogma. It was here that God became internalized as a Higher Power.

Going from thinking I was an expert on the way to God, to acknowledging I was a beginner in spirituality, the inner journey became my focus. Guidance began to be real and observable and I learned to trust. Yet, the heavy fundamentalist programming in **self-doubt** continued to plague me. (This seems to be more prevalent in women, as we are taught to defer to the wisdom of men over our own.)

Churches

I attended a liberal Lutheran church, where gays and lesbians were welcomed, and inclusive language was used. A newspaper reference to *A Course in Miracles* (ACIM) attracted me to a study group at Unity church. Although my first reaction to the course was, "This is heresy!" I felt guided to keep going.

The miracle is a shift in perception, which emphasizes forgiveness through a new way of seeing the other as oneself. In ACIM, *ego* is defined as the voice of fear and is alien to our true Self of unconditional Love. The patriarchal system's teaching of ego/body as our natural identity supported the "belief in separation" (which Jesus says is the core cause of human misery). ACIM presented a thought system that eventually would reverse my fundamentalist thinking. Soon I was going to two churches on Sunday mornings, Unity and my liberal Lutheran church.

My first taste of Hawaii was a Unity-sponsored event at a big island retreat center in view of the flowing Kilauea volcano. Alan Cohen was the featured workshop leader. In a helicopter flight to see the massive flow of lava from the air, I witnessed the steam and heard the sizzle as it hit the ocean. Alan led us in an early morning yoga practice. We tried nude bathing at a black sand beach nearby. Some rocks provided cover for a group of reticent women along with myself. In the force of the waves I lost my high school ring, and I can look at that as symbolic of the end of my delayed adolescence.

CHAPTER 11

SCATTERED, INDEED

A Delayed Diagnosis

My 1980 promise, *Everything Scattered will be Gathered,* was more fully understood when I read *Driven to Distraction* by Edward Hallowell, M.D., and John Ratey, M.D., more than ten years later, and diagnosed myself. Most of the 100 diagnostic questions for Attention Deficit Disorder, I answered positively. Not hyperactive, I was the dreamy type, most common in girls. My characteristics of ADD—*impulsive, scattered, unfocused* and *disorganized*—often resulted in devaluation of others and myself, as well as general dysfunction in daily life.

This discovery was actually a relief to know why I was academically bright, but unable to focus and function as easily as my peers. Instead of drugs, I used food to help me feel grounded and focused. My ADD also reinforced those feelings of shame, the lowest vibration of all feelings. Consulting ADD specialists confirmed my diagnosis.

Cause of My ADD

"Lily" invited me to a public session with a psychic channeler, Michelle Mayama. I had already listened to her tapes. When Mayama went into a meditative state and was connected to her guides, she asked for questions. I asked, "What was the cause of my Attention Deficit Disorder?" After a pause, she replied, "Premature cutting of the umbilical cord at birth." None of the books I had read referred to this, and speakers at the ADD conference never mentioned this, so I tucked the information away.

Later in Kauai, I was browsing Dr. Mercola's archives of articles on his website. In an article titled *The Epidemic of Autism and Attention Deficit Disorder*, the surgeon/author described the premature cutting of the umbilical cord by impatient obstetricians, a practice which deprives the infant's brain of the last flow of blood. This results in a premature disconnect. My birth began with a **disconnect**.

Effects of Not Knowing

Pleasing my parents wasn't a way to be popular with my peers. I felt awkward in many social situations. The ADD since birth was a factor as well. My conversations were scattered with too much detail, information, and inappropriate sharing of personal story I later regretted. Impulsive, compulsive energy is part of my ADD legacy. The unknown ADD made loving self more difficult. Had I understood this earlier in my life, self-forgiveness and self-acceptance would have been easier. My daydreaming type of ADD was an invisible disorder compared to the hyperactive type.

My ADD forgetfulness feels like Alzheimer's at times, especially with my inherited pre-disposition from both parents. The TaBIA practice has addressed Alzheimer's type symptoms and clarified my awareness. A balanced and healthy lifestyle has also helped, including new supplements for the brain. I use foods that new research shows as feeding the brain. Consuming processed sugar fogs the brain, yet I find it hard to eliminate as it is in almost everything. Awareness is key.

To be bright scholastically, and yet unable to organize my life and follow through with my ideas and inspirations, left me unfulfilled. Slow in performing tasks, I made easy jobs difficult. There was no consistency—at times when I was "on" I could move very quickly, as when expecting company, a strong motive for focused action. Procrastinating until the last minute, not aware of what I could do ahead of time, I became "insane" (according to my husband) and did a whirlwind job of cleaning just before guests would ring the doorbell. Chuck also noted my lack of time sense.

Chapter 11: Scattered, Indeed

My impulse to consume or chew something was so strong, I remember saying I could eat the paint off the walls. Later, I noticed this urge comes up whenever I need to initiate a new task. To shift my focus, I eat to ground myself. When I realized focusing was painful and a trigger for going to the refrigerator, even after a full meal, I could use my tapping process on this issue. My ADD was also the basis for my Compulsive Overeating (COE) disorder. Awareness gave me new options.

When getting my Masters in Social Work degree, I was directed to a remedial class on outlining. Outlining was something I simply couldn't do. Getting through college with excellent grades (graduating Cum Laude) was the result of cramming for tests, a form of hyper-focusing. After a test, the information evaporated.

With paperwork, I often don't have a clue as to where to put it, or forget I had a file or where it is, so I often have several files for the same thing. In stores, I ask for something and it may be right in front of me. Distracted by surrounding items, I can't see it.

No, It's Not Alzheimer's

Forgetfulness, made worse with ADD, is one of my most painful experiences. I recall a time in my office in a counseling clinic when I lay my head down on the desk, forgetting I had a client in the waiting room, and missed the appointment. Now I pause with automatic tasks, needing to be totally present. Friends often say, "Don't you remember when…" but I almost never do remember what they are referring to. I let them know that this lack of memory is something I live with and for them to not take it personally. The automatic recall is simply not there.

When going out to take care of shopping and appointments, lists were usually misplaced or left behind, or I didn't think to look at them. I have asked my unseen guides, notably my mother and my brother Luke, who are with me all the time, to remind me of what I am intending to do. Now, last-minute reminders pop into my mind, usually at just the right moment. I have used TaBIA on the symptoms, which diminished some of the ADD effects, and noted that some habitual patterns persisted.

Once, when I experienced dementia-like symptoms and Muscle Tested, I indeed had 50% of the conditions for developing dementia. After doing a TaBIA practice for several days, I tested at 10% and felt much more awake and alert.

As I sit before the computer with the Intention of writing, I have an invisible writing team that helps with recall and brings in the words I am looking for. (See "Acknowledgements.") I also Muscle Test the correctness of my thoughts. The Intuition comes first. I use the Muscle Testing for confirmation. My Self Inquiry Process uses intuitive questions that come up in the moment.

In the summer of 2014, I decided to see an Alzheimer's specialist. It was a chatty interview with a charming doctor and I knew it was negative before he said, "It isn't Alzheimer's, but you could use some Ritalin for your ADD."

Narcolepsy, or the tendency to suddenly fall asleep with hyper-relaxation or lack of stimulus, has endangered my life as well as others. In one driving incident, a miraculous (police) siren went off as I was drifting over the center line and heading towards an oncoming car. Pulling over, I sheepishly told the officer, I was heading home, only a few streets away, for a nap. He said to pull over and rest. I said, "I am awake now!" I thought, *where would I pull over on Kauai roads, typically without shoulders or next to mountain walls?* With ADD, it isn't rest I need; it is stimulation. I do not mean stimulants such as caffeine: drinking coffee does not prevent sleeping, and I can really enjoy chocolate without fear of wakefulness when I need to sleep.

The "self-absorption" I have been accused of and plagued with guilt over, is simply my struggle to function. I would internalize the anxiety. If not allowing myself to eat over feeling confused or frustrated, I might fall asleep instead, or take a nap.

Sari Solden, in her book, *WOMEN with Attention Deficit Disorder: Embracing Disorganization at Home and at the Workplace,* has this to say: "While all women may have some of the symptoms some of the time, in ADD, the symptoms are severe and chronic… Even so, ADD symptoms in girls can be subtle, quiet, hidden, and invisible." When undiagnosed, Solden writes, "Each year that passes, the difficulties are compounded, resulting in *secondary* emotional effects, such as depression, low self-esteem, under-achievement, and relationship difficulties." All this had occurred for me, yet I had no understanding until I had read *Driven to Distraction* in the nineties. It was a great relief to be aware of what I was dealing with, and to withhold judgment of myself.

CHAPTER 12

SEVEN YEARS IN MINNESOTA NORTHWOODS

Nature's Call

Moving in January, 1991, into a drafty old trailer home on a frozen lake was challenging. The plumbing had not been completed and an outdoor "biffy" or "outhouse" was a colder option to the chilly indoor bathroom commode. When I applied for energy assistance, my drafty place was insulated, making it more tolerable.

Local resources were soon found for snow removal and other survival needs. Winter neighbors were not close, as few lived in these "summer" homes year around. The 200-mile drive to the Twin Cities to visit my daughters and friends through harrowing snow storms where everything was white, is mind-blowing to me today. More than once, my car broke down and I had to walk to a rural farmhouse for help. One breakdown required an overnight stay in a motel. The challenge of survival on nature's terms, I learned firsthand.

Plans were drawn for covering my not-so-mobile home. A floor and a peaked roof were built over the flat trailer roof. It provided a sleeping loft, accessed by outside stairs in the large covered porch built with donated windows. An upstairs deck fronted the loft. I was quite proud of my amateur architectural plans, which the creative local carpenters fashioned according to my desires.

Space for Spirit hermitage

The idea of a spiritual, one-person hermitage inspired me to explore that possibility. An answer came from a brochure placed in my grocery bag at the Bemidji health food store.

I called the artistic builder who came on site to live while he built an unusual one-room structure complete with a small wood-burning stove and sleeping space for two, counting the tiny loft with ladder access. He didn't believe in square buildings. "Space for Spirit" was pie-shaped with a soaring peak. There was a spiral-energy feeling in its space.

I discovered that I simply didn't have the promotional wisdom, energy, and focus needed to have the space used as intended. Other friends who established retreat sites were not all alone. They had partners, teams or boards, non-profit status and recognition by the church. A guest, who did find my place, said something about it being "a best kept secret." It is not a viable dream for a loner. It was Space for Spirit for me. I felt that a powerful, supportive male would be a necessary partner for any such venture. That I lacked.

Car Karma

After my move to Garfield, it was not unusual to travel 40 miles to go to a square dance. I got used to driving alone at night for these occasions. It was at a square dance I met "Myron," whom I dated and fell in love with.

It was a winter night when I drove on the gravel road to meet him at his Bemidji home. My seatbelts didn't usually work until the car was warm, yet they were fastened when I hit ice and became airborne. The car rolled and I landed in a snow bank, hanging almost upside down. I managed to crawl out and walk to a farmhouse for help. "Kevin," my garage man, towed my car. It was totaled. He noted where there were no tracks in the snow, verifying my airborne experience. Though I usually recall my feelings from an impactful event, crises can cause me to hyper-focus on survival and numb the feelings.

Another used car was acquired. Six weeks later, I was in Bemidji, where after counseling I purchased a large amount of groceries before heading home. It was dark and raining on icy roads. I decided to travel the back roads, thinking it might be safer to travel slower. Even so, I hit glare ice and the car veered into a snowdrift. I felt panic as I was in an isolated area. No one in their right mind would be out on the roads. As I sat in the tipped car, I heard a familiar voice. A truck had stopped to help and I recognized one of the men as a carpenter who had worked for me. They took me home with my load of groceries.

Kevin declared, "Not again!" when I called him the next day. A year later in a "new" used car, I hydroplaned in daylight and slid into a ditch, causing considerable damage and expense to my car. A number of other close calls in my winter driving occurred and I was very grateful for my survival even if my cars did not fare well. It became clear to me that I no longer wanted to spend winters in the Minnesota Northwoods, no matter how beautiful.

More Lessons from Men

"Myron," my square dance partner, became a passionate lover. Quiet and reflective, he was interested in spirituality. He was sensitive to any reference to age as he was approaching retirement. Myron found out I was several years older than he was and distanced from me. In our last embrace, I asked if it was my age that was causing him to break up and he nodded, yes.

Next was a brief affair with "Lenny," an Indian, a "wannabe shaman" who was interested in staying on my property. Later, I observed that he was attracted to white women with property. He might still be living with the one he was breaking up with. Lenny smoked and his energy did not feel good. I told him I needed to end the relationship. He talked me into letting him come one more time. As he attempted to make love, I began to feel a sharp pain in my neck and told him he had to leave because the pain reflected my going back on my word. He questioned my interpretation, but finally left. I called a friend, who did massage, for relief.

In my appointment with a chiropractor as soon as I could get in, she said the muscle condition resembled a whiplash. In my readings about the use of will affecting the cervical part of the neck, I realized

I had betrayed myself. **The body knows** and tells us what we need to know, when we tune into it.

I met "Don" at a Square Dance Convention, where he walked across a crowded room to meet me. He was a retired coach. Don became a very caring and consistent boyfriend, who would accompany me to square dances and help me in other ways, even though he had to drive 200 miles to see me.

Selling my First Major Creative Venture

As lakeshore property became more valuable, I felt I didn't need 300 feet. I explored adjacent woods and asked the man who lived at the other end if he had a lot to sell. He sold me 150 feet at a very reasonable price. I proceeded to put my original site on the market.

My intention was to have more permanent housing with a safe heating system. (Toxic fumes were coming from the old gas furnace in the trailer and I was told there was a crack in the furnace.) So I wouldn't be entirely alone, I wanted a walkout finished "basement," which could be rented out. This was very doable on the high steep lot I had purchased.

The realtor was firm on her cut of the selling price. A lawyer and his detective son wanted to buy my property and put in their bid, considerably lower than what I asked for. My realtor warned me they would not compromise, so I accepted the offer. The hermitage would not be included and would be moved to the new lot as my temporary home, along with the outhouse.

The buyers insisted on a date sooner than I wanted. It interfered with a square dance convention I wanted to go to with Don. I went anyway. When I returned home, I worked very hard to pack up and take things to the new site. When they arrived with their packed trailer, I was still cleaning. They were angry. The meek wife of the lawyer said nothing. Exhausted, I broke down in tears and said, "There are three of you and only one of me." They further berated me for implying they were unreasonable. Don arrived later to help me complete the move. He had a way of getting the respect of the men and offered to help them. He told me the lawyer and son tried to discourage his relationship with me. I felt sorry for the lawyer's wife, feeling she was very dominated by both of these men. She never had a voice.

A new creation and another farewell

I stayed with friends on the neighboring lake until the hermitage was moved to my new site. From my hermitage, I watched them bring in the pre-manufactured sections of the house I would be living in. Don came and stained the natural siding and helped me get settled. It all came together, with a simple basement apartment to be finished later.

With Don, I noticed a distancing and he finally told me he had met a former student of his and wanted to marry her. He hoped I would find someone my age. Don was five years younger than me. Since I was attracting younger men, I noticed a pattern of rejection due to my age.

Spiritually, we had major differences. He insisted that God was male, and also said the one with the money has the power and makes the decisions in a relationship. Expressing concern for my wellbeing, he continued to call occasionally, including telling me of his frustration with his wife's secret smoking, something he had forbidden. Though I am grateful for the experiences I did have with him and his helpfulness, the heart resonance wasn't there.

Another experience with men bears mentioning. Three single brothers in my age group lived together on a farm nearby. They installed my septic systems and also included me in parties at their home. Two were gay and one was bisexual. Accepted in the community, they were quite proper. I appreciated their friendship.

CHAPTER 13

PROFESSIONAL UPGRADES, ROMANCE, MOVING ON

More Professional Enrichment

I continued to seek additional trainings to create more demand for my services—or was it to fill the hole of never feeling enough?

After my move to my second Garfield home, I flew to the big island of Hawaii in 1995 for a week-long accelerated hypnosis training in a Honolulu hotel. Excited about this opportunity to become a Certified Hypnotherapist, I hoped it would attract clients. This addition to my counseling services turned out to have mixed success in Northern Minnesota, which I attributed to my lack of promotion.

My continued study of ACIM fueled a desire for distinguishing my professional work with a spiritual focus. A Pathways of Light ad mentioned *A Course in Miracles* as the foundation for their courses leading to ordination.

Pathways of Light and a New Romance

Pathways of Light, a self-described spiritual college in Kiel, Wisconsin, was a 250-mile drive from Northern Minnesota. To attend a portion of their classes, I went and stayed for a week. There I met "Ted," already ordained, who was in transition and needing to find a new place to live. Strongly attracted to him, I invited him to live in my walk-out basement in exchange for Pathways training.

In his six months at Garfield, we were intimate as well as in a teacher-student role. He obtained some other temporary work.

Strikingly handsome, he attracted the surprised look of an attractive female acquaintance in a Bemidji grocery store. Her head turned to look at Ted, and then at me, her face registering a look of disbelief. The feeling it gave me was akin to possessing a prize trophy.

After several months the relationship became strained. He described my quick footsteps across the floor above him as a reminder of his mother. His unhealed feelings about his mother were enough for him to leave. The loss of a beautiful man, spiritual soul mate, and physical partner was cause for grief.

To complete the courses for ordination, I drove back to Pathways of Light in Wisconsin. Inquiring about Ted, I learned he had married someone, and later heard he had died. To find and keep a Physical, Emotional, Mental and Spiritual match in a partner eluded me. Yet, I knew it was all in divine order.

An Astrological Twin

"Betty," a woman I met at a conference for Adults with ADD, came to live in my walk-out apartment. She was my age and her birthday was identical. After a time, her core of anger surfaced, and she frequently snapped at me for reasons unclear to me. She offered to do Reiki on me and noted my anger, a reaction to her anger. The energetics of two people with ADD and identical birthdays trying to live together wasn't working.

What did prompt her leaving after several months was the occurrence of someone prowling around the house and shining a flashlight into her windows at night. One time we saw a distant light moving through the woods in the direction of the cabin of the man from whom I had purchased the property. He seemed somewhat peculiar in his isolation and his manner, and now I also felt anxious about continuing to live alone in this isolated place.

Letting Go and Moving On

The treacherous winter driving, my car accidents on ice, the window peeper, and Ted's leaving brought me to the decision to sell

Chapter 13: Professional Upgrades, Romance, Moving On

my place. A couple from Alaska wanted it as their winter home! They were very gracious and grateful for acquiring my home, my second major creation. Unfortunately, the hermitage became a storage unit, a commentary on my failed dream of attracting spiritual seekers for a retreat in solitude.

"Lily," a friend, had gone through divorce and found a large apartment in St Cloud. She invited me to move in and it became my transition space for about a year. It was close to Minneapolis and another Pathways of Light friend in St. Cloud.

Selling more accumulated stuff had to be done. My next move was going be to an apartment overlooking the St. Cloud River. It would provide some connection to nature.

CHAPTER 14

THE CALL TO KAUAI, THERAPIST TO COACH

Call to Kauai

In my private session with the psychic, Mayama, I told her I already felt so different, that I changed my first name, "Ruth," to my middle name, "Petra," named after my father "Peter," meaning "rock."

"Not rigid rock, but molten rock like lava," she said. Deciding to do an imagery session using volcanoes, she asked what I would like to release. "All the limiting beliefs I've taken in from my parents," I responded.

Without identifying them, I visualized the disappearance of my beliefs that no longer served me, into the volcanic fire. However, as I later learned, I would have to identify them and recognize when and how they showed up in my life. Beliefs are stored in our bodymind computers and become unconscious programming. This was the beginning, the allowance for them to be revealed to me so they could be released. It was "purification by fire"— a symbol of my transformation experience I could now embrace. It was also my connection to Pele, volcano goddess of fire.

The next day, Lily handed me application forms for Hale Kupuna on Kauai and said, "Petra, why don't you go to Kauai to write your book?" Lily's mother had moved to Kauai and was living in low-income housing for seniors. Ah, this could replace the paradise I had enjoyed in Northern Minnesota without the hazards of winter. I sent in my application.

From Therapist to Coach

Even my Pathways of Light ordination did not feel like "enough." At the ADD conference for adults, it was suggested that a trained coach was better-equipped to work with ADD issues than a psychotherapist was. So, in 1998, I enrolled in the Academy for Coach Training (ACT) based in Seattle, to first understand and heal myself and then to pass it on. . .

Money from the sale of my property was used to fly out and take the training. I was attracted to ACT because of their focus on *Living Your Vision*. I was the only one enrolled in this optional course. My instructor was a very spiritual woman who later became the director of ACT. I am grateful for the gift of her presence.

My CPC (Certified Professional Coach) certification would be completed by teleconference after my move to Kauai. Coaching was the last of my formal trainings. My first career of nursing was replaced by my Masters in Social Work toward the end of my marriage. Becoming an Ordained Ministerial Counselor by Pathways of Light (POL) quickly followed my Hypnotherapy training. I was never able to embrace the title of "Reverend." I had lived with clergy too long. Now my reason is that it fosters separation.

Awareness of the Most Valuable Training

The University of LIFE remains my best training of all. As I learned to listen to Source and later to non-physical beings, my training became orchestrated through my willingness to listen.

We all have the *Voice for Love,* the Holy Spirit within us. It is a softer voice heard during moments of quiet, as in meditation. The still mind is more receptive. When our Intention is to always be in touch with this inner guidance, we are in the mode of *prayer without ceasing.*

Synchronicities increase. It is really a partnership with the Higher Self that increases until we live fully from the *Vision of Christ.* Christ

Chapter 14: The Call To Kauai, Therapist To Coach

is the face of God (see ACIM) and we are meant to be the face of God on planet earth.

Not My Ego?

The ego is nothing more than a part of your belief about yourself (ACIM, p. 67).

The ego is the part of the mind that believes your existence is defined by separation (p. 69).

A Course in Miracles first targeted the ego as the false personality we constructed through the experience of entering a body. Veiled to forget our spirit identity in order to experience matter, we felt vulnerable, birthing fear and duality. Forgetting our Spirit Self, we created a sense of self as defined by our caretakers. As a blank slate, we took in the energy of our environment and interactions through our senses without any discrimination, for about the first seven years of life. This early programming became our primary operating system.

We all have egos. The recognition that the ego is not who we are is our **first step** to freedom. Fighting the ego doesn't work. We formed the ego to help us survive in the body, forgetting that our non-physical Source is more powerful. The ego has taken over the mind through our *belief in separation,* especially with religion. The ego is the voice of fear as contrasted to the Voice for Love, our true identity. This is a theme throughout ACIM.

To give up the ego identification, I needed to have an ego of my own! This came about with the releasing of the beliefs of my parents in my session with Mayama, and by embracing my right to choose for myself. This was only the beginning of discovering my own soul identity. This delayed process would put me at odds with those who had developed a sense of self in childhood, which is the norm, especially for boys. My experience is that some women have a delayed sense of self due to dependency on male approval.

Individuation Comes Before Oneness Can be experienced

Experiencing the sense of self as the individuated ego, apart from parental beliefs, is a pre-requisite for letting it go. It is important to distinguish ego from the soul expression of our creation. All souls are part of the One, and each is simply a unique expression of the One Self. Merging into oneness isn't the loss of individual expression as some fear; it is fear that implies separation and feeds the ego or the false self. The soul's unique expression involves our gifts, known or unknown, which we are meant to develop and express to the *Glory of God*, the bliss of the One Self. As One, we are like a diamond with many faces.

Choose to let the Higher Self be in charge and question the first egoic thoughts which come to mind. The ego automatically resists. It is the voice of fear and intends to be protective. Ignore it and listen to the second voice, the voice for love. The Voice of Spirit is usually soft and gentle, unless in an emergency situation, where it can be heard as an inner command.

A Move to the Unknown, My Next Transformation

Moving to Kauai became another act of differentiating from my former patterns and relationships. Trusting guidance was imperative. The door to profound change was open and I stepped into it. My purpose would unfold—there was nothing more to hold me back.

PART II

WILL BE GATHERED

CHAPTER 15

SEPTEMBER 1998 MOVE TO KAUAI

Hale Kupuna

Flying into the Lihue airport for the first time was truly a step into the unknown. Yet I knew this was home. I was excited. Two residents of Hale Kupuna met me—Lily's mother, and one who became my neighbor, remaining so since our first meeting and still a spiritual sister to me. I felt totally welcome and at home. Lily's mother was a thoughtful woman who supplied dishes, silverware, toilet paper, etc. My spiritual sister, Miriam, was a garage sale enthusiast. In my first week I found a sturdy couch to sleep on, matching chairs and table, and other items I am still enjoying.

Hale Kupuna is a housing complex for low-income seniors. Its interracial mixture mirrors Kauai, a meeting place for people from every corner of the world. The *Aloha* spirit is a beautiful preview of Heaven on Earth. Along with some local residents, many like myself from off island, are called to Kauai for personal reasons.

Pathways of Light

My ordination at Pathways prepared me to teach their courses based on ACIM, perform marriages, facilitate Self-Awakening groups, and ordinations. Within three years of my ordination, and after moving to Kauai, I performed weddings, facilitated a Self-Awakening group, and later ordained "Erin." Then I found myself drifting away from using the POL material. I pursued building a coaching practice until the writing bug became more persistent, along with my physical challenges.

Key Decision

One of many new experiences was with a couple, "Ed and Mary." Mary was a large woman who did healing touch, and Ed was a quiet, small man whose gift was accessing the Akashic records. This was new information to me. The Akashic records are a body of information about every soul on the planet. To access these records takes a gift of intuitive knowing given to those with a strong desire and intention. It is another resource for knowing one's Self and purpose here.

In a session with them, Mary would do healing touch while Ed would get in touch with my Akashic record. He told me I had "one more incarnation, but was at choice." My incarnation cycle could be completed in this lifetime. I decided then to complete karmic issues, and fulfill my purpose in this life.

Purification Precedes Purpose

This decision to fulfill my purpose helped me become aware of the role of purification in self-healing, already a focus in my life. Twelve Rays have been described as qualities of the Divine. Though all the Rays are important to the whole, we each are usually identified with one of the Rays. The Sixth Ray of Purification seemed to be my major purpose in this life. Purification is a necessary focus in our preparation for the New Earth. Yet, later I realized that purification was preparation for a very important contribution, the work of this lifetime, my last.

A Course in Miracles has much to say about purification. The aim of the course is about *removing the blocks to Love's Presence, our natural inheritance*. Realizing our Divine Essence while in the body (embodiment) is the soul's purpose of every person on the planet. The fifty principles of miracles give a greatly expanded meaning over our idea that a miracle is a spectacle that defies belief. A shift in perception is a miracle. As we reframe what the ego defines as "bad" into a valuable lesson, gratitude replaces the pain. This is a miracle.

When we are coming from Essence, miracles are natural. Miracles are habits defined as expressions of love. Thoughts from our spiritual level of experience, or our physical level, produce effects accordingly. Miracles transcend the body.

Miracles are always *affirmations of rebirth… they undo the past in the present, and thus release the future. Forgiveness does that. Forgiveness is the privilege of the forgiven.*

Miracles are everyone's right but purification is necessary first is the 7th principle in the list of 50 principles in chapter one of ACIM. This purification is basically the undoing of fear, the voice of the ego. This requires a daily practice, as we are all bombarded with fear thoughts from others and from our egoic minds. We can affirm our perfection when we accept our spirit identity and deny body identification. *Miracles reawaken the awareness that the spirit, not the body, is the altar of truth.* Some additional quotes from the 50 principles will help clarify:

#24   You are a miracle, capable of creating in the likeness of your Creator. Everything else is your own nightmare and does not exist. Only the creations of light are real.

#25   Miracles are part of an interlocking chain of forgiveness, when completed is the Atonement. Atonement works all the time and in all dimensions of time.

#33   Miracles honor you because you are lovable. They dispel illusions about yourself and perceive the light in you. They thus atone for your errors by freeing you from your nightmares. By releasing your mind from the imprisonment of your illusions, they restore your sanity.

#37   A miracle is a correction introduced into false thinking by me (Jesus). It acts as a catalyst, breaking up erroneous perception and reorganizing it properly. This places you under the Atonement principle, where perception is healed. Until this has occurred, knowledge of the Divine Order is impossible.

This allowing of a new perception happens with our willingness to see an experience with the vision of a forgiving heart, which allows the Holy Spirit/Voice for Love to be heard. This Voice is the voice of Jesus, who promised us a comforter before he left his body.

#38   The Voice for Love, *the Holy Spirit is the mechanism of miracles.*

CHAPTER 16

INTRODUCTION TO PAST LIVES

In my session with Ed and Mary, Ed said that in my last lifetime I had married an alcoholic who ultimately left me. I reflected on that as I noticed I was attracted to a new male resident in my complex. There was a familiar energy about him. I MT that he was my alcoholic husband in my last lifetime.

"Stu" and I connected through my asking a "fix-it" favor, and our relationship soon became sexual, including massages he loved to give and I loved to receive. We went on a memorable kayak trip together. He regularly went to AA meetings as he was an acknowledged alcoholic. The relationship ended with him having a slip and bursting into my apartment while drunk. Stu and I had no contact after that, and he reportedly continued to drink periodically until a crisis occurred which required a rescue and medical treatment. He went into a special program for addiction. Thus began my series of encounters with men from past lives.

As Ascension became my Intention, I have been introduced to many past lives through people I meet. Many are in my soul family and were partners and family members. I would encounter some whose energy was negative towards me, and through Intuitive Inquiry I learned I had a hurtful experience with them in a past life. Then I could use a form of Ho'oponopono as well as the Tap and Breathe I Am (TaBIA) process. As I briefly mentioned previously, Ho'oponopono is a forgiveness process that shifts the energy for both the participant and non-participant. TaBIA focuses on releasing

Physical, Emotional, Mental and Spiritual (PEMS) **blocks to Love's Presence, our natural inheritance,** as phrased in ACIM. These processes will be introduced later in depth.

ACIM, "A Better Meeting Place"

"Ernie" was a jovial and personable man in his fifties from an ACIM study group I started to attend. There was no past-life connection. My aware ego felt this was a good connection. We were on a group outing to Princeville to hear a speaker on Huna (Hawaiian spirituality). It was a long drive for me to go from Kalaheo to Princeville for these monthly meetings. He offered a ride from his place half-way in between, which I accepted. Then he offered a sleep-over and I hedged. Yet the next time, I came prepared to stay over, which delighted him. My choice came out of a feeling of scarcity and the logic of being with someone with similar spiritual interests. Ernie was well-liked and popular and a very faithful attendee to his AA meetings.

One of our adventures I can't forget was in response to my request to see a non-public beach. As we were driving on dirt backroads we saw a number of parked cars. "Oh, oh, a chicken fight!" he said. "Do you want to see it? It is brutal." I had heard about these illegal chicken fights that went on secretly, a Filipino custom. Still new to the island, I saw this as an opportunity to witness some underground culture, so I said, "Yes."

The man with the betting monies was a business owner, well known to Ernie. He anxiously asked Ernie, "Are you going to report this?" Ernie said "No." I was apprehensive but also curious. Ernie described the raising and training of these roosters' fighting instincts for cock fights. Then he told about the attachment of sharp knives to each cock's legs before the owners drop their roosters into a wire pen. The "sport" is for one rooster to fight another, until death. I felt guilt in being a witness to this and yet I knew my feelings could not stop the mayhem. It wasn't long before I asked to leave. Wanting to withhold judgment, I wondered if this tradition, prevalent in so many cultures, was an outlet which tempered the male instinct for relationship violence when feelings could not be expressed.

The overnights included sexual activity. His excess weight was a turn off, especially as pleasuring him was the major focus. When I said, "I can't do this anymore!" he was angry and there were no more dates. With sex his only interest in me, I felt I was simply another sex object. I also realized **nice, spiritually-focused men may still have the patriarchal attitude** that justifies using women only for their own sexual satisfaction.

In my anger at myself, I became aware of ways I used Ernie to feed my need to feel cared for by a man. His spiritual connections were no guarantee of genuine caring or intimacy. This became another learning experience.

CHAPTER 17

JESHUA

During the last 13 years I have learned to communicate with my observer/Higher Self and Holy Spirit. Through *A Course in Miracles*, I learned that Jesus/Jeshua is the Holy Spirit, so I image him always with me. On my wall is a large print of a channeled painting of Jeshua by a French female artist, a reminder of His presence.

Though the church of my early life emphasized, "Christ in you, the Hope of Glory," "Christ" referred exclusively to Jesus of Nazareth as the One and Only Son. In ACIM, and later in *The Jeshua Letters*, channeled through Jon Marc Hammer, Jeshua refers to John 5:23: *That all men should honor the Son, as they honor the Father. He that honoreth not the Son, honoreth not the Father which hath sent him.* We, "the Son," are the creation of the creator. As one with our creator, we participated in our own creation!

Jeshua, speaking through Jon Marc Hammer in the *Way of the Heart* series, states: *It is with great demand for attention that I speak now of this teaching. For those who build their temples and enter therein, only to give supplication to an image of Me created in the minds of Man, thereby thinking they 'honoreth the Son,' be it clearly known that they honor Him not. The Son is one, without a second. What does this mean? I am not the Son and you a 'second' which must be saved. I am not above you; I am the Son, as also you Are. For the Son dwells within the heart of all, whether in this universe or another, unlimited, without boundary. How, then, can you honor me, without honoring the Son within yourself, the Son that you Are?*

This is a profound teaching, reversing my fundamentalist programming. "The Son" is his generic term for both male and female. With this awareness, it became easier to look at my own image in the mirror and say, "I love you…an incarnation of the 'I Am Presence' I am coming to recognize as the 'Son of God'" This is blasphemy to traditional Christian thinking. And, so freeing.

Who is Jeshua?

In *The Jeshua Channelings* by Pamela Kribbe, Jeshua states, *I am the one who has been among you and who you have come to know as Jesus. I am not the Jesus of your church tradition or the Jesus of your religious writings. I am Jeshua ben Joseph.*

Jeshua lived as a human whose soul chose to live as Jesus, his future Self. This energy was difficult for him to hold in his body. He grew into Christ consciousness while on earth. Christ is Source energy. "***I came too early.***" Incarnated souls could not really integrate the Christ energy with their psychological and physical reality. *I do not preach and I do not judge.* He came as Jesus to demonstrate the vast power of Love.

He implores us to free him from the church's version of him as Jesus, and wants to be accepted as family, a friend, or brother. In explaining his identity on earth, Jeshua says that Jesus was the expression of his future self that was *the result of the infusion of Christ energy into the physical and psychological reality of Jeshua.*

The law of duality brought in a powerful reaction of the dark, which we are also seeing today with the intervention of increasing Light on the planet. Jesus came to awaken the lightworker souls on earth. Lightworkers were veiled and had karmic burdens to resolve.

The Message Jesus Intended

In *The Jeshua Channelings*, he says: *Among humans, there is a persistent belief that everything is predestined by some divine plan. Behind this belief is the notion of a dominant, omniscient God. This notion is false.*

Chapter 17: Jeshua

There is no outside authority but the probabilities resulting from our inner choices. Jeshua speaks of a collective energy of light, which made the decision to send Jesus. This collective energy of light is *an angelic realm deeply connected to humanity and earth,* it helped create.

Jeshua states: *My message is that the Christ energy is present in all human beings as a seed. When you look up to me as some kind of authority, you have misunderstood my message.* By this, Jeshua means that we are to go within and listen to the authority of the Christ energy already present. *I wished to invite you to believe in yourself, to find the truth within your own heart and not to believe any authority outside of you.* The official Christian religion has made Jesus an authority figure to worship and obey. *Quite the opposite of what I intended…to show you that you can be a living Christ yourself…return my humanness to me.*

Unlearning and Correcting the Patriarchal Distortion

Everything Scattered Will Be Gathered involves unlearning the ways of the Patriarchy, moving from the head to the heart, activating the thymus, the 'I Am' point of the heart chakra. That 'I Am' point is the seed of the Christ energy. Awakening our true identity which Jesus demonstrated requires removing the blocks in the emotional heart through forgiveness.

The bodymind has been programmed with much distortion and egoic perceptions of traumatic events. Purification or clearing this bodymind of the many emotional, mental, and spiritual viruses that plague us is necessary to fully activate the Christ seed within us. Purification, to the fundamentalist, is more about emphasis on separation, as in, "I'm a sinner, unworthy, deserving of punishment," which fosters the *belief in separation.*

Embodiment is the process of surrendering to the *I Am Presence,* the seed of Christ within us. It is allowing the Christ-Mind to rule the body instead of the ego. It is the opening of the portal to our Divine Essence by healing the emotional heart and listening to the still, small voice within us, known as the Holy Spirit, the Voice for Love.

Jeshua's personal gift

The TaBIA process was given to me as an Ascension tool to move out of the ego/mind-based consciousness in the head, into our core identity of unconditional love in the spiritual heart. Our core identity emerges when we heal the emotional heart through forgiving everything that has occurred, including in past lives, and our choice to be separate. The TaBIA practice has activated my DNA that was de-activated before I incarnated.

The Heart Awakening now occurring on the planet is the activation of DNA strands, which were de-activated before our incarnation. That de-activation by the dark forces is no longer occurring, and the "new" children are coming in with higher vibrations and spiritual gifts.

Use of Surrender

Accepting a schedule of interrupted sleep in order to write has been a learning experience. When I go to the computer NOT with the determination of the ego, but rather, *surrendered* to my commitment to purpose/intention, I am empowered to focus and stay awake. I thank my non-physical writing team for their presence. My energy increases as I move through a litany of appreciation for the blessings in my life. Gratitude raises my vibrations.

Embracing our Higher Self is a form of surrender. As we embrace our purpose, we are empowered and given directives. The ego resists. I hear prompts from within for quieting the ego—engaging or fighting the ego doesn't work. It is helpful to use TaBIA to release confusion, lack of focus, or self-doubt.

CHAPTER 18

THE WAY OF THE HEART

Way of the Heart family

In 2007, I was immediately drawn to a group who gathered to listen to Jon Marc's taped series of the *Way of the Heart* teachings of Jesus/Jeshua. They have become my spiritual family, meeting almost weekly. A channeler of Jeshua and founding member of the group, Peggy, was told the lineage would come together—the lineage refers to those who were connected to Jesus in his lifetime on earth. Intuition and resonance draws individuals to the group. The group has gone through Jon Marc Hammer's taped series of 35 sessions several times over the past ten years. Other Jeshua-related channelings have also been shared and discussed.

In ACIM, the Teacher's Manual reminds those on this journey of awakening that we teach as we learn our lessons in the curriculum of life which is set up according to **what you think you are, and what you believe the relationship to others is to you**. Everyone follows the world's curriculum until they change their mind. We become a teacher of God, not by believing in Him, but by seeing another as our Self. That is the message intended by Jesus. "You are as I am. I am as you are."

In the development of Trust in this Journey of Awakening, there are six stages we go through. Essentially, they are: Undoing, Sorting out, Letting Go, Settling Down (when we are assured of attracting companions to go with us before the next period), Unsettling, and the final period of Achievement, the stage of Real Peace. **Here is Heaven's**

state, fully reflected. It is the attraction of "mighty companions" I wish to illustrate with two channeled messages shared by friends in the Way of the Heart family.

The following might be called "a spiritual practice to build your core of calm."

Sananda/Magdalene, to Peggy

Dear Ones,

There is so much information passing through our realities these days, and it seems to be greatly accelerating. I would like to speak with you here, as these fear-based, yet sometimes true events may be forthcoming. We would invite you to go inside and feel the core of calm that you have been building there. We have been calling it "Holding your Resonance" and what is this resonance but a song, a scene in nature, an event, a place…

It is any of these which have given you a feeling that took you beyond the feeling of love. Can you recall that now, and remember how it made you feel? Practice ahead of a time when you may need it, to return to that one feeling…then when you are in a stressful situation or the unfamiliar suddenly appears before you, it is then that you will find holding this resonance will sustain your vibrational field. When you feel your field dropping back down into an old vibration that no longer works for you, use your resonance to sustain you.

Remember you are not alone. Remember that you promised to be here on Earth at this time of the Great Awakening, and remember: We love you, and Love is all there is.

When aware of having a bliss moment, cherish it, appreciate it, and add it to your vibrational field of resonance.

Princess of Maldek, *A Visionary Exploration of the Fifth Realm*, by Lisa Raphael

The purpose of Life is Life itself. Given that there is no past and no future, that space and time are illusions, that the interchange between densities and dimensions is an ongoing, continual process, that Source

Chapter 18: The Way Of The Heart

itself, the All That Is, is in constant flux, expanding, becoming through eternity, there can be no purpose in the sense of a goal, for a goal implies a specific knowable destination. Life's purpose can only be to live consciously and humbly in the unknowable present, which contains the past and future, and to trust the unpredictable flow of the forces of Creation wherever or however these move within and outside of us.

Jeshua's teachings from *The Way of the Heart series*

The Way of the Heart, The Way of Transformation, and The Way of Knowing, 35 tapes in all, channeled through Jon Marc Hammer, were recorded live over a 3 year period, 1995 through 1997. Jeshua notes that, "Just listening to these tapes with a 'little bit of willingness' provides all that any soul requires to fully awaken into 'Christ Mind'. These tapes along with the transcripts are the source of material designed to shift us out of our limited beliefs into new experiences through the refocus of our attention.

Your experience is always the effect of where you choose to focus the attention of your consciousness, its Self being unlimited forever. Jeshua reminds us that each reader or listener will create their own meaning—you "hear" *according to the perceptions that **you** have chosen to place value on.* We are here in an illusion of separation, the ego's perspective to make choices that create experiences. It we don't like what we have attracted, we choose again. The soul, after many unfulfilling choices, may choose to listen to the "still, small voice," which is always whispering a call to Peace, Truth and Love.

When our initial experience of life in a body turns into identification with the lower vibrational frequencies of material attachments, Jeshua says *it is the seriousness of the mind, which is the creation of ego.* This seriousness holds the vibrations of experiences you no longer want. You can choose to withdraw your value of the things you don't want. Recognize the value of *surrender* to the untapped wisdom within you. You begin trusting the invisible, the thought of perfect Love in form, what we are created to be. We are to communicate with that spark of Divine Light.

Jeshua says our duality has made the *split mind,* which has resulted in endless mind chatter from the noisy ego. Awareness of the ego as *not me* can invite the real me to emerge. "Shut up already!" is one response to the ego chatter, which can give the 'I Am' a chance to be heard.

When we identify with the insanity we see in our world rather than identifying with the Mind of Christ, we lose our innocence. Jeshua emphasizes **all events are neutral and we are free to see them any way we choose.** This neutrality avoids judgment. *Separation is an illusion.* It is fear (ego) that prompts this feeling of separation, reinforced by the Patriarchy.

The First Step on the *Way of the Heart*

Allow into the mind Jeshua's words: *Nothing, which you are experiencing is caused by anything outside of you.* We only experience our perception of the effects of our choice. This awareness removes victim consciousness. My difficulty with this is the ego's use of it to deny compassion and blame the victim. This truth's intent is rather to enlist the observer mind, to note without judgment the experience we are having. When we allow the interpretation of the event to come from the Voice for Love, our perception shifts. Our soul longs for meaning in this seemingly meaningless world. It keeps us on the Path. In our willingness to suspend judgment and allow not-knowingness, we cultivate trust that the answer will come—not from our egoic mind but from a peaceful place.

It is *that mind that trusts the Source of its creation that allows all things, trusts all things, embraces all things and transcends all things.* Jeshua describes the humility the first step requires with these words for us to say, "*I have done all this, I must undo it. But I have no idea how I did this. Therefore, I must surrender to something else.*" What a blow to the ego!

I encounter many who are seeking enlightenment as if it is an event. It is, rather, a process of Awakening to the truth of who we are. We are called to remember. Jesus never forgot who he is, and is now sharing the Way of the Heart to help us remember.

Cultivate deep love and respect for yourself, for you are not here to fix the world. We are to love ourselves wholly by purifying the mind and cultivating *a state of consciousness in which the Love of God is unimpeded.*

The Way of the Heart is the final pathway that any soul can enter. Jeshua is committed to teach us and enable us to live on this pathway, and states, "*I am merely to be your brother!*" He declares, *You are one with Source*, even as he was. He calls us to *willingness* to heal every obstacle to being the Presence of Love, possible only by accepting and loving yourself. Created in the image of God, we were given *infinite and perfect freedom.*

CHAPTER 19

INTRODUCTION TO CHANNELING

I was introduced to channeling by Ariana five years after coming to Kauai. Through my readings about this prophesied time on the planet, I have learned that there are many enlightened souls who have returned to earth to help us stop the self-destruction of an insane world. Living in Canada, Ariana would come to Kauai six months of the year where she held weekly gatherings on channeling. Word-of-mouth brought in those interested in connecting to the spirit world we forgot.

ARIANA SHERAN was born in North Battleford, Saskatchewan, Canada, in 1936. She was a secretary who learned to channel on her own by using her computer. In September of 1987, Cloverleaf Connection was spiritually born, and from that time on, newsletters, books, workshops, and retreats have been continuously offered to people of like mind. Ariana, and participants who have taken Cloverleaf workshops, are inter-dimensional communicators who channel messages of enlightenment and assistance for humanity from the Ashtar Command, the Spiritual Hierarchy and Ascended Masters.

Part of her mission was to connect with souls who had died suddenly and were stuck in the *astral plane*. The astral plane refers to a state of consciousness where a person is taken by surprise, and is sometimes unaware of leaving the body. The individual is not prepared to move on into the Spirit world. Individuals in the astral plane still have the thoughts and feelings they had on earth. Limited consciousness can keep them there for a time, and some get stuck.

Ariana's sessions to release these souls became known as Rescue Circles. Checking in with friends, family members, or beloved pets that died could be requested by any group member.

We released two of Kauai's eleven drowning victims from early 2013 who were stuck in the astral plane. My Inquiry process revealed the two that were stuck. Helping stuck spirits move on into the heaven world is the purpose of the Rescue Circle. Those who had become familiar with channeling could be involved as guided.

Specific non-physical entities assist Ariana and can be called upon in the contact process. Jael, the son of Ariana's friend, had overdosed and died. Part of Jael's mission in the Spirit world was to connect with others who died from overdosing. When Ariana asked to contact that person, Jael would respond. Ariana has a whole team of helpers in the nonphysical world.

My daughter Kari's husband, Jim, had overdosed and died. I gave a brief description of Jim and asked Ariana to contact him. Jael responded and made contact with Jim, who thought he was sleeping and could not wake up. When told to look for the light and go for it, he was released from the astral plane into the angelic realm.

Channeling as a Co-creative Process

Pamela Kribbe, in her book, *The Jeshua Channelings,* describes channeling and her meeting with Jeshua. Jeshua tells us channeling is "…a co-operation between a human being and a non-physical entity who acts as teacher…. The channel's mindset, awareness, and vocabulary greatly influence what comes through…. The channel is the receiver, the vessel, and therefore co-creator of the material." What is important in assessing its value is to ask, "Does it uplift, enlighten? Does it help you to love yourself more?"

Pamela was accustomed to getting messages from other spirit entities—meeting Jeshua occurred as a different energy coming through. Investigating by going into a trance state, she "saw the name *Jeshua ben Joseph*" in front of her inner eye. The ego promptly raised doubts and questions. The feeling of familiarity and inner recognition, however, helped her to accept this new connection. In my experience, a sense of familiarity usually points to knowing the person in a past lifetime. Pamela was a relative and follower of Jesus in his lifetime here. Through Intuitive Inquiry, I have discovered she was also a Magdalene.

Presenting himself as Jeshua instead of "Jesus" is his way of making it clear that he "was not the personality manufactured by the Bible and by tradition." Pamela describes his energy as "centering, grounding, and very powerful, devoid of sentimentality and drama." Jeshua informed her that his series of messages through her was especially meant for lightworkers, to help them "wake up and realize who they are." When awakened, they can help others move toward a heart-based consciousness.

Jeshua's Words on Channeling

Pamela describes herself as shy and holding back, quite terrified of becoming a public figure. Jeshua shapes his messages according to what the specific channeler needs to hear. Even so this message powerfully describes his preferred relationship to us:

Channeling is a way of getting closer to yourself with the help of another, a non-physical being. This being temporarily plays the role of teacher. The energy of the teacher helps you get to a deeper level of yourself. The teacher's energy lifts you out of the fears that keep your own light veiled.

A teacher shows you your own light…is more aware of your light than you are… As soon as this light, your inner knowing, is accessible to yourself, the teacher becomes superfluous. You are then able to channel your own light. The teacher does not have to act as a bridge anymore between you and your higher Self.

I am reminding you for a while of your own light. I mirror your greatness to you in the shape of Jeshua ben Joseph. In me, you see yourself, your Christ Self, but you do not realize this fully yet. I am like a frame of reference to you; my energy serves a beacon. I help you get more deeply acquainted with your own Christ self. It will slowly move to the foreground and I will move to the background. This is all right. It is as it should be. Don't forget: in this relationship, I am there for you; you are not there for me. I am not the aim, but the means. The rebirth of Christ is the awakening of your Christ Self, not mine.

I act according to what serves your greater Self. My aim is that you make me superfluous. When you channel me, do not try to make yourself small or invisible. I wish that you make yourself bigger, that you feel your true strength flow out of you and shine upon the world.

A teacher points at the road, but it is you who walk it. After a while, you find yourself walking alone, having left the teacher behind. This is a grand and sacred moment. The teacher will stay with you—will live on in your heart as an inner presence, but the separate figure will disappear.

We stay connected, but as you grow, you will see me less and less, and want to call upon me less, as a separate being. I will slowly become part of your own energy. And at some point, you will not know me as separate from you anymore. This will show that you have truly heard and seen me.

Forgiveness Beyond the Grave

Later, I asked for my father, Peter, who had died suddenly in the pulpit just before I met Chuck. In the apartment where we had our meeting, a lovely plant prompted a compliment from Ariana. After meditation, Ariana laughed and said a fairy had contacted her, the deva of the plant she admired. When Ariana asked her name, she said, "Just call me Lilia!" Lilia described the invisible devas and elementals in abundance on Kauai, from the blades of grass to the mountains. My father's work in the spirit world was with nature, which he so loved on earth. His interest attracted the devic kingdom of fairies, devas, and elementals. It was both delightful and very healing for me. Peter came through with the assistance of Kaatan in the spirit world.

CHAPTER 20

HEALING WORDS OF LOVE ACROSS THE VEIL

Spiritual Revelations Can Reprogram Belief

Fairy: *I don't know what is happening here, but I am feeling part of your group. I am one who tends the plants and am the main deva for this little plant on the coffee table.* [Giggling throughout!] *When you admire a plant, it really appreciates your interest. It is exhilarated! We, the fairies, are the spiritual energy that appreciates it. The plants just go along with it. They don't have the same kind of consciousness that we do.*

Hawaii's Devic Kingdom

Lilia, the fairy, goes on to say, *Can you imagine how many of us are on this island that you call Kauai, the Garden Island in Hawaii? There are trillions of us and we are tending this place of beauty. We are tending every place in nature—every stone, every leaf, every blade of grass, every flower; we are here.*

Some of us have much more spiritual energy than others. Ariana has been admiring this tree out here [referring to a large eucalyptus tree nearby]. *The spiritual energy tending this tree is a powerful being—like the tree—and as time goes on, that deva becomes very strong in love and joy. When you hug that tree you experience that love. There are other beings connected to the water in the streams that go by, and even the air. You are connected to this energy, breathing it and drinking it. We hope that the joy of all life gets through to you.*

You have a beautiful island in the ocean. Many devas are looking after it. You have one head honcho living in Mt. Wai`ale`ale. This deva is overseeing the spiritual care of every tree and every flower. It is an interconnectedness that is very tremendous when you expand your thoughts. The same holds true for all of the islands in the Pacific.

All of these main devas are connected to an even more powerful energy that oversees all of the Hawaiian Islands.

Creating Spiritual Energy To Assist Nature

Fairy: *I want to tell you where this spiritual energy comes from. When a person crosses over to the Spirit World as did your father, Petra, they go through certain processing and when they are all clear they come to a place where they ask, 'What can I do now?' One of the things they can do over here is duplicate their energy.*

When someone really loves nature and the outdoors, then one of the ways they can duplicate themselves is to bring in more devas and fairies.

Ariana: Your dad loved fishing; he loved the lakes. I am getting holy showers here. [Holy showers are the lovely tingling feelings that mean Spirit is giving a confirmation.]

Fairy: *He learned how to duplicate his energy and he gives this energy to the Devic Kingdom. It is probable he duplicated it many times.*

Peter's Mission Within The Devic Kingdom

After giving my father's name, I said he died in 1953 on New Year's Day while he was preaching in the pulpit of a country church near Veblen, South Dakota.

Fairy: *Your father has been working with devas for many years after he finished his processing. This has been his most joyous way to spend his life over there. It is difficult to explain; it is done with the mind. The Devic Kingdom can connect through telepathy. He has been doing this a very long time working with devas in very large places. A whole mountain range can affect the weather and growing conditions of the planet. This whole thing is a process.*

Ariana: Which Mountains? ...They are giving me a picture idea of George Washington in the mountains.

Chapter 20: Healing Words Of Love Across The Veil

Petra: That is Mount Rushmore in South Dakota, the state we lived in. This place is a work of art where the faces of four presidents were carved into the mountain…

Ariana confirmed his work with a large mountain area in South Dakota. Lilia says the work of fairies is done *in cooperation with those who have passed on from your planet…* Then Lilia asks for questions, and gives answers to several from the group. She explained: *Fairies are not depicted correctly. They are energy… little balls of light. There are not many devas where there is pollution.*

A question came up as to what could be done about the US military's test-bombing in the Marshall Islands which left so much destruction in its wake.

Lilia: *It is through prayer. Now you can visualize the chain of action from the Spirit World. It would give impetus to Petra's father, who could direct energy there. Prayer is as powerful as my connection with Petra right now. Many are affected.*

Miriam: Was there any positive purpose with those bombing tests?

Lilia: *It was an abomination! The universal energies of Light do not agree with what went on there. It was a grabbing of power by human beings but remember, there are no accidents in your world or in the Spirit World. Things like that which happen are lessons for the people.*

Petra Rediscovers Her Father

Kataan: *I have come to tell you of your father, Petra. Because of the circumstances of his death, it would be helpful for your peace of mind. Your father died suddenly, as you know. Sudden death is a difficult transition from the Third to the Fourth Dimension. A spirit can very often be caught in a never-never land of sorts.* [The astral plane.] *This happened to your father. He didn't stay there for long because of the prayers of the people in the church and his family. He was able to tune in and move on. Some souls that are lost are not able to tune in.*

With your father, he was caught in a circle of concern and went over and over his death until the prayers came through to him. After about four months, he was able to go into the Spirit World. Then be never stopped—he went through his transition beautifully. He remembered being in Spirit before. It was a time of retribution and clearing his karma. He did an excellent job of that. In Earth terms, it took about a year before he began his mission with nature.

He is very happy sticking to this work and has duplicated himself many times. His work is captivating his entire attention, whereas some spirits go from one thing to another. Mother Nature on Earth is such a huge entity and there are many opportunities.

Peter is thrilled to know you asked for him and would be delighted to be in touch with you through a passing thought, a spiritual touch, or through writing. He is inviting you; he holds out his hand to you."

After my expression of thanks, Kataan continued: *He wants to thank you for your love of the family. Even as a little girl, you had the family on your lap! He realizes a lot was expected of you and apologizes for any load that was too heavy for you. He sends you his love. He wants you to know he has touched in ever since he left to make sure his little girl is well. He wants you to know you will always be his little girl.* (This pulled up deep emotion within me in healing tears.)

Kataan affirmed my request to speak to him.

Loving Reunion Of Father And Daughter

Petra: Today, Dad, because of the message I heard from Lilia, I have a much different picture of you now. I love nature too and do thank you for encouraging us to swim and enjoy nature. I swim in the ocean because of your encouragement. The negative belief system I took in is not your reality. I am grateful we can have this connection now.

Peter (through Ariana): *It is a blessing. So many situations of the heart could be cleared up by this type of communication. Now as a resident of the Spirit world, Petra, I would encourage you to channel.*

Chapter 20: Healing Words Of Love Across The Veil

Petra: Knowing that you are there to assist me, I know it is possible.

Peter: *Yes it is possible. Every day the spiritual vibrations are heightening on the planet. Awareness is coming to the people. I would invite all of you present here to put some energy into channeling whether it is with a spiritual teacher like Sananda or with people in the Spirit World whom you love. They are all ready for communication with you, written or spoken.*

Petra: Another question. Are you in touch with my brother, Luke?

Peter: *Yes of course I am in touch with Luke, and with your son.*

Petra: Kirk. He is still living.

Peter: *You are wondering about the connection between those two. They are in the same soul family.*

I asked about my brother Daniel, Luke's twin, and Ariana said he was in some sort of denial and couldn't be reached. It reinforced the awareness that receptivity is important for the bodymind to hear spirit messages.

Butterflies As A Symbol Of Transition And The Earth Mission

Petra: Can you tell me about Rose, my mother? She died at ninety-three in 1993. She took your death very hard.

Peter: *Once one leaves the planet, the play-acting is over and you come home, in a sense. You see the big picture. Once she returned to Spirit, we were immediately reunited. It's a friendship thing. By the way, she is working with butterflies. Many people work with very specific parts of nature. She is working with butterflies.*

Petra: Wonderful! I really appreciate that; they are my favorite symbol of transformation.

Peter: *This is why she is working with them… We are very aware of what is going on over there and that we are all going to be together again without your experiencing death.*

Petra: I am open to that.

Peter: *You are getting help from other worlds… I am definitely a part of that and so is your mother. I am so glad we could have this conversation.*

When I asked, "Can I share about our visit with my brothers?" Peter cautioned me to be very careful and diplomatic, choosing a time when they are receptive. He emphasized *sharing with Joy*.

Peter: *I thank you for asking about me, Petra—this is the reason I could come through.*

Petra: Thank you for the gift of your presence. You have given me so much. I have wondered if you had reincarnated, but you are too busy! (Laughter!)

Peter: *I am not intending to reincarnate. The Earth Mission is totally intriguing and I am part of it here. I thank you, Petra, for holding the vision of love and light in all your interactions with people, friends and family.*

The conversation continued with my sharing the choosing of my middle name, meaning "rock" like Peter, becoming "molten rock" like lava. He loved it and went on to thank me for asking for him and to stay in touch, essentially saying we would *have to develop some kind of energetic knowing…you could feel me in meditation or I could slip into your writing.*

Peter also told the group, *Do not fear the Spirit World.* Peter closed our conversation by thanking Kataan for bringing him through, and Ariana for being a willing channel, and again declaring his love for me, along with love from my mother

Except for my summary parts this was spoken through Ariana Sheran in Kauai on

March 25, 2004, and distributed by Cloverleaf Connection.

My Response to Meeting my Father in Spirit

This had been a very tearful and profound healing session for me. After the very interesting message about the spirits present in nature—by a fairy, no less—I was amazed upon hearing of my father's work with devas, weather patterns, and the Mount Rushmore mountains in South Dakota. It reflected a tremendous change in consciousness from the father I knew, yet was consistent with his love of nature while here on the planet. When I heard my father's compassionate words of love, it brought a profound healing of the years of female repression via fundamentalist teachings that I had been so identified with.

When he asked in 2006 to write a letter to my one close childhood friend, "Rene," who had chastised me for departing from the belief system he taught, I was truly amazed. It was a beautiful gift to the growing awareness of my purpose on the planet to bring Light to the distorted message of Christian fundamentalism. Peter's personal testimony of his experience of transformation from a "hellfire and damnation" preacher to an assistant with Pan in nature, serves to inspire me and others. It is healing and forgiveness from beyond the grave.

"Peter Pan" has a very personal meaning for me, now. I recognize my purpose in partnering with my father, Peter, to bring a new message, "From Heart Attack to Heart Awakened. " He is doing what he truly enjoys from the heart, a lesson to all of us.

Ariana's Comments

"This channeling has a long and wondrous history. It facilitated a major awakening in Petra. She will be forever grateful for this channeling and those from her other family members. It came in 2004 when we were wandering around the island from one person's house to another to host the channelings. This day we were in Kalaheo. The whole thing was spontaneous and unplanned, joyful and, for Petra, highly emotional. While fairies danced, healing occurred between dad and daughter, across the dimensions." (Used by permission of Ariana Sheran and *Cloverleaf Connection*.)

CHAPTER 21

A TRANSMISSION FROM MY FATHER

A Special Childhood Friend

I was in the fourth grade when we moved to a very small rural town in Minnesota. "Rene," a sweet quiet girl in the class, became my best friend and the sister I wanted. We shared everything. Her parents were members of my father's church and were faithful attendees. We were in confirmation classes together and Bible camps. I spent a lot of time in her home, a much quieter and more peaceful place than mine. Scholastically, we also shared honors. She was the one most popular and became a cheerleader. Her gentle confidence contrasted with and helped balance my feisty self-consciousness.

We roomed together when we first got to college, but she eventually quit college while I continued with a five-year nursing program. Rene married a seminarian who became a missionary. She had eight children and in every way became a dutiful wife and mother. As I had moved away and she was mostly in South America doing mission work, our contacts were few. Occasional long letters described her life as a missionary, and connections with her adult children, one a doctor, two as missionaries. I lost touch for the most part, but my choice to get my Master's degree brought a letter of concern from Rene. It was a huge contrast to my present consciousness. As I mentioned previously, she wrote to chastise me, to admonish me about my life choices being out of line with "God's will."

My Father Transmits a Letter through me to Rene

As I prepared to answer Rene's letter of concern about my faith, I got a clear inner message from my father: "Let me write the letter." I prefaced his letter with the following:

Dear Rene,

Your letter at first felt hurtful, but I later felt sadness about the fearfulness you have about me. I realize we are worlds apart in understanding who and what God is, and who and what we are. I also realized how impactful my father's theology was on both of our lives—and yet how our responses involved choices that created very different lives.

We both were seekers of Truth about our maker and ourselves. This reminds me of the story of Truth likened to an elephant: A number of blindfolded men were asked to run their hands over an elephant and describe what was true about it. Feeling a tusk, one would say, "The Truth is hard and sharp," while another, feeling the side, would say, "The Truth is broad and expansive," and so forth. I think we were feeling the tail and saying, "The Truth is long and narrow… and it covers us, a dirty, stinky hole, so we better hang on." The difference between us is that I eventually let go of the tail.

This was part of a letter I set aside, asking for more guidance. Later, I went on to write: *My continued uncovering of the Truth and my healing has led me to hear my family in Spirit speak to me through writing. The blindfold totally fell off this morning as Peter, my father, in Spirit asked to write the rest of this letter to you, from his perspective.*

Dear Rene,

You are indeed a gem, and I thank Petra for allowing me to address you. Now we begin. Thank you for this opportunity to share what I now know about my life and work as a minister, specifically at your church. Indeed, my belief in hell and damnation resulted in many sermons with warnings against straying from the way of salvation as I understood it. My way of understanding the gospel stemmed directly from my view of

Chapter 21: A Transmission From My Father

early childhood emotional trauma which I had never dealt with. Indeed, I did believe and say to Ruth Petra, "Psychology is of the Devil."

Emotions have energy and, unreleased or suppressed, they have a tendency to explode in anger—or we turn against ourselves in the form of depression. I was chronically depressed to keep from dumping on others. The anger came out in sermons and punishment of my children. Fortunately I did not abuse my wife, Rose, physically, which is common with this kind of belief system and emotional suppression. Like a magnet, my guilt attracted all the punitive references in the Bible. Guilt screams for punishment. We can't punish ourselves enough. In a sense, I did so with Rheumatic Heart fever and my resulting heart condition, a perfect symbol of a heart closed to my feeling nature.

There were some things my fundamentalist brothers in the cloth were saying that I couldn't accept, so I saw myself as more moderate and loving, if you will. The core issue in our interpretation of the Bible was that we conveniently forgot the Bible states we are created in the image of God, and that like God, our true nature is Love and Spirit, not the damnation-deserving sinner I claimed to be.

Indeed, being in a body, and thinking that is what we are, contributed to teaching that we were intrinsically separated from God and each other. Actually, our Spirit is eternal; therefore we are eternal and Love that comes from the heart is our true nature.

When we don't clear our emotional baggage, so to speak, and forgive others and ourselves, we stay attached to our beliefs and thoughts in our heads to alibi everything we do. That is where the voice of fear operates, the devil spoken of in the fundamentalist interpretation of the Bible. Our fear of being wrong becomes very strong and our need to be right contributes to the need to control. The patriarchal church controlled through the production of guilt and threat of punishment if we didn't follow the beliefs produced by this denial of our true nature. Of course we had to put the devil of fear outside of us, because particularly as men, we could not acknowledge fear. That was easier for women to do who didn't have much worth in that system. Fear is simply a feeling to be acknowledged and released.

Literal interpretation of the Bible is to totally misread it. The New Thought churches can indeed use the same Bible—but with it interpreted metaphysically—and come up with an entirely different interpretation which honors our true nature. Some rightly call their church, the church of positive Christianity. The Bible is a tool for awakening and knowing your Source, which is within you, as Jesus said. The Bible is not to be worshiped. The Bible also was controlled by fearful men who omitted some important books that threatened their fear-based beliefs. Revelation continues. Jesus promised the Holy Spirit as your comforter, the Voice of Love within you that, from the heart is always gentle.

The voice of fear is associated with feeling separate from our Source/Creator and denying our God nature. Remember, Jesus said, 'The Kingdom of God is within you,' and 'greater things than I have done, you will do.' Jesus is one with the Holy Spirit within you, which will continue to teach you, but only with your willingness.

Ask and it is given. If you ask for bread, will you be given a stone? Of course, not. You ask for too little because you regard yourself as unworthy. Then you dishonor God, your creator, by belittling her Creation. This is not punishable—it's only a mistake to be corrected. 'Sin' means 'missing the mark,' so try again! Or choose again as Jesus says in 'A Course in Miracles.' When you see yourself as a sinner, you deprive yourself of Joy, part of your true nature along with Love and Peace. When you feel peace in your heart, you are connected to your Source.

Jesus demonstrated that his main purpose of the crucifixion was to "teach only Love, because that is what you are." It also was meant to show that death was not real, through the Resurrection.

Rene, I have instructed Petra to send this to you. I want to deeply apologize for giving my fear-based version of Jesus' message to your young and highly-impressionable mind. You dedicated your whole life and energy around this fear-based message that denies your wholeness, your wondrous essence. You have been faithful to the truth as you saw it. It

Chapter 21: A Transmission From My Father

has caused much grief for both you and Petra. When she promised to follow that inner voice of Spirit in her prayer, 'Teach me and change me' in the eighties, she willingly went through all kinds of emotional pain in order to heal and reclaim what she gave up for my belief system as a child—namely, her true identity. She held on to that false identity for many years and now is fully free of it. Her long journey through much pain has now made her a powerful teacher, which only now she is free to be.

Ask and it is given. Two years ago, through a gifted channel with beings of the spirit world, Ruth Petra asked for me from an inner prompting from her inner teacher, the Holy Spirit. I was thrilled to speak with her, and it was a great healing for her to hear of my love for her. No amount of Bible reading would have accomplished that.

I told her not to be afraid of the spirit world. There are many helpers here waiting for their loved ones to ASK for their help. Petra asked, and has truly received the 'bread of life.' Her mother and brother Luke are with her in spirit, empowering and teaching as they, like myself, have fully embraced the light and our mission to create Heaven on Earth. I urged Petra to learn to channel and now she has received words from both Rose and myself. This was only possible because of her continued focus on self-healing—allowing all 'blocks to the awareness of Love's Presence' to come up into the light for healing. She has been gifted with a powerful Process for healing that she can teach people to do for themselves, for Physical, Emotional, Mental and Spiritual healing.

E-motion is Energy in motion. Of course, fear-based Christianity causes you to deny your negative emotions, as it's 'not nice' or 'not Christian' to feel that way. Guess what…when you push those feelings down, they become illnesses, addictions, and depression, or the emotion pops out in unwanted behaviors. Paul said, 'The good, I would do, I don't do, and what I don't want to do, I do' (a loose translation). I had depression and sickness of the heart, because I denied my feelings.

May you accept these words as truly coming from the soul of the man you knew on earth as Rev. Peter Oas. This is a confession of error *that came from his unhealed heart while on earth. You may feel much grief and pain. I want you to know that you have lived a life of deep dedication to your path of service as a mother, wife, and teacher, despite the negative fundamentalist beliefs you accepted. It is very important that you let go of any judgment of yourself. You have done very well with the light you have. Just remember God made us in the likeness of Him/Her Self and you are a part of that One Self.*

Let 'Christ in you, the hope of Glory' be your Biblical foundation. The Christ Energy is our true Identity, which Jesus was the first to realize. The Christ or 'face of God' is your true Essence. Indeed Jesus is the Son of God, as we ALL are, who are willing to claim their true identity, men and women alike. There is much to learn about who you are. Look at everyone and see him or her as expressions of God's creation. Your realization of that is what makes the difference.

Many people are waking up to who they are. Petra has awakened, and this is her mission now. She has a Joy, Love and Peace in her heart that no one can take away from her. Yes, she can feel grief and release it. That is part of the healing process, which she welcomes. What you can feel, you can heal. I am speaking for her when I say she is ready and able to help anyone who is willing to ask for healing or help with feeling their feelings and releasing them. This no longer needs years of therapy. What she has been given can heal in minutes. She understands the pain that this letter could bring up for you. I have reassured her that you can receive this, because you do trust Jesus and he stands ready to support you.

What I taught you was a distortion of Jesus' message in its most negative form, as all the traditional churches had some form of the Error: the belief that we are separate from God, along with a whole lot of shoulds, dos and don'ts—fear-based rules that denied feelings. Feelings are your emotional guidance system. When you feel 'bad,' it merely calls for correction, not judgment and condemnation.

Ruth Petra took in a very harmful message from the Bible that I quoted as, 'In me dwelleth no good thing!' This has kept her from recognizing and using her gifts these many years. This programmed her

Chapter 21: A Transmission From My Father

mind at an unconscious level, so she wasn't aware of what held her back and kept her from valuing anything she wanted to accomplish. She has just released this destructive program, using the tool the God in her inspired.

She now is truly free to accomplish her mission on earth. For that, we are all celebrating in the Spirit world. Fear not: 'God has not given you a spirit of fear, but of power, love and a sound mind.' This is a verse that has meant much to Petra. Petra and I have a similar energy and now our minds are truly joined.

Yes, you ask, 'What about accepting Jesus as our Savior?' We needed a bridge to overcome our belief in separation and Jesus was that bridge. He did not mean for us to worship him, but intended to point us to our Creator Source, God. Incarnating into a body, we felt separate from our spirit identity. That is changing now as the Divine plan is for humanity to identify with their spirit and love identity within them, and allow the body to be an Expression of God in form, much like a painting is the expression of the painter, though not the painter herself. Know that God is Spirit, God is Love. Love is energy; therefore God is the all-powerful, all-knowing, and everywhere-present energy of love.

Petra is learning much from us these days. Trust what she tells you. She is always checking in with her inner teacher about the correctness of her thoughts and words. Her willingness to learn and to let go of all that does not serve her mission now is really speeding things up in her life.

She fully understands your intention of love in writing your recent letter because she had even a bigger dose of the programming you received, plus the pain of feeling my rejection of her gender at birth. I didn't value the female gender equally with the male. She took in the core belief of 'being defective,' which was reinforced by my Biblical interpretations as well as the culture regarding females. As she grew and competed with her brothers, I changed my mind, but the imprint of that rejection was left in her unconscious mind and continued to affect her feelings about herself.

Can you see the connections, Rene? You were accepted and loved from birth, so the negative programming Petra experienced wasn't experienced in the same way by you. Nevertheless, it contributed to self-limiting beliefs and fear-based thoughts you still carry. I am simply hoping this will expand your 'wine skin' and allow new wine to flow in to increase your joy, and accept that there are many ways on earth to connect with your Creator Source. You don't have to throw out your core belief in Jesus as your Savior; also accept Jesus as your brother and teacher. Include yourself as a beloved 'sister' of great worth and beauty and teach other women the same.

In closing, I want you to know you are surrounded by your family in Spirit with much love, along with myself.

May the Love of God surround you, the Peace and Joy of God be felt in you, and the Presence of God enfold you, Peter Oas

Letter, a Statement of Present Consciousness

Rereading this several years later, I was amazed how accurately it described my present state of consciousness and the Patriarchal system I emerged from. I sent the letter, but I never got a response from Rene. Later, when I asked her if she received it, she said she thought it was a joke. For this I am sad. I am aware that even angels cannot change some people's minds. That sense of *being right* is a very strong trait of fundamentalism, making change difficult. This energy blocks the wisdom of the heart. The need to be right fuel's the ego's control of the mind.

Through SURRENDER to the truth of who we are, we are given a deep knowing that bypasses the ego mind. It is the Peace of knowing *I Am that, I Am*. It is the *Peace that passes understanding*, the understanding of the ego mind.

We can have this knowing, even if our theologies differ, as Jesus reminds us in the introduction to *A Course in Miracles*: "A Universal theology is impossible, but a universal experience is not only possible but necessary." That experience is knowing the love deep in our spiritual heart is our divine essence and means of experiencing Oneness.

CHAPTER 22

BROTHER LUKE

<u>LUKE</u>

In Ariana's channeling group, I inquired about my brother, Luke, and after a period of meditation, gave information about him. Luke, ten years younger than myself, was the twin I chose to take care of when I was only ten. Tearful, I realized I had the grief of a mother, as well as a sister, when I recalled his death (June, 1983). He was a young 43, an athletic artist, enjoying kite-sailing and the outdoors. A conscientious objector, he had fled to Canada for a time as a young man. After he became an art professor, he was divorced following an affair with a student.

While driving over the Colorado Mountains with his girlfriend in order to live closer to his two sons who were living with their mother, they had a car accident. He died in his girlfriend's arms. A week **earlier**, Daniel, his twin, was driving on the same road when he suddenly broke into sobs at that spot, for no explicable reason.

Ariana connected with Kaatan who became the facilitator and said: *Luke is thrilled to speak to his sister. Luke wishes to give his love, affection and gratitude for his sister's early care. He is enveloping you in his arms. Because there was this connection, he decided to be one of Petra's guides in spirit for this lifetime. It was a heart-to-heart connection. Luke has been a 3rd eye connection ever since he went into his mission mode.*

Even though it looked like an accident, it was in his plan. He misses his loved ones, and is with them in other ways. Luke explains, 'It isn't as if we are spying on you. We hold the vision of love and joy for our family on earth. It is a touch of my energy with your aura.'

Kataan continued, *He has duplicated his energy and is with you all the time. With others, it is when he is prompted to touch in. He wants you to know they see you as an aura and as a light and can listen to your thoughts. The transition that occurred because of the accident was a surprise. But because of his very balanced attitude toward life, he went quickly to the heaven world and was met by his father.*

Kataan explained, *It is a very extended process with the remaining six bodies after leaving the physical body. Depending on the mental and emotional state, it takes weeks to years in earth time. Luke wasn't ready to leave the planet, so he found it difficult to shift his focus. He was very close to his sons and on his way to live closer to them.*

Luke is in the same soul family as your son, Kirk, and is connected to him. The soul family has deeper connections than human family, as Masters have created huge families of beings who are more connected than earth families. Souls are automatically in the 4th dimension after death. When souls have done their work, they move into the 5th dimension. Our love increases from one dimension to another. Love magnifies greatly in 4th dimension, increasing more in the 5th.

Now we can move through the 4th dimension while still in the body into the 5th dimension because of the earth's increase in frequency. The energy and connection to the nonphysical world has greatly increased. A second reason is the vast increase in channeling and soul-identity awareness. A third reason is the cutting of the power and control forces that have dominated the planet. Money will not be the driving force, as the heart wisdom becomes the master, and the mind its servant.

Kataan continued, *Luke is very much in touch with Daniel, his twin, who is still unaware of Luke's energy.*

Luke accepted my apology for being so uptight when he was alive. He encouraged me to keep on lightening up.

Chapter 22: Brother Luke

Ariana laughed and said, "Sometimes the whole family gets in the back of your car."

When I asked regarding my brothers, Luke said he *can hardly wait to thank them for listening to the tape with Peter and to see how this has made such a big change in Petra.* It was further explained that a major part of my family is in spirit with many on earth. *Spirit family wants you to know you are all together.*

Ariana continued, "Luke mentions something about art. There is an artist in Wyland studio whom Luke is working with, as well as many other artists. Anytime any family members are doodling, Luke comes in. The Alpha state is a state where he is there."

I had asked about the artist's awareness of Luke's spirit. Luke explained that the idea of channeled art needs to come from a friend. Luke is also working with his and my grandchildren, as well as children in disadvantaged lands. He works in the field of art, because *art* brings joy, a vibration to higher dimensions.

It was a refreshing channeling. I have become more and more aware of Luke's presence and intuit his energy with my electronic equipment, my ailing car, and with the energy symbol on the cover of my first book. It is my task to notice and ask intuitively. Invariably, I Muscle Test *yes* to his involvement. With my car, I would hear an engine noise that concerned me. The next time I drove, it would have disappeared. My old Subaru had good "pick-up" energy which was commented on by a passenger. For this I credit Luke!

CHAPTER 23

MOTHER ROSE

In our weekly channeling gathering, I had already heard from my father and from Luke. In 2006, I asked for my mother, Rose.

Rose' First Contact, March 02, 2006

Ariana: It is quite joyful for all to know that your mother and father in spirit are with you now to say "hello."

Our love is with you at this special time and we have a very excited person here. Petra, she is your mother, Rose. She is so grateful you have asked for her. She is overwhelmed with love for you. She is overwhelmed with gratitude. She is so excited that you understand Spirit.

She says you have come a long way. You have had a hard road. I gave you responsibilities way beyond your years as a little child. I look back at those times and wonder how in the world you coped. It makes you into the strong being of light and love you are today.

Petra, do you have anything to say to me?

At that point, I did reply, but when I later played the recording, I couldn't hear myself on tape. Judging from her words in response, my guess is that I apologized for not being there for her when she was in a nursing home 400 miles away from where I lived. My brother, Obed, had told me that she continually asked for me. The mini-strokes had affected her ability to express herself. I was preoccupied with my life at that time, living with scarcity-thinking and not knowing how to be with her in her state of painful dysfunction. Perhaps she provided a mirror to my own difficulty with self-expression.

Petra, no reason for guilt. You were there for me as a child, when I needed you. It is true, I would have liked to have seen you more in my later life, but after my transition, I realized what you were going through. I understood totally, and I was with you on another level. So guilt, be gone.

There is no room for guilt in your aura. Believe me, I love you. You did all a daughter could do for me. I took on a lot when I took on that marriage, when I had baby after baby after baby; I couldn't have done it without you.

I bless you and I honor you for seeking the spiritual side—for looking under the ordinary, for tuning into your dad and Luke. They send you love again for evermore.

I spoke and couldn't be heard. There was about three minutes of static on the tape recording before I could make out the words.

Yes Petra, you and I are so close…that if you choose to work on channeling, I would be good to begin with. Channel verbally, channel by writing… channel for me to come through poetry—whatever would fit in with your lifestyle. The easiest would be to begin with writing.

In these sessions, if speaking verbally is possible, I encourage you to do that.

Again, my response was inaudible. Rose, through Ariana, continued: *It is true, you may wonder if it is your own thoughts, or thoughts coming from another. The truth of it is that you don't have any thoughts of your own. They are all inspired. If it is a definite message, you will notice that it is a heart connection. I can tell you one of Ariana's tricks. She doesn't mind if Spirit catches her somewhere in the house and wants to give her a message. If an idea goes around in her head three times, she knows it is Spirit! Yes, it is spirit and she answers.*

"I do think of you often when I go through an old recipe," I responded. She continued:

We can also come through song—as in a song you learned or heard when you were growing up. If you hear a song going around in your head you will know it is me. I am very interested in this. I hope we can make it a project together.

"Thank you for coming today," I said. "Is there something you would like to tell the whole group?"

Yes, I can expand on the butterfly project if you wish. [I gave an inaudible assent.]

Of course you know there are hundreds of thousands of forms of life on your planet and also hundreds of thousands of butterflies—such a planet of expanded and glorified life. I have chosen to work with the butterflies on your planet in a spiritual way.

It is a very simple thing I do from spirit. I am not there physically to help the butterflies. The butterflies need help spiritually. All life on planet earth needs help spiritually.

My particular interest is those gorgeous blue butterflies from Brazil. Do you remember them? They are iridescent…a phenomenal blue color. Those butterflies sometimes fly all the way up to Canada. At one time, Delphiana and children in her classroom caught one of those butterflies. I am involved with the entire life of those butterflies, from the time one begins as a fuzzy caterpillar, the time it goes into its cocoon, to the time it emerges wet and sleek until it dries and flies.

And what do I do? <u>I hold the vision!</u> I just hold the vision. That is my job and it is something I love. I hold the vision in many categories of the butterfly's life. Not just one, but all of them, and they can tune into this.

For example, I know this sounds kind of silly, but imagine a butterfly just dried its wings for the first time and then wondered what to do. It wouldn't know what the wings were for—unless someone told the butterfly. It automatically tunes into spirit, which is me—holding the vision of the butterfly flying. Because of that connection, it knows how to fly.

There are so many of us working in spirit, on little projects like this, which becomes the whole world to us. This is just one aspect of the many things I do, but it is an important aspect. In my way of thinking, the beauty on the planet is very important and these butterflies enhance that beauty so fantastically.

"Thank you mother, for sharing that," I said. "Are there other things you can say to us in these chaotic times to help us 'hold the vision'?" She replied:

This is the way we work in the finer dimensions. [Here, I omit a detailed section.]

You are tuning into the finer dimensions—all the way up to ten dimensions. This is the spiritual way to help the earth. This is a part of your light work, because you can come from a finer dimension. You can help and influence the planet just as I do, but it takes <u>Intention</u>. It definitely takes intention. It takes intention for me working from spirit. It takes intention for you working from meditation.

You need to be in an altered state to do this, however. Your thoughts and words from the 3rd dimension can reinforce that. The action takes place from your mind—when your mind is in the finer dimensions. Do you understand?

"I am beginning to."

How about the rest of you? To hold the vision you need to be very pure, very sure in a space of love. I know Ashtar comes and tells Ariana these things and he says not to be wishy-washy, because if you change your mind, spirit doesn't know what the heck to do. Spirit is always helping you.

If you hold the peace in the world, it is magnified a thousand times, if not more, by those in spirit. If one person is working in meditation, it is worth a thousand affirmations. You are very special. If you choose to take some time out of your life to do this work, I honor you. I send my love to you.

"Thank you so much, mother," I said. "I will really focus and connect with you through poetry or song, as I know I struggle with a very scattered mind. I thank you for however you can help me with that."

Chapter 23: Mother Rose

You are so welcome, Petra. I love you so, so purely. Meditation is the best time to connect with spirit. Remember to 'keep the words' from Spirit. That is why Ariana keeps the tapes going, and types them up. All of us in spirit know this is a very difficult time for you—so keep the words, not only for you, but for whomever you share it with. If the words are there, you can share. If you don't have the words, it is only an experience. That's all it was. So please keep the words.

"Thank you. I appreciate that and will remember. Anything else?"

Yes there is, and thank you for asking. There is a question of soul families.

"Yes, I have discovered several people to be in my soul family through Muscle Testing, and wondered if it is important to know that? To what purpose do we have soul families?"

It is only in your enlightened times that you would be interested in soul families. Normally, people in the 3rd dimension would have no clue about soul families. They don't learn about it until after their transition. Now, with the veil's thinning and teachings of metaphysics since the 1800s, these things have come through. People find it very interesting. Much has been channeled by this one [Ariana]. *I will see if I can expand it, taking ideas from her mind at this point in time.*

When projects of populating the earth came into the awareness of many ascended masters and teachers, some decided to work with creating life on the planet. How did they do it? By Holding the Vision, of course. Holding vision, they manifested in the 3rd dimension in marvelous ways. Ashtar and Athena, a couple in spirit—twin flames—worked together to put the people and animals on the planet. They were not the only ones. Many more were involved. They did this through their mind and down through the dimensions.

As life began—years later, it manifested that these lines of families had traits that were similar. As in Sananda's family; his family coming down the dimensions had different traits and different coloring. Then all the people got mixed up and nobody cared. The masters had finished putting life on the planet.

Ariana started collecting pictures of people who were really close to her, and noticed similarities, so she became very interested in the soul family aspect. Your Soul family doesn't need to be your physical family. It can be a family on earth, but mostly is in spirit. Who guides you and teaches you from spirit is your soul family. That connection will go on forever and ever.

When you return to Spirit, there will be a great reunion. First you have your family party, then your soul family party, and then the animals will come. Absolutely phenomenal!

Petra, there is a little trick we use in spirit. That is, tuning into Universal Mind. I am not all knowing, but I can tune in. I can tune into your mind and tune into Universal Mind. I can put two and two together and answer any question you want to ask. That is the reason we say, 'Practice going within. Going within will give you answers to all things.'

"Thank you so much," I said. "I know it is goodbye only until we connect again." Then, I asked, "Is there anything else?"

Petra, I want you to know there is a connection between myself and Ariana's mother, who is in my soul family. This woman and I helped you and Ariana get together.

"Thank you!"

Ariana said, "Holy showers!" Then she continued channeling:

Our soul family has a master named Cha ara. They called him the inventor of the rose. He held the vision of the rose. Ariana's mother has worked with the roses and now they are working on the planetary aspects that will come forth with the change in dimensions. I am very pleased to give you this revelation. Thank you. Goodbye. This channeling has been given to all of you.

Claire, in our group, started to speak. "My mother has wanted to say something to Petra. It will give Ariana's throat a rest."

Petra and everyone here: How important it is that you and everyone on earth disentangle yourself from guilt, regrets, pain, and all things that bind up your energy to prevent you from being fully present as light workers. It is easy for me to say, because when you pass over, you are freed from all those emotional shackles that hold you back, drain you and keep you from being who you can be.

Those of you who do their emotional work on earth transition so easily. Here, when we think of anyone, we can duplicate ourselves, so it is not a distraction to be called upon. Simply ask and call the name of the one you want and they are there. I spent most of my life trying to right the wrongs of the past. Forgive yourself and forgive others. Do the personal work to free yourself. Spirit works it out.

Ariana: Oh, that was wonderful. They engineered the whole thing about lightwork and holding the vision. About Rose, I know she was working with Cha ara.

Acceptance, Support and Empowerment

My mother's words were so accepting and comforting and erased the guilt I had been feeling regarding her last days on the planet. Her deep wisdom was so welcomed in our group of all women. She gave us a lot of practical advice and her impassioned *Hold the Vision* message will be with me always. The strength of her character and her life was a beautiful model for women. I felt her deep love for me, and her joining me as a personal guide is most assuring. Truly I am never alone.

CHAPTER 24

RECEIVING THE TaBIA PROCESS

May 2006, Using the Four Keys to the Queendom

Receiving Jeshua's ***Four Keys to the King/Queendom*** happened naturally in my desire to create an original tapping process for self-healing. The first Key was my **Heart's Desire** to have a tapping process for the workbook I was intending to write, instead of using the well-known Emotional Freedom Technique (EFT). In the second step of **Intention,** I tried to create it from the learned information in my head about EFT and PEAT, an advanced program on tapping. It worked for me, but was confusing to my clients. Then I **Allowed** myself to set it aside for six weeks. When I returned to my Intention, I fully **Surrendered** my thoughts and asked to have the third eye and the thymus (the "I Am" point of the heart chakra) included in the tapping points. Neither of these points are in EFT or PEAT tapping processes.

Having learned the value and power of breath and the high vibrations of gratitude and appreciation, I included these as well. When only four points were specified, I asked Spirit if they were enough! It was simple—as I requested! Though I did not realize it at the time, Jeshua was giving me a significant release process. This head-to-heart process embodies the shift we need to make into the 4th dimension. It allows the heart to be the master instead of the ego.

As another plus, I later learned that stimulating the thymus strengthens the immune system. The *Tap and Breathe I Am (TaBIA)* process was born in May, 2006. TaBIA *releases the Blocks to Love's*

Presence, called for in ACIM. Love's Presence is the Higher Self within our spiritual heart which helps us become miracle-minded. However, *purification comes first* (one of the 50 principles of ACIM). The TaBIA process very specifically gifts us in changing from ego-awareness to heart-awareness, from ego to Essence.

The Significance of Each Step of the "*Tap and Breathe I Am*" Release Process

This process can be easily memorized when you are aware of the importance and value of each step. Think of applying TaBIA whenever you have an issue affecting your *Peace*. It can be Physical, Emotional, Mental or Spiritual, or a combination. You don't have to classify it. Just note any discomfort, distress, judgment of self or others; anything that is not Love. You then formulate your "Even though" statement, which you will be stating out loud (where practical). Saying it aloud conveys a stronger intention to acknowledge the issue.

"Even though" statements of the Issue

While writing this section, I was feeling discomfort in my chest. I intuited it was a digestive reaction as I had taken some medicine with a small amount of food prior to sitting down at the computer. I decided to TaBIA the distracting discomfort. "Even though I am experiencing this discomfort in my chest…" I stated this aloud while lightly tapping on the 3rd eye, side eye, and under the eye, before taking a breath of acknowledgment, and completing the TaBIA process. Relaxed, I burped and felt better. This example may seem trivial, as burping is considered natural and automatic—my intention is to show that you can use TaBIA anytime, even to speed up natural processes.

"PEMS," the acronym for Physical, Emotional, Mental and Spiritual, helps us look at the whole person as we look at our patterns of behavior to become self-aware.

At the **Physical** level, where our *issues are in the tissues*, results will be slower to manifest. My arthritic stiffness, mobility, and strength issues improved with TaBIA over a period of several months. I went

Chapter 24: Receiving the TaBIA Process

from getting up at night to use the bathroom frequently, to once a night, and occasionally sleeping through the night, over a period of months. Also, a side effect of my TaBIA use came out in comments like, "You look younger every time I see you!"

Creating an Intuitive Inquiry Process to ask for the spiritual source of specific pain patterns in the body has led to greater self-awareness and inner knowing. The pain can be seen as a reminder or cue of something we need to learn, forgive, or change in our life.

Even when we haven't identified a specific cause, our willingness to remember Source and "I Am" identity can help us through the pain. It focuses on doing our inner work before addressing outer causes in the environment, lifestyle habits, and relationships.

Look for the *issue in the tissue*. To illustrate, repression of expression over lifetimes resulted in my thyroid cancer. The body was expressing the blockages in my throat chakra, which eventually became thyroid cancer and resulted in the removal of the thyroid gland. This repression had to do with my gender as well, and a complete hysterectomy was the result of the effects of devaluing the feminine.

We avoid emotional pain, even unconsciously, and so ignore and overlook this fact: Society and the medical profession are stuck in Patriarchal, third-dimensional, mechanistic thinking. Even if we are aware of this, it isn't something we figure out in our heads. Intuition can reveal the cause of physical issues. Using Jeshua's Four Keys will speed the process: I **desire** to know the cause. I **intend** to find out. I will **allow** myself to accept the cause without judgment. I **surrender** to my Higher Self, my I Am Presence for the solution.

Three of my brothers have had knee replacement surgery, so it would be easy to blame my knee problems on heredity. Some could point to a physical trauma. My inquiry process and Muscle Testing pointed to **Emotional** issues. (*Vibrational* may be a better term now as we have been able to measure the energy levels of the emotions.) Dr. David Hawkins was able to determine the frequency or vibrational energy range of emotions in his "Map of Consciousness," found in his book, *Power vs. Force*.

The *Feeling Frequency Guide* is my adaptation of that map, with emotions ranging from shame, guilt, fear, egoic pride (all head-based emotions), to courage, love, joy, peace and surrender—the heart-based emotions of the Higher Self. As he stated, I found I could get the same measure of energy through Muscle Testing as Hawkins did. In my model, one can add spiritual qualities such as forgiveness, surrender, and other qualities along with the vibrational level of tools such as the TaBIA process. See the *Feeling Frequency Guide*.

The ego-based lower vibrations weaken our immune system. The lower vibrations of anger, fear and depression need to be acknowledged—they are pointers to something we need to look at and process. Denying these feelings does not get rid of them, and chronic denial is especially hazardous. Recognizing the thoughts that triggered the feeling, and shifting our perception, is the process called for.

This is called Living in process, which involves feeling awareness, inquiry and release, usually in some form of non-blaming expression. The TaBIA process as a spiritual practice keeps us clear of stuck emotions. Our vibrations shift to an *at ease* feeling rather than staying stuck in a *dis-ease* feeling.

During my Intensives with Anne Wilson Schaef, she noted that in doing the emotional work of feeling the feelings and expressing them, the healing and release, or forgiveness, occurred. Indeed "forgiving everything that has occurred" is a key to Ascension from the 3rd dimension of consciousness, through the 4th dimension of Heart Awakening, to the 5th dimension of Oneness. We can't afford to carry resentments. They are toxic and keep us stuck.

Mental beliefs matter. Bones are the body's basic structure. If we believe we are our ego, our spiritual core is affected and our bones are weakened. We are not our bodies—the body is an amazing computer reflecting our consciousness. The bones are connected. When there is a disconnect from Source, the body reflects that also. The structure of the body reflects the mental, emotional, and spiritual structure of our life. Our "belief in separation" is the root cause of all illness and human misery, according to Jeshua.

The beliefs we were programmed with by the Patriarchy in the 3rd dimension are now showing up in self-destruction. As we become aware of them, we can TaBIA them to clear them from our unconscious. Many of those unconscious beliefs will simply disappear when our Intention is to live from our I Am Presence, our divine Essence. The key belief under all negative beliefs is our belief in separation, represented by the ego.

Examples of common negative beliefs are: "God is a male Being separate from me," "God judges and hates sinners," and "We deserve punishment." All the dualisms—good/bad, strong/weak, fast/slow, either/or—are softened with a perceptual shift to both/and and win/win.

Beliefs about one's self, such as "I can never be good enough," are common results of Patriarchal parenting. The belief "I am defective," stemming from paternal rejection of my gender, at birth, fed my feelings of inferiority. Any success was looked at as not real, or undeserved. Examine your beliefs and become aware of those that limit you. Undoing our obsolete programming will give us plenty of "Even though" issues to tap on.

The **Spiritual** issues are interconnected with the emotional and mental patterns. Discern—from the heart—those feelings, beliefs, and behavior patterns that affect your Peace. Any judgments need to be released. Failure to ask for help, or to give help when it is asked for, may be spiritual issues. The prayer "change me, teach me" brought plenty of issues into the light for me to release. Simply ask to see the blocks to your Love, Peace and Joy, which is your natural inheritance. Allow the blocks to come into your awareness without judgment.

Three points on the face: The "third eye" refers to our spiritual vision; the "side eye" point is just below the temple, and refers to insight. The point under the eye is the "neediness" or "fear" point. After declaring the issue, begin lightly tapping on the three points—about seven taps on each point with the index or middle finger with one hand on one side of the head is sufficient. PAUSE and breathe a breath of acknowledgment of your issue before tapping on the thymus.

The **fourth point is the thymus in the heart chakra,** a powerful reminder to move out of the head, to our heart for solutions, for a new perception, which changes everything. Then, while tapping lightly on the thymus on the sternum just below the collarbone, say, "I remember, I am one with my Source, I am that, I am." This is a declaration of your identity.

Continue tapping the thymus (your *I Am* point) and say "I love, accept and forgive myself, my bodymind, and personality, and I release [restate issue] to Source." Breathe a breath of release.

The two breaths—the breath of acknowledgment and the breath of release—are important to embodying what we are saying. The use of the word "Source" instead of "God" is also an intentional departure from the Patriarchal God (a being outside of us) to the creator Source of all life, the unconditional love within us. We are all Children of All that is.

The gratitude and completion gesture with words provides a high-vibration closure.

The completion gesture of joining the thumbs and fingertips in an arch accompanies our gratitude for the release and concluding affirmation, "I am Holy, whole and complete!"

When I objected to the word, "Holy," I got a very clear "Don't change it!" The significance of this is in reference to the unconscious guilt we all carry through our belief in separation, felt by our choice to descend into matter. In feeling separate, we add on more guilt. *Holy* declares our core innocence. May *I am Holy, whole and complete* become a daily affirmation as you let go of your day and go to sleep.

Chapter 24: Receiving the TaBIA Process

In making the statements given for tapping the thymus and doing the completion gesture, declare these statements as a command. Ask boldly and claim the authority you have been given.

The TaBIA Practice and Journal

Having a TaBIA journal and diary combination helps you track your work. You simply record your issue, followed with a number from one to ten, which indicates the severity of the issue. I then draw a heart to indicate the move to tap the thymus in the heart chakra. Three dates with a blank after them indicates the three days I am to tap on a particular issue. I can use Muscle Testing, or an imaginary ruler from one to ten to indicate progress in lowering the intensity to zero. If not at zero after three days, let it go. More time may be needed. Allow integration.

Write an affirmation correcting the issue just released. A declarative command stating the desired outcome empowers you to manifest what you want.

If you hurriedly recite the TaBIA process without feeling it, the heart is not touched. Return to **be fully present** to what you are saying, and the energy will do its healing work. Sometimes my pattern of doubt prompts me to ask Source, "Am I really clear of that pattern or belief?" and I am assured I am. I simply need to live from the truth of my divinity. Tap on the doubts and resistance. The ego will finally weaken and give up, and let the heart be in charge.

Let the TaBIA process release your unconscious *belief in separation*. This is core. From there you can apply TaBIA to anything, any time you feel less than peaceful.

Physical Pain Prompts a Healing and Commitment to Purpose

In July of 2006, I felt like I was 90 years old. I didn't have the strength to get up from a chair without reaching for support. My bone-on-bone knee pain prompted several alternative measures that didn't work: Synvisc, arthroscopy and prolotherapy. According to the doctor who did the arthroscopy, I was facing double knee replacement.

I had been given the *Tap and Breath I Am* process from Jeshua in May, right after connecting with my mother in spirit. I was using TaBIA on my emotional issues and realized it was important to share this process; yet I was quite distracted by the condition of my body. With a bargaining plea, I prayed, "I will share the TaBIA process if I can walk normally without having this major and expensive surgery." Immediately, I felt a surge of energy go through my knees. I gradually felt stronger and let go of my cane. The painful locking up of my knees faded away.

The TaBIA process became a spiritual practice. It replaced the Emotional Freedom Technique I had been using. TaBIA became the centerpiece of the Purification process, the first "P" in my book, *A Journey of Ps and Cues to Inner Peace and Power*.

CHAPTER 25

THE TAP AND BREATHE I AM (TaBIA) PROCESS

Introduction Added from Jeshua, February 20, 2007

The planet earth has been given a reprieve on its accelerated journey to self-destruction due to the rising consciousness of those awakening to their true identity. The fearful egoic energy of the need to control and keep its self-serving values in place has been unmasked, and its rush to use force to prove its power is bringing on its own demise.

Ascended Masters and galactic forces are sending energy to all those committed Light Beings on Earth to join with each other in support and healing of self and the planet. All that has been kept secret is coming to the light. The spirit and power of Love is released through quantum forgiveness. This is needed at the Cellular level as the new energy coming onto the planet requires new bodies, which are already being rewired.

Embodiment of the Christ (Love) energy in the heart and cells is the birthing process of the new human Being and the New Earth. This first requires a release of the old on both the planetary and the personal level. 'Love is letting go of fear.' It is simple to say, yet hard for many to do in the midst of the chaos and massive suffering occurring now.

Inner Peace is the beginning of true peace in the world. Inner Peace can be had by changing our perceptions of everything that we see and hear which fosters fear. It is a journey from the head to the heart, which is the only level Unity can be experienced and achieved. TaBIA illustrates and accomplishes that. Therefore the feelings need to be addressed and acknowledged at the head level and released at the heart level through declaring oneness with Source and affirmation of one's identity.

Complexity is of the ego. TaBIA has been designed with this in mind. Do not dismiss its power or value because it is simple. It is to be incorporated as a Spiritual Practice. Twenty-one days of committed focus and attention will bring tangible results and awareness of its value when in consistent use. Clearing is a continuous process to undo years of negative programming. Years of therapy are no longer practical. TaBIA shifts the energy at the cellular level and empowers one to Partner and depend on Source and integrate their experience.

This identification with Source prepares one for the activation and expansion of DNA by this incoming energy of higher consciousness. If this energy exchange occurred without this preparation, the physical body couldn't survive. Now tapping into the bodymind's programming can occur very rapidly with the TaBIA process, in partnership with Spirit.

This Embodiment is the coming together of Spirit and biology. It is Reconnection to our original awareness of Source. It is the expansion of Being into the invisible world. It is not the only process available—many more complex processes are offered. This is unique in its simplicity, effectiveness, and completeness. It is within the reach of everyone.

Undoing the ego with this simple process will bring up resistance, even in the "enlightened" person. So, tapping on the resistance may be the first issue to tap on. The bodymind will express this resistance in the form of sleepiness, cravings, procrastination, distractions, doubt and distortion of this Practice. The ego has unlimited disguises. Know your ego.

To do this Practice, use the Four Keys to the Queendom: Heart's Desire, Intention, Allowing, and Surrender. Remember I Am with you always, in all ways, Jeshua.

Tapping connects with the bodymind computer and changes scripts at the cellular level. TaBIA clears the bodymind for new programs. Perceptual shifts occur. As mentioned, TaBIA heals Physical, Emotional and Mental issues on the Spiritual level. *All reactions have roots in the past.* The *Tap and Breathe I Am* process works with Source energy on seven areas to:

Chapter 25: The Tap and Breathe I Am (TaBIA) Process

Relieve Pain and other Physical symptoms; activates the thymus and immune system

Clear Emotional charges by changing Perception

Reduce Stress

Eliminate destructive Patterns, Scripts, Beliefs and Addictions

Heal Cellular Memories in Present and Past Lives—this is Quantum Forgiveness

Alter Genetic Codes for Physical, Emotional, Mental or Spiritual illness

Open the Spiritual Heart and identify with Source, the I Am That, I Am

Go ahead and try it now. Choose a specific issue in one of the above areas. Identify a feeling.

Example: *Even though I have this unconscious core belief and feeling that I am separate from Source, others and nature...* Intuit intensity from 1 to 10, or Muscle Test. Say the issue statement while lightly tapping the first three points—the third eye, side of eye, and under the eye—five to seven times each (either hand, either eye).

The Ten Step TaBIA process:

1. Tap third eye (**point between eyebrows**) and say *Even though I feel, have, judge,* _____
2. Tap outer side of eyebrow on temple (**insight point**), continue saying, *about* _____
3. Tap under eye (**neediness and fear point**), while completing the issue statement.
4. **Pause and breathe deeply, a breath of acknowledgment.**
5. Tap thymus (**thy muse**) mid-chest just below collar bone and say:
   - *I remember I am One with my Source*
   - *I am that, I am*

- *I love, accept and forgive myself, my bodymind and personality*
- *I release this [can restate issue] to Source*

6. Breathe a conscious release and measure the new intensity from 0 to 10.

   Note any reduction in intensity.

7. Gratitude and Completion: Put fingertips and thumbs together to form an arch.

   Say: *I am grateful for this release. I am Holy, whole and complete!*

   ("Holy" declares the core innocence of your divine essence.)

8. Repeat cycle with the same issue for 2 more days, saying:

   Even though I still feel_____.

   If not at zero intensity after the 3rd day, note in your TaBIA Journal.

   Let it rest and integrate. It will come up at a later time, probably in a form closer to the core issue.

9. Keep a TaBIA Journal. Simply state your issue. Note intensity from 1-10.

   Write the dates for the 3 days, adding a small blank line after each date, and check off as you complete the issue.

10. Declare or state a command or affirmation correcting the issue.

Review of TaBIA Benefits

Feelings, beliefs, habits, and past experiences are stored in our bodymind computers.

Tapping key points while acknowledging the issue releases unwanted programming.

Source-inspired TaBIA is unique in several ways:

Chapter 25: The Tap and Breathe I Am (TaBIA) Process

- Simplicity, self-forgiveness and affirmation of Self-identity.
- Perception shifts as TaBIA moves us from head to heart, Source of true wisdom.
- TaBIA activates the thymus, our *I Am* point in our Spiritual heart, and stimulates the immune system.
- TaBIA corrects the programming in our bodymind computer, addressing the cause of any PEMS illness discovered through Intuition and the Inquiry process.
- Powerful vibrations are embodied in TaBIA's gratitude and completion statement.
- TaBIA is an Ascension Purification tool to become Ageless, Awake, Aware and At One.
- TaBIA helps maintain higher states of vibrations as we quickly release ego vibes and shift from ego to Essence.

Examples of My Use of the TaBIA Process since 2006

Bear in mind that my early tapping processes focused on obvious issues based on initial awareness. With honest self-inquiry, awareness accelerates with each release of a resentment, pattern, pain, judgment, limiting belief, or grief.

Examples from my 2013 journal include the following "even thoughs," typically repeated for three days. The numbers in brackets indicate the intensity of the problem, from one to ten.

- Even though I resist moving my body,[6] "I remember…" (Went to 2 on the 3rd day)
- Even though my energy feels depleted… [7] (varies and is released in the moment)
- Even though I have these defensive thoughts and feelings about…[4] (zero on day 3)
- Even though I worry about____ and feel frustrated in trying to help. . [9] (Note our co-dependencies.) In time I was no longer subjected to this person's neediness. It has taken about

nine months of TaBIA work precisely because this person was a daughter in a past life. Your Inquiry process can reveal your past life connection to a person.

- Even though I feel inadequate and doubt myself… [7] (reduced to a 1 at present)
- Even though I feel compulsive about eating when I have to focus… [8] (still a 4) This is a cue about the power of addiction and why a program of accountability is necessary.
- Even though I eat when I can't focus or prioritize my tasks… [9] (now a 4 as I may eat with full awareness!)
- Even though I still have traces of feeling defective, stemming from the gender rejection at birth trauma… [3] (to zero)
- Even though I resist focusing…[6] (to 2)

When my grandson "Patrik" (Hawaiian spelling—means "noble man") came into my life, his patterns and personality triggered memories of my ex-husband and my relationship with my four children. What an opportunity for further purification. Some of the lessons have been quite painful. One lesson, which involves programming common to many women, is the fundamentalist response to responsibility. It is judgment and expecting the worst. This gave me many opportunities to tap on these old patterns rooted in a faulty sense of responsibility. My grandmotherly concerns were interpreted as controlling. The TaBIA practice helped to change my way of being,

CHAPTER 26

THE INTUITIVE INQUIRY PROCESS

Key to releasing anything which no longer serves us is a Self-Inquiry process. Muscle Testing dedicated to the Holy Spirit's use assists greatly, especially if we have stifled our intuition or don't trust it. It is not a substitute but rather a confirmation of intuition. Whenever "pain" alerts me to a condition, an event, a relationship, etc. , I ask some basic questions. It is helpful to remember our Intention to move from the ego self to the divine Self when we are asking inwardly. We are speaking to the Spiritual Heart, which the TaBIA process is designed to awaken. Some key questions are:

- What can I learn from this experience?
- Is this pain pointing to a memory, a belief, pattern, habit, behavior, or past experience I need to forgive, release, or correct?
- Is it in this life? Or in a past life?

I Muscle Test each question. The following scenario took place after my use of the Inquiry process for several years.

<u>Persistent physical pain</u>

Shooting pain in my left thumb and base of my hand has been the subject of many Inquiry processes. I learned that choosing a vocation that doesn't represent my heart's desire can attract a mishap. Preparation for a nursing career (my first vocation) required chemistry, a subject that baffled me as I never had chemistry in high school. A broken test tube cutting a nerve in the left thumb has often resulted in pain when I try to grasp something with my hand, or for no known reason. A major lesson was that the pain reminded me of something I hadn't fully grasped, or which would be painful to realize.

TaBIA and pain relief ointments were tried. The occasional pain increased to almost constant pain one October evening in 2012 before I went to bed. The following Inquiry process took place.

"Does this persistence of pain in my left hand indicate I have something more to clear spiritually and emotionally?" MT *Yes*.

"Is it a past-life issue?" MT *Yes*. "Is it guilt over something I did with this hand?" MT *Yes*. More intuitive questions resulted in the following awareness:

<u>An Ancient Lifetime and Karmic Replay</u>

I was a male—a father in India—and I saw myself sitting in a boat with my left hand pushing the head of my six-year-old daughter under water. Because she was an extra mouth to feed and I wanted to punish her for insubordination, she was drowned. The guilt persisted as a cellular memory through many lifetimes. My father's rejection of my gender at birth in this life was a karmic completion of that experience, where I became that little girl, drowning in Christian fundamentalism.

It came up because I was ready to know this. Tears confirmed the feelings of remorse. That six-year-old is my inner child that was suppressed and depressed in this lifetime. Emotional pain occurs almost every time I read of child abuse, and sometimes tears. I am also aware of trying to suppress my very active daughter, Kim, in her early years.

My immediate response to this six-year-old child was Ho'oponopono. *Forgive me, forgive me, forgive me, I'm sorry, I'm sorry, I'm sorry,* while tapping on my third eye, side eye and under the eye. I took a breath and tapped on the thymus, saying, *I love you. I love you. I love you.* Fingertips together, I said *Thank you, thank you, thank you.* Then I spontaneously used the last line of the TaBIA process, *I am Holy, whole and complete.*

Everything we judge in others we have done in some lifetime. Now the TaBIA process has far more meaning in the declaration of self-forgiveness. Self-forgiveness includes other forgiveness when we begin to see others as ourselves. I can say to my father, Peter, "Indeed, You are as I am. I am as you are." Peter's journey in spirit is being replicated now in my life in the body. His work with devas and the energies in nature cues me to honor, respect, and heal through connecting with nature.

That same evening, after I used the TaBIA process, the pain dramatically lessened, and then disappeared. The healing process had begun. Even though I have some reoccurring pain which calls for patience, I have much gratitude for this revelation. I know some would not want to know or own their past-life experiences—yet, it is one of the most effective ways to let go of our automatic judgments and to experience Oneness with others.

Letting go of judgment does *not* mean to withhold accountability and the judgment of the courts where indicated. But as this story demonstrates, there are consequences of guilt—physical/emotional/mental/spiritual effects—that result from pushing experiences out of our awareness. It is not the deed itself that affects the quality of our beingness, but our deceptions, judgments, and unawareness. Those that carry a spirit of genuine humility have the awareness of their own culpability.

A practice of Self-Inquiry helps us to practice discernment or wisdom in every situation. Intuitive questions to ask oneself will come easier with practice. Examples are: "Will this utterance be helpful for all concerned?" "Is this thought coming from fear, or love?" "What are my motives here?" "Am I willing to be vulnerable?"

Loving oneself and accepting the "I am as you are, you are as I am" spiritual awareness allows one to speak the truth in love, and experience oneness at the level of the heart.

CHAPTER 27

PERSONAL TRANSMISSION FROM ROSE

In following an inner prompt, the following includes part of mother Rose's transmission.

Rose 2/11/09

Our thoughts have mingled for some time now. Yes, let the symbol of the Rose, its Purity and Power, nurture and protect you now, whether from Perelandra Rose essences or from its ancient meanings. (I have been using Rose Essences from Perelandra.)

You have received several cues calling for writing a cookbook. It is a call to begin where the people are, as Jesus often took care of their physical hunger before he delivered his message.

So do not think you are compromising yourself. You have had some fears about this. It is always your will that is paramount. You can always question your Inspiration as you intuit and Muscle Test.

Yes, the inspiration is mutual. You have learned truths which benefit my consciousness as well. Though thrust into the light of eternal truth, souls here still benefit from the wisdom of our counterparts on the earth plane. There is no substitute for experience. Cherish it all in the wisdom of the heart. Yes, the rose is also a symbol of the heart, a symbol of love.

You will not be alone in this endeavor, as Jeshua, Luke, and I will be with you in this writing. Indeed you are transmuting your own eating disorder. So many are struggling with that. That will be one of the themes. You have the tools. And you are enough. It is this feeling of "not enough" that drives one to eat compulsively. Even Oprah struggles with that feeling while being constantly in the limelight.

Yes, you can combine that transmutation with your simple, main purpose of recording the joy and fun of creating in the kitchen with the energy of a helping soul. The sharing of your wisdom in the Physical, Emotional, Mental and Spiritual areas can spice up your cookbook, while demonstrating the balance needed.

As a child, you helped me in the kitchen. Now I am helping you. It is such a joy for me, this time together. Indeed we were like sisters in some ways. In our family of seven males, our feminine energy struggled for expression. You lived with male domination in the family as well as in the culture, and you wisely rebelled against the arrogance and high-handedness of male behavior. Though your anger at the male species colored your relationships on the job, you have tempered that with much compassion.

Your self-healing momentum will continue, and every stumbling block on your path will melt away. Yes, pieces of your memoir will show up in the cookbook as well. That will be part of its appeal.

A disciplined writing schedule has eluded you. Mornings are best, as you know.

The potlucks are your opportunity. The encouragement of your cooking by others is no accident. They are also interested in uncomplicated and healthy eating. I can contribute short bits and will prompt you from time to time.

You are in for some surprising shifts in energy. Let your process be easy and effortless. Remember, struggle is from resistance and impatience. Desire, Intend, and Allow, Allow, Allow. Surrender to the process of allowing. TRUST, is your key also. Passion provides the energy to persist with patience, and to share when appropriate. You will be living more of your Ps and Cues in this Process. The whole creation of the Ps was a Playful idea. Enjoy. Struggle doesn't belong here. [This resulted in first completing my 2010 book, *A Journey of Ps and Cues To Inner Peace and Power.*]

Chapter 27: Personal Transmission From Rose

I know the potential feels overwhelming and seemingly more than you have energy to carry out. Simply focus on flow, and all will be taken care of in divine order. Trust the feeling of flow and ask for correction when you don't feel it. The turtle wins the race as it moves steadily onward in its own time. Align yourself with your Purpose and flow will happen. You are creating your own reality and all manner of support will show up. Though you feel there are more tasks than you can possibly manage, trust the flow and release what is not yours to do. Simplify, simplify. You are learning not to get caught up in other people's agendas.

Your service will happen naturally as you share your self-healing and inspire others toward their purpose. That is a tremendous service. Your body will also become the body you want to share with a lover who shares your purpose. Visualize a firm, healed body of a 50-something. Claim it as yours. Give yourself the rest periods the body asks for. You model what you want to teach.

Begin with the Four Keys—write them out for "Cooking with Rose." You have a team of helpers and wonderful tools to accomplish this.

Heart's Desire, Intention, Allowing, and Surrender

Rose ended the transmission with more declarations of love and support. I wrote out the Four Keys: *Heart's Desire, Intention, Allowing, and Surrender*, before setting the project aside.

The content of these channelings in my nocturnal calls to the computer would often be forgotten. The *Cooking With Rose* manuscript, with its health care information and recipes Rose and I have created together, had to be put aside in order to complete *Everything Scattered Will Be Gathered*, a delayed project which Jeshua urged me to complete first. The sense of urgency I felt is due to this book's application to the birthing of Heaven on Earth, the focus of our Ascension process. Purification comes first and calls for rapid means such as TaBIA to let go what doesn't serve us. I have also tapped on my resistance to writing.

With my cookbook project in the back of my mind, I find myself collecting healthy-eating ideas, and create or modify recipes, making them gluten-free and close to sugar-free, as well as raw. One time, at a health expo, a Chinese doctor did an ear diagnosis and told me to "eat black foods." Black foods benefit the kidneys (key organs to continued wellbeing) so "black food cuisine" could be part of the cookbook.

My focus on a healthy lifestyle and eating patterns that serve me best, is preparation for this writing. Food habits are not easy to change. I welcome the awareness that comes with this delay.

CHAPTER 28

DEEKSHA

Two friends who went to Oneness University in India for training in giving Deeksha, the Oneness Blessing, introduced Deeksha to me. Deeksha involves laying hands on the head of a person seated in front of you, with the intention of transmitting divine energy. The initial three-week training involved a lot of release work regarding family and the past, to prepare the blessing-giver to be a clear channel for divine energy.

Bhagavan and Amma are the Hindu couple who initiated this work. They are said to be God realized since birth. The Deeksha, or Oneness Blessing energy, is deeply felt. It is said that it enhances brain waves by increasing frontal lobe activity.

When a trainer came to Kauai in 2008, offering a shorter period of training with no travel or housing costs, Jeshua told me to take the training as he laid hands on people's heads. East and West have come together in this practice. Now I can give and receive the blessing with these friends, and occasionally with a larger group in a monthly full-moon gathering. It can provide a healing experience for any who accept the blessing.

<u>Sexual Abuse?</u>

As I heard client's stories of the effects of sexual abuse in their childhood, I was grateful that even with six brothers, I couldn't recall any. Indeed, my spitfire defensiveness prevented that. Ample warnings from my mother made me especially wary of male sexuality. Later, flirting did not feel safe to me, and I was uncomfortable with men unless we had a common intellectual interest.

Then, in a Deeksha healing event, I became aware for the first time of memories which were from infancy. I discovered that my father had fondled me sexually as an infant. My information from intuition is that it so frightened him, he then withheld all affection—the normal, assuring affection I so needed from a father in my early years. My reoccurring desire to be held by a loving man is coming from this deprivation. This is a hunger felt at the cellular level by many women who grow up without a father's love and healthy affection. It can contribute to promiscuity and issues around authentic intimacy.

I did feel his love later in childhood. He had a heart condition, which prompted a doctor to tell him he would never live to see his children grow up. After I had broken my leg at age eleven, I recall him carrying me up a flight of stairs. Only love could prompt him to do that.

Oneness, the Ultimate Intention of Deeksha

The training for Deeksha (Oneness Blessing givers), includes processing past hurts, resentments, and faulty parenting. My choice to know myself and focus on self-healing has accomplished this.

A daily spiritual forgiveness practice of connecting from the heart with Source becomes *Prayer without ceasing*. This will empower anyone to lay on hands in blessing another, sending healing energy to persons, pets or plants. When Oneness is our Intention, and we have done our forgiveness work, we are ready to hear those inner prompts. Ask permission, and proceed.

Oneness erases class, status, hierarchy, and specialness—or anything that would block "I am as you are, you are as I am."

Bruce Lipton, author of *The Biology of Belief* and the field of *Epigenetics*, states that further cell studies indicate we are One.

Could we simply define God as the Oneness we all are?

Chapter 28: Deeksha

We Chose our Script

We all have feelings, denied or not, and the capacity for inner knowing. Awareness differs according to the veiling and choices (not all ours) before our incarnation, and the use of our will after we are incarnated. We chose our script according to what we wanted to experience, and then were veiled as part of the game we were to play on earth. My son, Kirk, from my Soul family, chose addiction, which took his life. Yet his loving spirit prevailed.

Coming from the perfection of Spirit, all loving, we wanted to experience contrast and limitation. Our Soul wanted to participate in the game of Life in the body. We already had Soul families and wanted to experience families in form. Indeed, bumping into each other veiled added fun to the game. Can you see the truth in the statement, "Seriousness is a disease!"?

Fundamentalism denies us this natural playfulness. We have even killed one another over differences in beliefs. The illusion of separation became our reality—we forgot we are simply playing a game we chose to play. Awareness of our Oneness is key right now in the Ascension to higher consciousness. Jeshua tells us we are God and pure consciousness in our One Spirit identity, and we chose individual expressions as Souls in order to have those experiences.

Out of this choice to embody, our soul felt separate from other souls who chose to express differently in a body. The belief in separation was born. The Patriarchy, in their denial of the feminine and their own feelings, further emphasized our separation from Source, from nature, and from each other. Unlearning and undoing, and forgiveness and Allowance along with our Heart's Desire and Intention will bring us back into a place where we recognize our Oneness.

Shifting Dimensions without Death

Surrender, the 4th Key to realizing the Queendom within, is simply to experience the One Self while still experiencing duality. When we recognize *time* is also an illusion, we can experience our multidimensionality. The increased frequency of the planet makes this possible. My awareness of past lives and karmic completions reflects this frequency shift. We can move through the 4th dimension of heart-awakening to the 5th dimension of Oneness without going through death of the body first.

Some will resist this Ascension in consciousness and will continue to function in the 3rd dimension. Accepting this fact without judgment is part of our realization of Oneness. We will no longer expect support from 3rd dimension family and friends. Instead, allow a spiritual family to be your support as you join one another through heart resonance.

Giving and receiving Oneness Blessings can bring us closer to the awareness of our Oneness with the realization of our God identity.

CHAPTER 29

GUILT, CHUCK'S TRANSITION

Silencing the Guilt

"No place to come home to," was a comment I heard from my son, Jeff, when I decided to sell my lake property. I reminded him that none of my children chose to visit me during my seven years in Northern Minnesota. Kirk did visit just before I sold it.

My relationship with my oldest daughter in Minneapolis had always been fragile. She was very bonded with her mother-in-law, and let me know that. Florida and Michigan, the homes of my other three children, was reason enough for not visiting. The idea of a family reunion in my beautiful space was only a thought in passing.

It would be much later that I would understand their lack of interest. I stayed focused on self-healing and expressing my purpose, whatever it seemed to be in the moment, often just surviving, a prevailing attitude since my divorce.

On Kauai, I would attract several women friends who never had children. I wouldn't be reminded of my own disconnection by grandmothers showing me pictures of their grandchildren.

A Friend Offers a Transmission

It wouldn't be until 2011 that I would fully accept my move to Kauai, without guilt. A transmission offered by my friend, Lisa, given in 2011, gave me tremendous relief. Lisa had a gift for typing words from a nonphysical team who responded to the thoughts of a subject who would focus non-verbally on personal issues. The answers came from "The Group," with no further identification. Except for her typing, we sat in silence as I focused on current issues.

Lisa Raphael Transmission 5/8/2011

We are SO pleased that you have decided to connect with us today! This is indeed a different way of communicating.

First of all, we want you to know that you are completely on track, so to speak, in everything you are doing, reading, accomplishing. Do not dismiss your 'muddledness'—it is part of the process. When you feel and read about Mary Magdalene, you are of course quite correct, the only thing is that what you are feeling and receiving is coming from many, many more energies, beings, 'beamings' if you like, than the multiple aspects of the biblical Mary. Indeed, Petra, did you know that you have had a very strong spiritual female energy and energies with you from before your birth into this incarnation???

You have chosen this path at this time very deliberately, and with the help of the deliberations of many, many soul brothers and sisters in many dimensions and in many places in the multiverse.

One of the reasons we encouraged this transmission today through Lisa is that she is more aware and accepting of the intergalactic factors playing themselves out in the spiritual evolution that is accelerating all over the planet, within human consciousness.

*Our basic guidance at this point in time for you is… do not distract yourself with self-diminishing thoughts about ADD or so on…your task right now is to allow the **expansion** of your consciousness, your world view, your heart to reach deep, higher and wider.*

*Can you consider the lack of responses from your daughters as a **positive** sign? **not** a sign of any guilt, misunderstanding or other 'mistakes' on either end… but a way to encourage you to separate further from your ties to human family. Your true family in Spirit is where your attention be best spent.*

When you are muscle testing (which is a wonderful thing to do,) be careful, too. At times, you may want to preface [MT] with, "Can you

Chapter 29: Guilt, Chuck's Transition

answer this question accurately at this time?" You will know when it is important to do that first.

*Your husband, as he is leaving, is sending you **so** much love and appreciation for all your years together! As he moves in and out of the other dimensions, he perceives your devotion from a whole new perspective... it is part of his life review that is ongoing.* **Feel** *his deep love and caring... and admiration for the courage with which you have been conducting your life, during the marriage and since the divorce. His direct communication is not yet available through Lisa at the moment.*

In the Spiritual realm with which you are communicating, there is no <u>one</u> entity, name, energetic. Yet, we are all aspects of the one, the All That Is—that transcends time, space, boundaries, belief systems, planetary systems and galaxies.

That is all for now. Namaste

Effect of Transmission

What an encouragement! I am in awe of Lisa's gift and the reassuring words of the Group.

The reframing of my relationship with my daughters was amazing. Knowing I am on track, despite my distractions, is empowering. The connection to my ex-husband through his aware spirit that his misconceptions are being cleared is so healing of our disconnect. The energy of Oneness in the Group's message is also instructive on what we are to become as One.

My Husband of 32 years Transitions: March, 2011

Because of my persistent prayer, *teach me, change me*, it was easier for me to emotionally release Chuck when he chose to marry Sharon, a nurse and his soul mate. I was sad to hear of his decline in health after they had enjoyed over 20 years together.

Chuck had been seriously ill for several months with a heart condition, diabetes, and kidney failure. I would call and speak to him briefly. The kidney dialysis became too painful and he chose to remain at home with Sharon, his wife and caregiver during his final weeks. When she said he was slipping in and out of consciousness and could no longer take phone calls, I chose to write him the following letter in February of 2011.

Dearest Chuck,

I want to share my feelings of gratitude for the 32 years we spent together.

You gave me space to grow and taught me much through your patience and non-reactivity.

You tried to fix and relieve my pain and couldn't share your own. For that I am deeply sorry.

We had a very co-dependent relationship. I felt our teens needed a father first before a pal, and you tried to meet my unconscious need for a caretaker though I consciously wanted a partner. It was a very confusing time for me.

I didn't realize my dependency on you until you had the courage to leave. It came in response to my prayer, 'Teach me and Change me!' Though, I was devastated, I deeply knew it was for our highest good. I thank you for taking that step as I couldn't at the time.

I am grateful for your happiness with a loving, caring partner. Though I thought that would be a solution for me, it was not to be, and Self-healing became my life purpose. Now, I truly feel joyful and complete with many partners in spirit. I have found my ultimate purpose on the planet during this Ascension time, and continue to be taught by Master Jeshua along with other supportive masters and my many spiritual friends here on Kauai.

You can look at your life and say, 'Well done!' You are prepared to let go and join your spirit family who are eager to welcome you. Whatever your choice, simply know I am grateful for your part in my life. The best is yet to come when we fully awaken to our One magnificent Self of pure Love.

Peace, Petra Ruth

Chapter 29: Guilt, Chuck's Transition

In 2010, Chuck's younger brother, John, had a heart attack when he went to visit Chuck in the hospital and died shortly after. This affected Chuck greatly, as they were close. Now his entire family is together in spirit.

Chuck made his transition about the time of Lisa's reading. My main regret is that I couldn't be present at his memorial in Kenyon, Minnesota, his birthplace and our wedding site. My son Jeff who was already there with his family called and asked me to come. Old friends of our years as a couple were also there. I had already sent my words of appreciation for my life with him. His body was cremated and had ashes buried in the Memorial Garden at Zion in Ann Arbor in 2011.

A Channeled Message from Mother Rose

Some parts of the following message mentioned persons I had just encountered. In designated areas I altered the transcript for confidentiality reasons.

Rose, 11/06/11

You awoke with itching… not from mosquitoes, but from itching in childhood in this lifetime and a past lifetime we also shared. I was an adult acquaintance and you were a child. I was a friend of the family and observed the trauma. It involved criticism from an unrelated adult male. He was an authority figure. The criticism deeply affected your self-esteem. Yes, it was related to your female sex. It affected your sense of value as a female, and you chose your rejection at birth by your father, before you came in. Your script was a set-up to heal that trauma of being devalued for your femaleness.

Your Martha personality [refers to my past life as Martha, with Jesus] *preceded that criticism, so you were already conditioned to serve males in some way in order to be valued. That is what made the criticism so hurtful. Yes, you were a prostitute in some lifetimes, precisely for this reason. You overvalue compliments from men. This sensitivity was behind your feelings toward* [the two women visiting a mutual male friend in the hospital] *who, in their demonstrations of caring* [along with the patient], *ignored your presence. You strongly felt less value in their presence, and particularly resented one* [who was more aggressive and assertive than you.] *They elicited* [the patient's] *appreciation. Your article was ignored, which had involved considerable effort on your part. It was also meant to be shared with this male brother from a past life in private.*

That primary trauma of not being valued by men has fueled your self-consciousness. The stab of pain you just felt in your left foot, just now, was a reminder of those traumatic memories. That initial hurt affected your confidence and you devalued your own presence, also a factor in other's acceptance of you. These criticisms tend to generalize to any source.

Yes, the pain in your left thumb and neuroma in your left foot are both related to your sensitivity in how you receive. Absolve yourself of your self-criticism and don't take anything personally. These are effects of the Patriarchy you can now deprogram. All this processing and releasing is preparation for being an ageless presence in this time on the planet. As you respect yourself, you will respect others.

Yes, it is the One Self, your identity, that is orchestrating all these learning experiences.

This is part of the Ascension Awareness process: bringing everything up into the light, so it can be healed. This is key to your message.

Even though the article series you are contemplating seems so alien to the contents of these weekly magazines, take the initiative in preparing the series. Everyone needs to be given the opportunity to wake up. [Then, several paragraphs of instructions, expanding an idea I had expressed, omitted here, as I didn't follow through.] *Channel your itching into a creative process.*

My purpose here is to show how personal and practical your assistance from spirit can be.

CHAPTER 30

KIRK'S TRANSITION, DECEMBER 2011

Kirk Leaves the Treatment Center

"Sam," a counselor and friend of Kirk's at the center, became attracted to Sue, a woman 20 years older than Kirk, who came in after a DUI (Driving Under Influence). She had recently inherited a great deal of money, but had a number of health issues. Sam promised to marry Sue if they secretly left the center. Neither had a valid driver's license and Sam persuaded Kirk to drive. En route, Sam asked Kirk to take care of Sue if anything happened to him. Shortly after, Kirk found Sam dead from a cocaine overdose, with Sue's money in his pockets.

Kirk assumed responsibility for getting Sue to her brother's place in Florida. On the way, they became attracted to each other and decided to set up housekeeping. After committing to the care of Sue, he would call me on a fairly regular basis, always kind and loving. Caring for Sue had become his purpose and motivation for staying sober.

I was grateful for the conversations we were having by phone, the connectedness I felt, yet I noticed that Kirk would only speak of Sue's health and was evasive when I inquired about his own. So, when I received news in December of 2011 that Kirk had collapsed and was in a delirious state in a Florida hospital, I was not shocked. Hospice had been contacted and they said it would be a matter of days. Aware of his suffering, I spoke to him in spirit and gave him permission to leave. I reassured him that Luke, my brother in spirit and in his soul family, would be with him in his transition. Feeling a soul connection gave me far more comfort than a physical connection with his body.

It was some comfort to know he and Sue had enjoyed eight peaceful years together. She told me to wait to come until a Memorial service could be held in Minnesota or Michigan, near his siblings, in the spring. On December 16th, his spirit left his toxic body. Cirrhosis of the liver had finally taken his life at age 52.

Portion of my Christmas Letter to Friends and Family, 12/20/11

…Kirk, 52, our oldest son, collapsed early December and left his body December 16th. Shocking as this is, I am comforted by his gifts revealed by Spirit. It has enriched the meaning of Christmas for me. I have felt a connection with his spirit and a peacefulness, knowing he is free of his painful toxic body. He is reunited with his father, Chuck, whose death he was still grieving.

Kirk was an alcoholic, beginning in adolescence. An affinity for alcohol can be inherited and is frequent in adoptees. Judgment is an automatic response by those who do not suffer from it. Spirit revealed that Kirk felt he was a misfit in the church world he grew up in, and befriended others he perceived as like himself. A sensitive and loving man, he was traumatized deeply by the judgments of others. He felt loved by those he chose to be with and would judge no one. He remained outside the church, except for the Christian treatment center, in which he had three separate admissions for treatment.

After months in treatment, he left with Sue, who had some health issues. He made a commitment to care for her and they have been together for 8 years. He had a relapse three years before his death and was told he had cirrhosis of the liver and wouldn't live long. He didn't tell Sue or anyone else. He didn't drink or complain. The rest is history.

What I tearfully realized was that in finding a purpose for himself, he was faithful to his commitment, and was determined enough to abstain from alcohol, his one pain-reliever.

Chapter 30: Kirk's Transition, December 2011

I see the primary block to Love's Presence is our judgments. His love in our conversations and in his life is testimony to his non-judgmental nature. Let us remember his legacy.

I have learned that one can have greater intimacy with family in spirit than family in the flesh. We are never alone. I sense their presence wherever I go. Perhaps, this is how death loses its sting...

The tears didn't come until later. They were more in awe of the love he lived despite his illness. The sympathy of others didn't seem appropriate! Knowing I could access him in spirit gave me a sense of joy that canceled any grief I might experience.

Sue, his partner, couldn't live without him and joined him nine weeks later, according to information from her sister-in-law.

CHAPTER 31

PAST LIFE ENCOUNTERS

Strong Reactions in Meeting Anyone Can Be a Cue

I felt revulsion in meeting one elderly man, particularly by his attention to me. He was beloved by others. My intuition and Muscle Testing indicated he incested me in a past life. I avoided him and told him not to touch me and said it was a past-life thing. He did not comprehend. Compassion will replace the loathing I have felt as I remember he is only playing a role in a play. We choose the parts we play before we incarnate.

Using the TaBIA healing process on my feelings has diminished their intensity. As I choose to hold him in the light, I know I am safe. My focus is on healing the memory I carried from that lifetime, using the tools I now have.

Even though he is not aware of that lifetime, working with my process has cleared the karma for both of us. Forgiveness is the answer. Incest is another characteristic of the Patriarchy. Females are considered fair game for sexual exploitation in war, society, or family. There is actually a new law in a mid-eastern sect that makes it "legal" for men to rape women. Many societies condone extreme exploitation of women. Patriarchy is still greatly affecting the planet.

Embracing Past Pain Frees the Present

When we are willing and ready, the pain shows up. Now, when this occurs, I have tools to free me. Awareness that we have done it all helps to prevent judgment and allows us to forgive ourselves and others more easily. One of the lessons I have learned is that I don't need to have this past-life father figure understand his offense in order for me to experience peace; it is my consciousness that is my responsibility.

To accept responsibility for my own peace is a difficult lesson as we are so attached to the belief that making the other understand the pain they caused is going to make us feel better. We suffer needlessly by this dependence on another's consciousness in our attempt to make the pain go away. Jesus words on the cross, *Forgive them. They know not what they do,* is a powerful reminder. Forgiveness is not excusing the other, but freeing us from the energy of that hurt. Jeshua has reminded us that it is ignorance and fear stemming from our veiled incarnations that causes the mistakes.

The impulse to exact vengeance or attempt to force guilt upon another is associated with ego satisfaction and does not serve us. To deny the ego may feel like a deprivation at first. A true shift in consciousness eliminates the need for the other to understand, as the bliss of Oneness begins to be felt. Shifting to the perception of our Higher Self becomes a practice that brings its own reward. TaBIA can help release our resistance.

My Circus Connections

At one of our channeling meetings, two women who are working together discovered they were in a past lifetime together as a family who owned a circus. I discovered I was a niece who worked in the circus as a trapeze artist. This circus lifetime also explains my childhood fantasy to be a trapeze artist. I was a tomboy and hung from low tree limbs and fantasized being a circus performer. Becoming aware of that lifetime with them helped explain the bond I felt with them.

Some New Arrivals on Kauai Feel Familiar

In 2008, "Ray" showed up at Unity. A new arrival on the island, he was handsome and engaging. I felt a connection with him immediately and MT that we had a past life together as well. He was homeless and went from shelter to shelter. He had money issues, yet he gave

Chapter 31: Past Life Encounters

workshops on prosperity. He went by several last names, one relating to money. This is only one of the contradictions I noticed. Ray was ten years younger than me, but there was a definite mutual attraction. I gave him my TaBIA process, which he used briefly.

Peggy, friend and channeler of Sananda/Magdalene, gifted me with a reading concerning the past life between Ray and me. It was a positive reading of my marriage to a sailor who was usually absent, yet with a strong soul connection.

Ray asked me to a tasting event at Blossoming Lotus. It was a standup, crowded, milling around affair. A younger woman caught his eye and he spent the whole time flirting with her. I felt hurt and angry and visited with other people as he was clearly unavailable. Neither of us had a car at that time so I told him I had to leave to catch a bus. He insisted that his new friend would take me home. I reluctantly accepted and sat in the back seat while they conversed on the way to my place. Later he told me nothing happened between them. After an overnight encounter with him, he returned to the mainland. There was a brief email exchange, then, I no longer felt any interest in him and was complete with this "charming sailor" affair.

Night Travels

A psychic spiritual teacher on the island volunteered an observation that in my spirit's night travels I was visiting a young man in South America and wanting to help him. At a Deeksha full-moon gathering at the beach, I met a new arrival on the island. He greeted me formally with a quick kiss on both cheeks, the greeting of another culture. His name was an obviously chosen spiritual name. When we gathered around the bonfire at the beach and he said, "I have to sit down," I sensed an energy of recognition. My MT indicated he was the man I was checking on in my night travels. Excitedly, I looked up "twin soul" and was sure he was it. I embarrassed myself with my disclosure to him of my twin soul belief—he was polite but not interested.

On Self Inquiry from a neutral rather than a needy place, I learned he was from my soul family but not my twin soul. Close to the age of my son, I mentally let him go as a potential partner. We greet each other socially. His presence is humble, peaceful and loving. On further Inquiry, I have never been his romantic partner, but I learned that we were female friends in a past life. Without a memory of that lifetime, I am simply getting information from my intuition, verified by Muscle Testing.

2012 New Years Day ("Carlos")

"Carlos" first contacted me by email and said we had past lives together. He had found me on the Pathways of Light website. At a Unity service on New Year's Day he showed up, a young man who was very enthusiastic and outgoing. He was effusive with "I love you" greetings to just about everyone he would meet. In his emails, he first stated he was going around the world with an intention to go without pre-planning and little money, expecting everything to be provided. He had been a powerful manifester in his business, and was very confident about manifesting anything he wanted.

Extraordinarily mindful of the Law of Attraction, he refused to say anything negative, and he reacted immediately to any shared process of mine with a vigorous, "Stop it!" It caught me totally by surprise as I deeply value my process of coming into a shift of perception out of a place of lack. He never allowed himself to feel or acknowledge lack. It felt contrived and unreal to me.

A female friend of mine firmly rejected his approach. The contrast in response to him was instructive. My own reaction was ambivalent. Our different reactions reflected neediness (or absence of need) for male attention and approval.

He landed a job with a man from Unity who was building a new house for himself. Carlos was very confident and capable and was permitted to live in the partially-finished house while he worked on it. For transportation he used the bus, his bike, or hitch-hiked, always getting a ride with just the right person. According to his story he had an illustrious history, heading a large successful construction company but losing everything in a divorce process "under a judge who hated me." Through my Inquiry Process with Source and Muscle Testing, (MT), I confirmed that in a past life he and the judge were antagonists.

A Past-Life Re-Connection with a Contract

Though attracted to Carlos, much younger than me, I was reactive early on to what I perceived was male privilege. He reacted by distancing himself from me. Even though we were not a couple, the following message from Jeshua may be instructive, especially to couples.

Jeshua, 1-18-12

Now we begin. Carlos is hurting. You have done nothing wrong except take him by surprise. He is a natural manifester, and is learning limits to his power over others. He has had many privileged lifetimes. You are correct in understanding the contrasts, and that part of your assignment together is navigating differences for a common goal.

The duality present in the male/female relationship will be changing to an egalitarian one. He did consent to come in and serve you at our request. Since he is very capable, he expected the assignment to be easy and assumed his usual take-charge style. The focus needs to be on a common vision, plus the exploration and navigation of male/female differences. His assumptions on his role are confused, as are yours. The key is willingness to listen and learn.

Remember the glue that will keep you on course is a common vision of being Love, Light and Peace, and enJoying the Process. Respect each other's guidance. Using the Four Keys as a process you both can ground yourselves in will be helpful. He will need to surrender the "how."

The challenges are male privilege and your fundamentalist programming of female powerlessness and self-doubt. Sharing what you value is important. Trust the process and let go of power and control. The learning potential can best be realized through gentleness and understanding. Acceptance of differences in each of your processes is needed. Awareness of the levels is key. The ego is still operating for both of you and cannot be completely ignored. —simply recognize it, and choose again. Yes the male ego is the more sensitive, because feelings aren't understood.

Your Heart's Desire is for healing the rift between you, and to accept the contract you have with Carlos. Neither of you know what that entails. You didn't accept his version of the contract. Your dream indicated there was no room for you in his version, because it was Patriarchal [Described in Part III re Carlos]. *I am here to guide each of you into a new way of relating as male and female.*

An approach for any female in relationship with a male could be, 'May I tell you how I can feel safe and equal with you?' Neither of you feel safe with each other. Exploring this alone and then together is your first task. The absence of judgment is a given for feeling safe. Sharing in this way will help you avoid making assumptions. Creating safety for sharing is an Intention you both need to hold. The 3rd Key of Allowing is to trust the process and avoid control. The 4th Key is for each to Surrender to your I Am Love Presence.

I am with you always, in all ways. Jeshua.

Impact of Our Past Lives on Current One

In an early email, Carlos had said he had come to teach me. To me, this reflected male arrogance. I felt devalued. I noted he was the same age as Kirk, my son who had just transitioned. I briefly felt the spirit of my son's love, knowing he would have dutifully cared for me if he had not been so impaired. Through Self-Inquiry I learned I had five lifetimes with Carlos. In one, I was his Queen mother; he, my princely spoiled son. He said that in a past life, he was a Hawaiian king and I was a male friend. In the other three lives, I had one as his lover, and was married to him in two lifetimes. It was the energy of the last marriage that I needed to release, according to my guidance from Jeshua. As always, I can count on Jeshua to come through with a message I need to hear.

Chapter 31: Past Life Encounters

Jeshua 1-25-12

Now we begin. Be in Peace. The energies you were feeling as you were awakening were from your night wanderings.

I wish to speak of your soul contract with Carlos. You have nothing to fear. You have had many lifetimes with him. Fear stops your remembering. Yes, you had several lifetimes as lovers. There was a lifetime you were involved in Christian fundamentalism. He was not. You were planning to marry as he had impregnated you. You died in childbirth, along with your son.

When Carlos returned to spirit, he reunited with you. Yes, you had other lifetimes together after that—two as husband and wife. He was a good husband in the first of the two lifetimes. You were unfaithful. He divorced you. In the last lifetime together 300 years ago, he was abusive emotionally and controlling. He had a number of affairs. Helplessness was a dominant feeling you carried. This is the lifetime you are feeling now with him, which makes trust difficult. Yes, there is karma to be cleared between you from that lifetime. You are to clear your traumatic memories with TaBIA.

The contract involves healing the Patriarchal wound, and experience a new way of relating as male and female. His push to be your teacher comes from male domination, not from Spirit. Purification of past patterns is necessary first, before any satisfactory work can be done.

Your fear that he will resist learning from you is reinforced by the traumatic memories of that lifetime. Your anger also is rooted in that lifetime. Clear that first before beginning to address your current experience. At this point, trust is impossible.

You need to set boundaries and confront from a clear place. Carlos's task to recognize his role in many lifetimes is now obsolete, and he has to clear his memories, forgive Self, and become willing to learn a new way of being male. Be firm and gentle with him. When the clearing is done first, learning new ways of relating will be easy and fun. You are feeling lighter already.

In reading the 'Anna' books, you are coming to realize I had many women teachers. This is necessary now in your Heart-Awakening 4th dimension. There are men who have become students of heart wisdom, yet women must lead the way. So accept your role, and note how the Patriarchy has wounded men as well as women. Unlearning the old ways is the focus now, in order to make room for the new. Deleting old programs from your bodymind computer that do not serve Oneness is your primary focus.

Lighten up. This task is easier with humor than with seriousness. Unlearning is easier in the vibrations of Love, Light, Joy, Peace, and Gratitude. There need be no judgment in the realization of the many injustices embedded in the Patriarchy. Forgive everything that has occurred. Forgiving Self is first. Without collusion, Patriarchy would have been over long ago. Yes there were alien dark forces that came on the planet, who are now being banished. Blaming them does not serve you. Self-awareness and release work will serve you best.

Your alarm is ringing in a new day. Hold the Vision of Heaven on Earth and your thoughts will fall into line. Your Intentions matter. You are mightily supported by non-physical forces that are sending you love. You are never alone.

I am with you always in all ways, Jeshua.

I was soon to learn Carlos was treating me like he treated me in our last marriage. It was this I needed to reject. I had stayed in that marriage for the sake of "security," a pattern common to many women, one I no longer wished to repeat. My lesson is to never accept a marriage for the sake of security. A mutual purpose is now my Intention for the basis of any committed relationship.

Female Process

Incensed by his male arrogance and lifetimes of male privilege, I sent him a series of insightful emails about valuing the feminine process in response to his scolding words.

Chapter 31: Past Life Encounters

In an early email, I said we had come together to release the karma, the energy of a mother toward a son she had spoiled and made into a King in her life. I wrote:

…We were emotionally enmeshed. How that has affected our relationships in this lifetime is for each of us to intuit with the help of Spirit and our guides. (As I reviewed this later in 2012, I realized I had repeated this pattern with my son Jeff.)

For us to communicate the truth in our heart to each other and honor each other's process would correct this. It will take focus and divine direction, i.e., you from your father in spirit and I from Athena, as well as from Jeshua, our Higher Self, our Soul Essence. The 'I Am Love' Presence is God, the One life energy of the Universe. We both have the same Heart's Desire and Intention—to be Love and Light, Peace and Joy.

My reaction to my gender rejection at birth, was to become competitive with my brothers, excelling scholastically and functionally. I became incensed by the idea of male superiority.

When I was caustic and abrasive with men I cared about, I was surprised at the effect of my words. It was your attempt to be Source for me that triggered a reaction of not being valued for what I can offer in an egalitarian relationship.

I have been receiving information that a new way of relating is coming to the planet. We have an opportunity to learn this through our awareness of Ascension. It is an exciting time. We can use our wounds as an example of contrast.

I sense that this is going to require patience and a willingness to change perception. For me, it means to use TaBIA to release my anger, understand the male programming, and patiently teach that our process is to be respected and to trust the process of the heart. May we embrace our path and heal our 'belief in separation…

I never received a response to the content of any of my emails. He merely said, "I love you"—to me, that was a way of ignoring it. I felt devalued, not loved.

Contrast

Carlos attended meetings with Ariana and exhibited a persona that felt unreal. "I love you" was a stock phrase he used to initiate or use in a conversation. It felt like an avoidance response.

My hope that my emails would inspire a conversation between equals was disappointed. It was obvious he felt enlightened and had nothing to learn or change. No further email inquiries from me went through. He had left Kauai and was on his way around the world. I wished him well and felt complete with him. Our contrasting male/female mindsets could not find common ground. We were both strangers to the life experience of the other gender.

As a female I value process, which is often judged as negative in the Patriarchal system and by some "positive" thinkers. This denial of what is, fails to recognize the power of our unconscious programing which requires gentleness to bring up into the light. This is a process of becoming aware. Saying 'Stop it!' doesn't do it for me though I find myself saying it to myself! There is a place for 'Stop it!' when we revert to old ways that no longer serve us, and we know it.

As a result of my Intensives with Anne Wilson Schaef, I value *Living in Process*. It was the theme of her Intensives. She would often remind us. "Trust your process!" God is a verb, God is Process, God is Love. This is in contrast to the God as a noun, a male being outside of us. We are not separate. How different our world would be if we honored God as the unconditional love process within us. I deeply value my experience with her work.

Connecting from the Heart

Carlos returned to the island and attended the same spiritually focused functions that I did. His purpose is still to travel to every country, manifesting the means as he goes. He came back to Kauai for some respite from the cold. The energy was somewhat different between us. At one encounter on the beach with several from his spiritual family, he greeted me with enthusiasm. As he used his stock phrase, "I love you!" he began coaching me on my expected response,

Chapter 31: Past Life Encounters

"I love you, too." I felt uncomfortable in the presence of two young women who were obviously interested in him and giggling, perhaps at my discomfort. I wasn't responding correctly, according to Carlos. Later, at another meeting, I finally told him of my discomfort from his pattern of editing my words in casual conversations with him and he apologized. It felt 'pono' (right).

I feel complete with Carlos and any past-life issues. After giving him feedback, he no longer edits my conversations. He, with a girlfriend who was his spiritual equal, were a delightful couple in any gathering where we were both present.

Absence of Self-Honesty

The "I love you" messages are disarming, and while there may be situations where that is quite appropriate, the phrase often felt phony and used as a dismissal of my feelings in a situation, as well as an avoidance. It reminds me of, "I will pray for you," which, when it comes from someone you are trying to communicate with and experience clarity, can feel like a one-up position by that person. It is like my friend, Rene, who felt I had left the fold and was a lost sheep, promising to pray for me. There is judgment involved. The feelings are avoided and it becomes an incomplete communication.

A complete communication involves the clear sharing of feelings by both parties as well as addressing the subject matter. Otherwise it feels unfinished and incomplete and we are not being authentic and honest. As light workers, this is important to understand and be aware of. Love and prayer are powerful energies which can be abused as cheap words. I feel loved when I am heard and accepted. The **language of the heart** is the feeling of resonance.

Sharing the truth of our being via an open, forgiving and accepting emotional heart allows the deeper connections to be felt from the Spiritual heart. This means that privileged males need to really hear the female experience. Carlos is a master of the Law of Attraction. Yet, I value feeling heard before I affirm the level of perfection in all things. Feelings are energy and they don't disappear with denial.

Holding the Intention to honor and accept the experience of the other as well as your own, can bring us into genuine harmony. This is the Vision I hold for birthing a new humanity.

A Physical Reflection of Unfinished Healing with Carlos

Shortly after meeting Carlos, a pimple appeared on my left cheek, festering and oozing for almost two years. As it persisted, to me this was indicative of cancer. An appointment for diagnostic testing and a biopsy revealed basal cell carcinoma.

My Inquiry process revealed a Spiritual issue. I have referred to Carlos as a privileged male with considerable judgment attached. When I asked if I had lifetimes as a male, I was told I had five such lifetimes, two were privileged. Then I realized it was my guilt I was projecting onto Carlos. According to my Inquiry, asking with permission, Carlos has had no lifetimes as a woman, so his missing that experience calls for my patience.

My initial action was to TaBIA my past life guilt for three days. This alone would not clear the problem. Before my diagnosis I tried several alternative applications with mixed results. One healer suggested Black Salve. This did start to dry up the lesion. When the kind doctor said he should remove the lesion, my strong desire to have it off my face gave consent. After the surgery, I started to feel guilt for my lack of assertiveness, as I felt the Black Salve would have taken care of it, and I feared a scar and disfigurement with surgery. As it turned out, a month later it was barely noticeable.

Despite my resistance, going to a doctor, getting a diagnosis and undergoing successful surgery was part of completing the Physical, Emotional, Mental and Spiritual aspects of this issue. I felt totally At One with Carlos. This healing is complete.

CHAPTER 32

MARTHA, MY PAST LIFE WITH JESUS

Correction of Perception

Up until the following message from Mary Magdalene, I thought I was her sister, Martha.

This channeling was received June 16, 2015, after I had already submitted my manuscript to Barbara Dee at Suncoast Digital Press. It is not clear which Martha the Bible referred to. My guidance tells me I am the Martha (aunt) that Jesus spoke to in the Bible reference. This Martha "never married and later managed her brother, Joseph of Arimathea's country residence in Bethany." There may have been two residences, one "country" and one city. It is not clear in my source, *Anna, Grandmother of Jesus*. I was very much a part of my niece, Martha's life. I felt her energy and experienced it accordingly in this life. Allow the experience to be what it is.

Mary Magdalene: 06-16-15

Now we begin. We recognize you are taking some bold steps in the writing and publishing of this book. We want to encourage and affirm your intention. It is easy for you to doubt yourself. You can look at your memory issue as a blessing as the ego is less present, prompting your trust in us to supply the information. Indeed this issue is but a reflection of your focus on the 4th dimension, making it more difficult to live in the 3rd dimensional world.

You had identified yourself as a Magdalene and as my sister, Martha. You are now realizing that you were my aunt, Martha, and not my sister. My sister, Martha, was named after you.

You, in this lifetime had so identified as my sister in that lifetime, we waited until after your reading of Anna's account in <u>Anna, Grandmother of Jesus</u> to bring in a correction. Both Marthas were Magdalenes.

Yes, you were a partner to Judas and your experience and guidance to meet him as "Al" in this life was totally authentic for you. I, along with Yeshua, was 21. My young sister, Martha, was quite mature at 15, when she joined the Magdalene order. All the Magdalenes went through certain initiations. Now, in the absence of these initiations, you have the personal promptings of the Holy Spirit through your own unique life experience. These are indeed your initiations.

This is the time for bringing in the Divine Feminine. It does indeed begin with Purification… You have a ministry of bringing in the Divine Feminine and using <u>The Return of the Magdalenes</u> as a primary source of support…. We are complete for now.

<u>As One, Mary</u>

My Probable Martha Identity

In the Relationship Chart of Appendix A, from the back of the book, *Anna, Grandmother of Jesus*, I discovered that after Anna had a son, Joseph of Arimathea, she had a daughter, Martha, 26 years younger than he. "She never married and later managed her brother's country residence in Bethany." She was probably the Martha who Jesus spoke to in the Bible story. I have interpreted my experience to be that of the much younger Martha, named after me. The Biblical account does not mention Aunt Martha, or that the Martha he spoke to was the Aunt Martha. The following is what I felt and experienced before this recent discovery.

Completion of My Past Life as Martha

Through Intuitive Inquiry, I discovered that I was Martha in Jesus's lifetime. This realization has clarified my purpose for this lifetime to complete her mission on earth.

My present awareness of Martha as my soul's physical incarnation during Jesus's time on earth, notes some similarities with this lifetime,

Chapter 32: Martha, My Past Life With Jesus

such as her inability to bear children. Adoption was my passionate choice to fulfill a longing to mother children.

Very little is said in the Bible about Martha, the sister of Mary Magdalene who married Jesus. *Anna, Grandmother of Jesus*, reveals an Aunt Martha, who Mary's sister is named after. It was Aunt Martha's preoccupation with food which was repeated in my eating disorder and focus on food. Our current and standard version of The Bible does not talk about the aunt, who was the Martha in the story that Jesus spoke to.

I have her passion for healthy food. Remembering Mary's better choice, I have set aside the cookbook project to "sit at Jeshua's feet" and hear the message he wishes me to share in this book, first.

In rereading Martha's life in *Anna, Voice of the Magdalenes*, I am amazed at our similar qualities. As more of my fundamentalist programming is deleted, I am uncovering the Martha in me. The *Anna* book describes the many activities of Martha, which include her following Jesus's teachings. Her work in caring for the sick, and also as hostess for her wealthy and well-known father's guests, contributed to her focus on physical needs. She didn't understand Mary's affinity for the esoteric and the resonance between Mary and Jesus.

In my increased awareness of my Martha soul identity, I also feel my Martha life's unfinished business as my purpose to complete in this lifetime. This has been confirmed many times for me, especially after reading Martha's story. Ending her karmic cycle as Martha, I am choosing to complete some aspects of that lifetime. This is my experience.

"Martha of Bethany" is a channeled dialogue between co-author Claire Heartsong, who took on the persona of Martha in that lifetime, 38AD, and Catherine Ann Clemett, a chapter in *Anna, The Voice of The Magdalenes.* It was very moving for me to feel my lifetime as Martha. She was staying in grandmother Anna's hermitage, which Martha describes as a humble hut in contrast to the spacious home in Bethany which she had to flee, along with the other close followers of Yeshua (Jeshua).

The Martha I identified with, was born at Bethany in 3 AD, and was the daughter of Joseph of Arimathea, Anna's oldest son. Joseph, a wealthy owner of ships, had built the Bethany home for his second wife, Mary of Magdala, Martha's mother. Mary, Martha and brother, Lazarus, lived there. Near Jerusalem, it was visited often by their cousin, Yeshua, who later became betrothed to Mary. (Biblical references found in Luke 10, John 11 and 12, don't mention the betrothal.) In 56 AD, Martha returned to southern France after living in Britain and France, and died at age 85. Through Claire Heartsong, Martha describes Tor of Avalon and Chalice Hill in England as the sacred place of ceremonies and initiations for Yeshua.

Martha goes on to describe her mother as a Magdalene high priestess, who taught her from birth about the Great Mother's ways, which Martha found exciting and beautiful. Isis was referred to as the Great Mother. Isis, an ascended master, was the Goddess that inspired the peaceful ways of the Atlantis period. The priestesses seemed to have powers that the male priests didn't experience. This was part of the jealousy felt by the male priests, who eventually corrupted the Atlantis peace with their lust for power and control, causing its sinking into the sea. (In a reading after I came to Kauai, I was told I had been a priestess in the temple of Isis.)

In a profound statement, Martha says, "I know those who have soul Awareness beyond their mind's concepts, and who are present with their breath, are much happier and calmer than the ordinary people I meet." The Aloha spirit involves the *ha* or breath as the presence of Love, or heart connection. Living from the Spiritual heart, in the *now* moment of conscious breathing, is a practice taught by Yeshua. The breath is therefore included in the "Tap and Breathe I Am" (TaBIA) process.

Martha goes on to say that the alchemical practices of the Magdalenes were too difficult for her to understand. Her impatience

Chapter 32: Martha, My Past Life With Jesus

with the time and energy these practices entail feels familiar. We return to the embodied state, lifetime after lifetime, to complete our original assignment in coming to earth. The TaBIA process is Martha's alchemical practice in this lifetime, a completion of her original assignment.

The Essene practice "cleanliness and eating only vegetables, fruits, nuts and grains" would be helpful today for obese America. Martha tried to eat only raw food, but cold weather called for compromise. These are goals I have today, though my blood type O seems to call for meat at this time. In our Heaven on Earth, our diets will become more and more vegan and raw. In past times, fasting and cleansing practices were routine with the change of seasons.

Martha had an ability to speak, read, and write Hebrew, Aramaic and Greek, as well as communicate in other languages. Joseph of Arimathea hosted people from many places with whom she could converse easily. Later lifetimes brought the experience of repressed expression. The language of the heart, a transmission of energy through the I Am Presence, is the Universal language called for now.

I am amazed at how much she and her family traveled without our modern means of transportation. Their mastery of many disciplines and general knowledge makes our culture look backward. Martha spoke of the training in Druid wisdom and the many stories from Yeshua about his time with them in Avalon, when he was a young teen.

Martha thought of Yeshua as a beloved brother and describes her heart connection: "…where I know he knows me and I know him… sometimes, I can attune to him and he helps me relax. I can breathe and let go of my worries and my cares." To me, this resonates as a beautiful practice of *prayer without ceasing*. As "a beloved brother" is exactly how Jeshua would like us to regard him. It is also the way I would like to regard most men.

Martha's Sexual Nature

She related that the energy in Yeshua's touch was like no other energy she has felt with men. Martha went on to describe her promiscuous behavior in her early teens and her mother's concern. This led to her father arranging a marriage with an older man she had no interest in.

She was only 16. When this husband discovered she was not a virgin, the marriage was invalid. Aware that wives caught in adultery were stoned to death, she suspected her influential father had protected her.

She speaks of her mother: "…a priestess of the Great Mothers Isis and Ishtar, tried very hard to teach me a different way to use my sex…we worked with the elemental energies of fire, water, earth and air. We sometimes took various herbs that opened our minds and bodies to more energy. We learned how to breathe consciously and recite words of power. We used certain oils to anoint our bodies so that we had more stamina and flexibility… We danced until we attained ecstatic states of trance… I slowly learned how to use my life-force as a way to benefit others …"

Martha goes on to describe the humanitarian causes that she and Lazarus undertook. They provided temporary housing for the homeless, unwed mothers, orphans, battered women, and the infirm, with her father's expansion of their large home. Their intake of lepers included Simon, the leper, in whose home her sister, Mary, anointed Yeshua's feet with spikenard oil (valuable perfume).

She relates her sadness about the secrets she lived with. Some of the maids who worked in her father's home had their own secret sexual lives and taught her about herbs to take after a missed period. Later, when Martha wanted to have children, she was barren, unable to conceive, her greatest sadness. In my present lifetime, pregnancy didn't occur, which turned out to be a blessing, as I've written about in an earlier chapter. My abnormal right kidney displacement (since birth) became a non-issue due to Chuck's lack of sperm. The adoption

Chapter 32: Martha, My Past Life With Jesus

of four children, including two Afro-Americans, became a rich experience in our lives.

Martha was asked to write and did not. The call to write has been with me for years. I made an attempt in childhood, and since have filled numerous unreadable journals. Heavy criticism from writing group members, and problems with outlining, focusing and organizing my material made writing distasteful. I made numerous commitments, only to lapse. My best time for writing is to awaken and write after 3 AM, stop at 7 AM, and go back to bed until 8:30 AM. Then I felt more disciplined. When I have slept through until seven and have tried to write during the day, there are too many distractions.

What I have discovered is that when I surrender and simply go to the computer with the Intention to write, I feel the presence of my "writing team"— Jeshua, mother Rose, Luke and Pam. Pam was a writer/editor and a friend in Kauai who died in 2004. Pam was also my mother in another lifetime. Later, Athena also came in to assist me.

In dealing with all my perceived handicaps, I periodically complain to Jeshua about picking me to do this writing. Feeling his smile, I am reminded to simply surrender to the process and listen. Struggling is another form of resistance. We engage the ego and the voice of fear when we try to figure it out.

Staying on Purpose

A partner could be helpful, or a distraction. Trust Source to provide what is needed. Recognizing and meeting our needs is a creative endeavor and part of necessary self-care as we embrace our purpose. Passion for a partner can be re-directed to "Passion for my Purpose in expressing the message I have been given."

We are never alone. When we commit to our soul's Purpose, the *commitment* will magnetize all the assistance we need. Remember the Four Keys: feel the Heart's Desire, focus your Intention and will to listen for directions, and Allow what shows up to be part of the divine plan. This calls for the Surrender of the ego to the Higher Self, our true spirit identity.

CHAPTER 33

THE MAGDALENES

Meeting Magdalenes on Kauai

After learning that there were women disciples, called Magdalenes, I began asking about reincarnated Magdalenes. Through Intuitive Inquiry, I have identified ten of the original Magdalenes, including a tourist wearing a necklace representing Mary Magdalene. I asked Spirit the purpose of identifying them and their presence on Kauai. I sensed Mary's presence and desire to communicate with me. The Magdalenes represent the Divine Feminine, which is to lead the way to a new humanity.

Recognizing our role refines our purpose and provides support. Any woman focusing on the Divine Feminine is a Magdalene. What that means in expression, service, and teachings is to be developed according to guidance. The restoration of the Feminine Presence requires purification. This calls for the release of all the disempowering messages in our programming.

THE MAGDALENE PRAYER

Aloha Jesus, Prince of Peace,
Remind us of your words, "The Kingdom of God is within you."
You valued the one called Mary Magdalene,
Who anointed you.
Today I honor her as the Chalice of the Divine Feminine,
The Queendom within.

Everything Scattered Will Be Gathered

Our Beloved I Am,
Our Holy Mother,
The Voice of Love in our Heart.
The Divine Feminine within.

May we allow all feelings to flow
And may our hearts desire
Love and light, peace and joy.

With any fear or feeling of separation
May we ask for a shift in perception.
May we feel acceptance and gratitude
For gifts of forgiveness and release,
And wisdom from lessons learned.

Cries of Enough from Mother earth,
Earthquakes and weather extremes,
Get our attention, our awakening
To our mindless pollution
And disrespect for her gifts to us.

In partnership, gratitude and love
For her blessings and healing resources,
May we share her gifts so all may be fed.
Acts of love flow easily from Source,
Intuition and Resonance guide us
And keep us from choices of error.

We birth and use our gifts
As we listen within.
Surrender to the One Self we are
Frees us from the illusion
Of separation from Source,
Separation from nature,
And separation from each other.

Chapter 33: The Magdalenes

The Queendom of our Being
Our Beloved I Am
The Glory of our Light
The Power of our Spirit
Abide now and forever
With all life as One.

Amen.

The I Am

By nature, the male energy is outwardly focused. It individuates and is that part of Being that focuses on Doing, creating into form. The **I** manifests. The female energy is inwardly focused heart energy, inclusive and oceanic in nature. It is the **Am**, which hears the Voice for Love, the Higher Self. Flowing and joining are its characteristics. **"I Am" is the mantra of male and female joined as One.** It is the divine masculine and feminine energy in perfect equality that Sananda/Magdalene represent. This gives focus to our Ascension in consciousness.

Submission to the male as the head was the rule emphasized in the church. The heart was subject to the head. Hear again the words of Jeshua—*Let the Heart be the Master, and the head becomes a useful servant*—meant for both men and women. By nature, heart energy is the feminine energy which informs the masculine energy in the solar plexus, the power center, to manifest the desires of the heart. When the emotional heart is cleared by the free expression of feelings without blame and forgiveness is a spiritual practice, the Spiritual heart, the Voice for Love, is heard. It is the Source of true wisdom. The ego tends to rule the head and is dominated by male energy and the voice of fear, which assumes a controlling role, unless it is ruled by heart energy, which allows choice.

Jesus, Known as Yeshua to his Partners and Children

Yeshua first married Myriam of Tyana after meeting her at the well before his first journey to India. Martha relates, "Before he returned to India with Myriam the second time, he became betrothed to my sister, Mary." With Myriam he had three children.

Myriam and Mary adopted another child fathered by Yeshua. Mary was barren until a miracle of healing occurred on the night of the Last Supper, when Sar'h was conceived. Later at Mount Bugarach in France, Mary had Lizbett.

Mary was known as Mary Magdalene because she was born in Magdala. She became a leader of 12 female disciples, including Martha, and they were called the Magdalenes.

Anna's Comments in *Anna, The Voice of the Magdalenes*

It was a practice among spiritual masters to practice high Tantric alchemy, also practiced by Yeshua. It was troubling to the channeler, Claire Heartsong, to hear of Yeshua's polygamy. The idea of polygamy could overshadow his intention and accomplishments. Claire chose to relax and trust the process. Anna goes on to say, "…speaking openly about Yeshua's multiple partners is not about condoning licentious sexual activity, or any sexual practice where love is absent." Yeshua, himself comments later that he does not recommend polygamy. Though he treated both women with great respect and honored them equally, he realized the potential for conflict and hurt is so much greater.

The fundamentalist teaching that Jesus was celibate carries the implication that sex is sin and beneath the spiritually pure life of Jesus. "Not understood is the esoteric practice of Tantric alchemy, which includes the conscious cultivation, retention and channeling of life-force energy through the body, with or without a partner, for the attainment of spiritual enlightenment."

Sex for Jeshua was not a lust-based, genital-focused sexuality. Great karmic harm has come to many individuals and many generations because of this ignorance. Because of the lust-based understanding of sex, "erring in the way of extreme austerities, or blatantly indulging harmful self-gratification, promiscuity, and all manner of human bondage" has occurred. The transmission of life-force energy (or sexual passion) as practiced by Yeshua and the Magdalenes was always accompanied by "loving mindfulness and deep care for one another's wellbeing." Not just in the moment, but for their lifetime and lifetimes to come for those who reincarnate.

Light conception, as used in the Anna books, is consciously conceiving children to bring a unifying matrix of Light, to facilitate awareness of Oneness. This may or may not include sexual intercourse. Therefore, virgin births are possible! Jesus' birth was a light conception. Others in his family were also light-conceived.

The temptation for jealousy between the two wives of Yeshua became a spiritual challenge they each undertook, resulting in a very loving relationship between them. Read this amazing book for a vision of heaven on earth, and new ways of being together in peace, love and harmony. Martha affirms Anna's vision where men no longer use women, earth, or war for their aggrandizement. And women no longer need to find their identity in their relationship with men. They can partner as equals in a spirit of cooperation rather than competition.

Awakening to the Magdalene Energy

Intuitive Inquiry has increased my awareness of the reincarnation and connecting of the Magdalenes. My sleep patterns go from the usual getting up two or more times a night for bladder relief, to sleeping until a nonphysical presence awakens me. This morning I MT that Mary Magdalene wished to give me a message.

Mary Magdalene, 1-10-2015

You have heard a professor speak on Buddha and Jesus, comparing similarities, and repeating the Patriarchal version you no longer accept. You need not fear your talking to the speaker with a desire to sow a seed of correction. Again, you have become aware of the depth of the Patriarchal programming which ignores women and the heart energy.

Everything Scattered Will Be Gathered

You are questioning what to do with your awareness. Continue to focus on the primacy of listening to the Voice for Love in the heart, and trust your Intuition. That is the feminine.

To most male scholars this is a foreign process. Education is necessary and much patience is required to sow the seeds of change in a society steeped in the dependency on the ego mind to find the answers to one's questions. This is the path you are on. You have many spirits interested in assisting with this shift to heart wisdom awareness.

This is a latent energy in men which some are eager to learn. A compassionate approach, acknowledging their male programming by a Patriarchal society and church, will help them forgive this obsolete structure which has greatly affected the expression of the Divine Masculine.

Simply tell this professor of comparative religions that the version they have studied is obsolete.

Jesus declared his continued presence in promising the Holy Spirit, the Voice for Love present in every heart birthed on the planet, individual expressions of the One I Am identity. The Buddha didn't provide that. That inner voice is the voice of truth, in contrast to the egoic voice in the head. **Truth resonates and needs no outer proof.**

The seeds of truth are present but ignored because of the dominant emphasis on the "outer." It is the awakening of the heart that has caused many to leave the church with its dogma and 3rd dimensional consciousness. The assumption that Jesus and his apostles started Christianity is another block to accepting the truth that is now coming forth.

For now, keep the professor's name available to you. He has your card. Your use of Ho'oponopono can lessen his fear. Yes, he is another to whom you would give your book. Indeed you are aware of the pain some will experience when the light brings forth the truth—their entire lives have been devoted to serving the Patriarchal version of Jesus. You have been alerted to key quotes from Jeshua to share. You will be given more. These quotes will empower them to accept the truth revealed by the light, revealing all that has been suppressed by the Patriarchy. As you review these quotes you will be given one that is most helpful to the person you are sharing with.

We value your checking in on priorities in the use of your time. May all lightworkers do so. When you identify a lightworker, telling them so is an encouragement. You have tools to share, which are very helpful. You will be given energy to do all that is yours to do. Accept help. A new way of being is the task for all awakening soul, so facilitating change is primary. It is the embodied expression of the divine that needs to change. Your core essence and identity as the One Self needs no changing. It is the realization of this that is necessary at the soul (mental/emotional) level as well as the physical level. This is consciousness. Here, a distinction has to be made as some lightworkers are confused, thinking the soul is perfect and not in need of change. Soul is an expression aspect of the One Self.

You are feeling our immense gratitude for your willingness to serve. You have many creative ideas coming to you. Some will work and some won't. So as you share them with us, we will encourage you to follow through on those appearing most effective to us. Remember to have fun and use humor to melt the resistance to change. Remember Jesus' words, "a universal experience is not only possible but necessary." Writing a separate paper on the Universal experience with J's help would be a valuable introduction to heart awareness and higher consciousness.

As one with Jeshua, know I am on your writing team as well. More will be revealed.

As One, Mary Magdalene.

CHAPTER 34

JESHUA AND MARTHA SPEAK TO ME

The Jeshua Messages

They began with Inquiry and became more regular in 2010. Usually awakened during the night from a pleasant dream, I would intuit and Muscle Test to confirm it was Jeshua. An early one in 2010 affirmed an Intention to share the Purification work of Ascension through the use of TaBIA as my primary contribution. His messages always began with, *Now we begin.*

The following is an excerpt of his comments, which usually filled a page at the computer.

…A clear intention is important. You are establishing a niche and the initial focus needs to be the least threatening, and specific to the primary need you are to fulfill—that of Purification.

Be gentle with yourself and persistent at the same time to choose your boundaries. Not everything that pops into your mind is inspired. 'I am here only to be truly helpful' will invite in the wisdom of the Holy Spirit within you.

He usually closed with *I am with you always in all ways, Jeshua.*

I have received many more messages nocturnally. (Some are at the end of Part III.) Please know that this experience is available to any who are open to communication with the non-physical world, i.e., master teachers, teams, angels, transitioned entities who are interested in a connection with you. Test the spirits. I use Intuitive Inquiry. "Who is speaking to me?" is a standard question, if I am not sure. In my case, I will back up an intuitive answer with Muscle Testing. This is not necessary, however. Muscle Testing became an answer to my self-doubt.

The Lost Key

One night, when the *Way of the Heart* group read the chapter on "Martha" from *Anna, the Voice of the Magdalenes*, it felt very familiar. On trying to leave to drive home, I was unable to find my car keys. It was dark where we parked our cars and we searched the ground between car and house with a flashlight as well as the front seat of the car. Meanwhile, Peggy, who has channeled Jeshua for 30 years, had already left, then phoned back to the hostess. I was not to go home, she said. She received a message that she was to come and get me so I could stay with her for the night.

After sleeping two hours at Peggy's house, I was awakened. I had my Neo (portable word processor) and was given the following message from Jeshua:

Now we begin. Indeed, you were not to go home. Not because of any danger to you, but because of a connection needed through Peggy. It was no accident that the chapter tonight was about Martha. Does it have a ring of familiarity?

Yes…this is about you, as Martha, and your future life here. Martha knew she ought to write and did not. It is this Martha energy you want to release with TaBIA. She was also a Scorpio. Your sexual energy is similar, but much more restricted by your programming. You are meant to channel it. She was a gifted conversationalist in several languages. In one lifetime she/you were severely traumatized for expressing your truth. This will change. TaBIA the many issues around expressing.

- *"Foot in mouth"*
- *Silenced for speaking up for the unjustly-treated, and protesting Patriarchal offenses*
- *Defamation of your reputation by those offended by your words*

Chapter 34: Jeshua And Martha Speak To Me

Judas is a soulmate of Martha. They were lovers. His spirit wants to reconnect with Martha in this lifetime, in the body. That is you. He is at this time on island, single, looks about 70. No, he doesn't have a clue about who he is. Be a magnet for him and he will show up, most unexpectedly.

Yes, your brother Luke was one of the incarnations of Judas. He is working on this reconnection. We are pau [complete] *for now. In summary:*

- *Free the Martha resistance to writing.*
- *Enjoy the sexual energy as a creative force.*
- *Your ease in the Esoteric will increase.*
- *You have your 'practice.' More is not necessary.*

It was Peggy's habit to go into her rose garden early each morning to meditate and frequently channel Sananda/Magdalene. I went with her, knowing I was to connect with Martha. While Peggy focused on her connection with Jeshua, I listened for Martha's message. Martha is the soul identity I readily identify with, even though I had other identities in previous lifetimes.

Message from Martha

"Aloha Martha."

Aloha Petra, Yes, I am here within your bodymind to complete the incarnation cycles I began. You recognize the energies even today of my resistance to writing. I made you an introvert to make it easier to settle down and write.

You also feel my sexual energy and the longings of centuries. Know that I/You am here to melt the wall between male and female and experience Oneness. Your work in the kitchen mimics my lifetime then. I/You will again experience the embrace of Jeshua in the embodied soul of Judas.

All is moving very quickly on earth and your energies, vibrations, will match earth's rising frequency. Clear all that no longer serves you in all Physical, Emotional, Mental and Spiritual areas. I will help you. Spiritual cleansing is part of your mission.

Yes, it was I who kept you from finding your key. As your consciousness merges with your Soul identity, your uncertainty will leave.

The Martha reading in Anna's book states Judas was enlightened in a following lifetime. In this current incarnation he chose to be heavily veiled as to his identity. Though enlightened, he is unaware of his lineage. He is coming to the island. You will know him, especially now that you have been alerted.

Peggy, my gracious hostess, returned me to my car, where I found my key left in the trunk lock. Gratitude for the orchestration of my life accompanied me on my way home.

Mary Magdalene and her 12 Women Disciples

Peggy, a reincarnation of one of these 12 women, initially said to the *Way of the Heart* group that the lineage of Jesus (followers in his lifetime) are coming together on Kauai to help birth the new humanity under Sananda/Magdalene's direction. Jeshua tells me there are seven of the former 12 women who have found the *Way of the Heart* group, some who do not yet know of their connection to Jeshua. Therefore I am not to reveal more names, except for the following:

Alia Gets her Wish—A Conscious Death in Community

Alia was a friend who opened up her home as well as her heart. She initiated our friendship, and I often stayed overnight with her rather than driving home at night after a meeting. In addition to her Cranial-Sacral work, she was an alchemist, and creator of herbal essences out of pure oils. She gardened and produced some herself. Her pain relief oil for sore or injured body parts is very effective.

In early spring of 2013, she told me of a tumor in her lower left abdomen. She had used her healing potions and Spiritual tools for a time before going to a doctor. When she did, it had already metastasized. When many other healers and friends tried to help,

Chapter 34: Jeshua And Martha Speak To Me

she refused. She had become aware of being called home, and was determined to stay out of the hospital and let her community of friends surround her and be with her. Her daughter came for a brief time toward the end. A morphine patch became routine. She stopped eating. A psychotherapist friend had organized a care group, which became an amazing community as her body lingered on for six weeks after she stopped eating. It was said that the loving energy of those who sat and cared for her is what prolonged her stay in the body. She frequently spoke of Jeshua. Some of the caregivers knew her in her lifetime with Jesus.

I had invited my grandson, "Patrik," to live with me, which necessitated a major move into a two-bedroom apartment in Lihue, where he could attend high school. This so consumed my time and energy, I could not be with Alia. She lay naked (her preference) on her bed for four months with 24-hour care by volunteers and hospice. Through "Go Fund Me" (an Internet program for requesting money), she received enough to pay the rent and for her daughter's trip. She was very specific in her requests for care.

As soon as I completed my move and enrollment of Patrik into high school, I volunteered to sit for five hours. She had been without water for a month and we all marveled that she was still breathing. Psychic information was that she feared the tunnel associated with leaving the body. She was barely conscious. I assured her of Jeshua's going with her, and encouraged her to leave the body that no longer served her. She transitioned an hour after I left, when another caregiver took over. I know she is present to me when I speak of her or to her. I feel she has forgiven me for not being with her more in her final four months. She has a mission to return and help with the New Earth. I am assured that I will know her when she shows up.

Mary Magdalene Breaks 2000 Years of Silence

Consciousness of Magdalene energy is growing. An increasing number of women are channeling Mary Magdalene and leading workshops on the Divine Feminine. General information is to do what we love, which is becoming aware of our Heart's Desire. Focus on expressing through dance, song, art and voice in ritual and ceremony is happening. Hula, popular on the islands, is a beautiful expression of the heart. Slowing down to allow flow and intuition, our natural way of being, is now honored.

Opening up conversation regarding the significant role of Mary Magdalene has revealed many women already aware of her importance and their connection. They simply have not felt free to talk about it. Those still attached to the church's denial of her true essence and role will resist this information.

CHAPTER 35

JESHUA CONNECTS ME TO JUDAS

Judas, the Most Misunderstood Disciple

The one Martha loved "almost as much as Yeshua," she would have married if he had been willing. Judas Iscariot. He later became a devoted disciple of Yeshua, and Martha then became a "Magdalene consort" of Judas. Yeshua's inner circle of 12 men worked with the 12 hidden women called Magdalene consorts. These couples worked together "as an energetic unit throughout Yeshua's and the Magdalenes' formal ministry," especially in ceremonies and the healing and teaching of large audiences. Our patriarchal Bible says nothing of these women.

Judas did not fully grasp the message Yeshua taught about the inner King/Queendom of God. He had great expectations of Jesus using his power to overthrow Roman rule. When Yeshua did not live up to Judas' expectations, he felt not only disappointed, but betrayed. Judas was influenced by his own harsh father and other Zealots, who lived at Qumran, an Essene desert monastery. They saw the Messiah as one who would rid them of the Romans.

Martha knew Yeshua's message focused on the Kingdom within. He taught that we came to earth not only to serve God, but to BE God, a Presence whose "essence is both emptiness and the awareness of pure BEING and LOVE."

Judas was asked by Yeshua to play the betrayer role. Martha knew that Judas was greatly loved by Yeshua. Though Yeshua was giving him much support, others did not understand the "dark" role he was to play. The inner conflict Judas already had, plus the judgments of others, deepened his depression, and he hung himself after the crucifixion.

Jeshua Alerts Me

Jeshua had informed me that an incarnation of Judas, Martha's lover in that lifetime, would come into my life. I was given an image of a man with grey hair and a beard. Three days later, my friend "Malia" and I decided to go to Salt Pond to swim, despite the heavy rain. We waited in the car a couple of minutes and the rain stopped. (When I ask the sun to come out, it usually does.)

As I was taking off the clothing over my bathing suit, a man walked over to us. He had grey curly hair, a beard and mustache, and was considerably younger than I had imagined.

"Is this the man?" I Muscle Tested and received a firm YES.

We conversed and as Malia and I went into the water, "Al" said he was going to put on his suit. While swimming, I saw him standing on the beach watching us. I was surprised that he didn't venture in. As I emerged from my swim, Al said, with amazement, "You are really good swimmers!" Malia said she was really hungry as she hadn't eaten. Al immediately offered to take us out to eat, and chose to skip swimming.

This was the first of several observations that indicated he might be afraid of the water. He stated that he preferred to go in for only five minutes and stay where he could touch bottom.

Later, my Inquiry via Intuition and MT indicated he had a past life where, as a teen, he was drowned by his brother. At an appropriate time, I informed him of this and shared the TaBIA process for healing the cellular memory and his fear of the water.

We went to *Grinds*, a popular eating place where we could have fish and salad. Malia was the conversationalist. She asked questions I would hesitate to ask. Much of his interest and conversation was about his recent attendance at a UFO conference, and his visit to

Chapter 35: Jeshua Connects Me To Judas

the crop circles in England as he showed us pictures of them. He was very interested in the stories of Big Foot and the Sasquatch beings in his area, and wanted to reassure people there was nothing to fear from UFOs. He hoped to communicate with these beings.

Al asked for my phone number, which I gave him, along with my card. We parted and he returned to the Waimea Cottages to join his in-laws, related to his ex-wife, his "guide and angel," as he referred to her. He revealed that they traveled together.

My First Date with Al

Two days later he called. He wanted to take me to the special place in the canyon I had described to him. Monday, with a prepared lunch, I drove to Waimea to meet him. It was a beautiful clear day for excellent views of the canyon,

In our conversation about his divorced wife, whose family was gathering in Kauai, I asked him, "Doesn't she object to your encounters with other women?"

"Oh, no," he said. "She is 88 years old and sex between us stopped 20 years ago." I then realized he wasn't kidding when he said he was attracted to older women. She "just doesn't want to know" about his sexual encounters. They were traveling buddies and enjoyed each other's company. I learned he was 51, younger than my son Kirk, who had just transitioned at age 52.

At "13-Mile Road" we took the narrow, paved road down to the spot I had discovered in my first year on Kauai. It was my special place, an exclusive pine forest that reminded me of the beautiful Scotch and Norway pine which I had left behind in Northern Minnesota. A short drive on a dirt road took us to a private lookout of canyon, ocean, red-sculptured earth peppered with young lime-green pines. The stillness was magical. We sat on some rocks and just took in the view until interrupted by several small planes flying low overhead, reminders we were close to a military base.

As we sat next to each other, he made a sexual move and said I turned him on. He kissed me and enquired about my health. I said something about this being "too soon," got up and went to set up our lunch on the rocks.

After lunch, he asked if we could meditate together. I was surprised and delighted by his suggestion. As we sat on a rock, back to back, in silence for a few minutes, I decided to tell him that my last sexual encounter three years ago was painful. He was distant during the rest of our Kokee explorations.

Arriving at the location of my car, he became conscious of the time, saying he was expected back by five to be with the family for the evening. Drinking and talking was their agenda. He said goodbye without a hug and hurried to his car. It was anti-climactic, in every way.

In our initial conversations, I had disclosed my source of guidance for meeting him, our past life with Jesus and *A Course in Miracles* as a primary revelation of Jesus' message. I promised him some reading materials. We had arranged to meet again.

After my Wednesday morning meditation meeting, we met at Salt Pond. He had a late breakfast and wasn't ready for the lunch I brought. He read the ACIM materials I brought for him while I went swimming. Later, after eating, we became separated when he went to the end of the beach to swim in a shallow place before looking for me. As we said goodbye, I reassured him I was physically okay.

Saturday, I took my friend Malia swimming. Al showed up and said he was walking to the far end to swim where the water was quiet and shallow. I said I would swim over there. When I arrived I coaxed him to come out into the water and stand next to me, remembering his need to be sure he could touch bottom. I remember his beautiful brown eyes and knowing smile as I approached him and felt his body and embrace. He quickly got out of the water and we got dressed. Malia waited while he invited me to sit in his car a few minutes. He kissed me, saying, "You turn me on," and asked to come to my place.

Chapter 35: Jeshua Connects Me To Judas

I declined. I didn't want a "slam, bam, thank you mam" encounter, knowing he had to be back with in-laws in an hour or so. Intuitively, I knew his strong desire came from an ancient cellular memory of our lives as Judas and Martha. My desire was similar.

A Disappointing Encounter

When Al walked into my apartment on a Monday around noon, we stood looking at each other. Without further conversation we went to the bedroom. Pain prompted an abrupt shift in energy. A committed relationship would have allowed patience and skill to restore some of what I had lost through inactivity. Yet, this was something I felt I had to do. Even though disappointing at the physical level, this served me as a completion of our past life experience.

A Lesson in Love

The next day was the last day I would see Al before his departure. He called and said he wanted to gift me with a TV and DVD player. I had mixed feelings as it had been a major accomplishment for me to let go of TV. There was no room for it in my living room, so I hastily cleared my bedroom desk. He came early afternoon with a beautiful new thin TV and DVD player, and set it up for me with a very impressive DVD, "Quantum Consciousness."

I watched it while he left and was gone for an hour to retrieve a part he had forgotten. I felt awed and grateful for his generosity. He patiently attempted to teach me how to use the control/remotes. My intention is to use this technology to promote my purpose, not delay it.

We shared a couple phone calls after that and emails with words, "Keep in touch!" I have come to realize this was simply another completion process. There is no further processing needed of our several lifetimes together. Al had just finished gifting me out of his well of love! This realization gave me another Cue for deletion of a bodymind program—that of equating sex with love—which does not serve me. This is how *living in process* serves one. Allow. Allow. The more we release, the more the curtain dissolves that conceals the authentic Self. This past life encounter came right after the one with Carlos was completed.

An Exciting Possibility

At the Wellness Expo, while I was speaking to an author friend and his wife at their display table, an Asian man approached and greeted the author. As I was complimenting my author friend on his promotional work and writing, I added my wish for a promoter to assist me. "Malu" heard me, turned to me, and said, "I will promote you!" Malu and I proceeded to talk and exchange cards. He represented a company that promotes people through helping them use video emailing.

He was remarkably patient in coaching me in front of a computer camera. Though I had almost memorized my script, I would go blank in front of the camera. I couldn't stand to look at myself. Malu reminded me, many times, to smile. Repeated tries did improve my performance but none were acceptable to me.

Intensity of Fear Recognized

This became a focus for Self Inquiry and new lessons. Speaking in front of others brings high anxiety and I would freeze. Inquiry revealed that I had several lifetimes which suppressed my expression as a woman. Punishment was mostly in spiritual cut-offs, with resulting emotional pain. This past life issue is reinforced by this life.

TaBIA was used to release that early programming. Knowing and articulating the value of my work is an ongoing challenge, not only for me but for many women coming into their power.

After learning that my willing promoter was Chinese-Hawaiian as well as a martial artist, I've named him Malu in this book, which includes "Peace" and "discipline" in its meaning, qualities characteristic of a martial artist. When I took on guardianship of my grandson, Patrik, in 2013, I introduced them to each other. I intuited a connection between them and my Inquiry revealed their past life as Chinese brothers.

Chapter 35: Jeshua Connects Me To Judas

Malu and I have similar needs, goals, and interests, with different skills and talents.

He is a uniquely conscious man. My Intuitive Inquiry informed me he was an Indian teacher of Jesus in that lifetime. Inquiry also indicated he was my brother in a past lifetime and a friend in another. In guidance from Jeshua, I was to stay focused on my purpose with Malu and not get carried away by my attraction to his gentleness and humility. I can see Malu as a loving brother. It is an opportunity to practice and learn a way to experience heart resonance and a new way of being together on the planet. Malu is in my soul family, but not a soul mate.

Circumstances have distanced Malu and me, and I have put promotion efforts on hold. Any exceptions to that vision of having a promoter partner come from past patterns, attitudes, and beliefs I have not yet cleared. Sometimes we are not ready for what we ask for. Part of our readiness process is to return "home" and deal with what we left behind.

There is a pattern of financially stressed and/or circumstantially unavailable men crossing my path. They are spiritually conscious men and may be connected to one or more of my past lives. They seem to be mirrors to my own life. According to Jeshua, at this writing I have connected with six of seven male soulmates on the planet—we are not limited to one!

CHAPTER 36

FAMILY (DIS)CONNECTIONS

Undertaking a trip to visit my children on the occasion of the Memorial service and burial of my son Kirk's ashes, became a major event of completion. There is nothing so powerful as a family reunion to bring up unhealed stuff.

Preparation for Trip to Ann Arbor for Kirk's Memorial Service

I was blessed with the following nocturnal message from Jeshua, May 22, 2012:

Now we begin. There is nothing to fear. Allow yourself to be in flow. You have nothing to lose but your peace. That is most important to you now. Everything is in divine order. Continue your TaBIA work as you notice unhelpful patterns coming up. Being in your power is simply knowing you are loved. Stay with your heart. The opportunities before you are many, but the most important task is to be in the Now. Showing up in your I Am Presence will handle every situation that arises. Anxiety brings in the ego which immediately tries to figure it out.

Trust the process. You have voiced your intentions. Spirit hears. Notice all the occasions you have allowed fear to come in. There will be many who can help you use the cell phone, while on the journey. Your ego loves to dump everything on you at once and it only triggers worry. 'What comes next?' can be a habitual question that Spirit hears and will cue you. You will have many opportunities to experience new responses when in peace that can surprise you.

Regarding your compulsive sharing when you have a gracious listener, no harm was done. Yet you did not feel good afterward, which is a cue.

Since your intention is to become conscious of the choices you make, TaBIA this pattern. It comes from the need to explain or justify things that occur. Yes, it is discretion that will be sorely tested on this trip. Yet, don't be in fear, seeking the most loving way to respond. As you center in your I Am, ground yourself with your many high vibration phrases such as, 'Peace Be Still and Know I Am God.'

If you first recognize the anxiety and TaBIA the low vibration, the I Am shows up. This is an important detail to teach—remember to clear what gets in the way and your true Essence shows up without efforting. This is the biggest contradiction to fundamentalism that says our true nature is 'unworthy sinner.' Your self-judgment does not serve you. TaBIA this automatic ego response. Becoming conscious is just that, becoming aware and letting go what no longer serves you. This is the work of Ascension.

Mind your Ps, especially Patience, Persistence, Purpose and Playfulness. Stay with your core Intention, Allow and Surrender to Source. What an opportunity to practice discretion.

Remember I am with you always in all ways,

Jeshua

A Missed Connection

This trip to be with family had some unknowns for me. Communication had been cut off by Kim, my oldest daughter, for reasons unclear to me. Kari, my youngest, was quite dependent on her as the foster mother for her son, Sebastian, my grandson whose high school graduation I planned to attend.

The first part of my trip was to Ann Arbor, home to my son Jeff, my grandson, Patrik, 13, and my granddaughters who were in their early 20s—Tricia with son, Cayden; Kim Kari, with son Kimani. I feel most connected to Jacinta, mother of Jeff's children, who is the family communicator and a motherly presence to all, including my son, Jeff, the father of their three children. They never married.

Chapter 36: Family (Dis)Connections

Seated in the back of the plane and unable to get out in time in Los Angeles to get to the Detroit gate, I missed my connection to Detroit, MI. After an apology and a free breakfast I was able to get on the next flight to Detroit.

Family Secrets

Jeff and his girlfriend, "Shar," met me. Jeff had never revealed anything about his marriage to Andrea and I didn't ask. I felt very out of the loop and went along with the flow. According to Jacinta, Andrea had finally left after an on-and-off marriage. This all occurred, unknown to me. I didn't question or show surprise, as I have been excluded from the events in my children's lives (including their address changes) since my divorce. Only births would be reported to me. This pattern of secrecy began with Chuck's alignment with our children during their adolescent struggles.

We waited at the baggage carousel and…no suit case. I didn't realize it had gone on the missed plane. When we went to baggage claim the third time, the suitcase was brought out. Jeff informed me I would be staying with my granddaughter, Kim Kari (named after her aunts). Quite intuitive, Jeff said Kim Kari wouldn't have the food I was accustomed to eating, so we stopped at Trader Joe's where I purchased what I desired. We arrived at Kim Kari's apartment where Jacinta, Tricia, Kim Kari, Patrik, and my two great-grandsons, ages three and four, were waiting.

Overlooking a scenic river dotted with geese, I enjoyed a wonderful view from Kim Kari's bedroom window. Kim Kari gave me her bedroom while she slept on the couch.

I brought the Christmas presents that had come back to me, undeliverable at an old address, and these were now opened. I cooked quite a bit while I was there as Kim Kari worked the whole weekend, and Tricia was caring for her four-year old son, Kimani. Friday I prepared stir-fry for everyone. In the evenings I had some significant conversations with beautiful Kim Kari, now a working mother who

I had last seen as a child. Her goals included training in the culinary arts.

She revealed a secret which "everybody [in the family] knew" about Chuck's forced move to Michigan from Minnesota being due to a parishioner's involvement with Jeff, our black son. I was told that Jeff resented the move. I hoped to get the story from Jeff when I could be alone with him. I never got the chance to talk with him about this "secret."

I could recall no clue from my husband (or anyone) about any such issue with a parishioner prompting our move to Michigan. His pattern of secrecy had excluded me far more than I realized. My openness was a fearful thing to Chuck. In my psychiatric work I had learned that family secrets are very much a part of the addictive system. Revealing them in a non-judgmental setting allows healing. Since that is my Intention, I trust the Allowing process to bring anything else into the light for healing. It requires no conscious effort on my part; only Surrender of the ego (the voice of fear) to the voice for Love in my heart.

My grandson Patrik whom I had not seen since age four, was now 13 and looked a handsome 16. He very much wanted to come to Kauai. He referred to reading "The Daily I Ams" poem in my 2010 book, and asked me to help him with a poem for school. I had given all my children my book, *A Journey of Ps and Cues to Inner Peace and Power*, and never received feedback or thanks from any of the four. I have begun to realize how unfamiliar my consciousness is to them, another sign of the disconnect in their teen years. Patrik gave me hope for a meaningful connection.

<u>More about Jeff and Me</u>

Though adopting Jeff was the fulfillment of my desire to mother a little black boy, it didn't mean he would share my consciousness. He displayed many macho attitudes as he took on the characteristics of an adult male. Estranged from his wife, Andrea, he has retained

Chapter 36: Family (Dis)Connections

Shar, a girlfriend who he takes to family gatherings, which is politely tolerated. It felt strange indeed.

I experienced Shar as assertive and caring, and she was the first to support me at the Zion Memorial Service. She can cut through and correct Jeff's macho behavior with her calm observation and assertion. In my Intuitive Inquiry of Spirit, I learned she is his soul mate and they have had past lives together.

Charming and lovable, Jeff avoids discussion of anything personal. Male privilege, something I abhor, has shown up in my black son. As his mother, I wondered how I have contributed to his attitudes and behaviors. I had favored and excused him as a dyslexic child, as well as in making a bold declaration of acceptance of his race and inclusion in our family. This lesson is becoming clear to me. For my role, Self-forgiveness through TaBIA can shift the energy in this scenario. Without judgment, I can observe the cause and effect of my parenting.

My Daughters, Kim and Kari

Kim's decisive action to go to Florida to get Sebastian (age nine) after the judge took him from Kari during her heroin use, stands out as an amazing example of doing the right thing. Growing up with Kim and her husband, Markus, Sebastian is a confident, well-adjusted, and mature young man, already in his own business following his high-school graduation.

"Cut-offs." Severing communication by temporary or permanent distancing of adult children is common in families where addiction has occurred. My daughter's choice could be seen as a blessing in disguise. For one thing, it lessoned my guilt for my move to Kauai. Sharon, Chuck's widow, has beautifully undertaken the grandmother role, for which I am very grateful. And, Sharon has reminded me not to abandon my grandmother role.

Kari, my youngest daughter who I favored as a child, has survived her former heroin dependency to be reunited with her son, Sebastian. She is working as a trainer in a fitness establishment. Each of my adult children has their own script, level of consciousness, and choice to follow their heart. I wish for them the healing of forgiveness, and fulfillment of their heart's desires. My role is to surrender to the I Am Presence within me and to fulfill my purpose on the planet with the support of my **spiritual** family. Even so, I've allowed the grieving to come up, and send love to my children and grandchildren.

The years of separation from Kari during her struggle with addiction have left their toll—her connection is stronger with her sister, Kim. I decided to let go of my expectations, and flow with the connections I have. It was a joy to meet my great-grandsons, Cayden and Kimani. Mikala, the third great-grandchild, arrived after I left. A beautiful girl, I'm told at 1½ years she started to speak in sentences. I look at these new children coming in with more activated DNA as the leaders for our promised *heaven on earth*.

When I first met Jeff's son, Patrik, at age four, we immediately took to each other. His mother said that over the years, Patrik often talked about going to Kauai. Handsome and shy, he again expressed an interest in coming to Kauai, and it then became my Intention to make that possible. In my inquiry process, I asked spirit about a past life connection and intuited that we were Hawaiians—he was a very loving, caring uncle and I was his niece. Now roles would be somewhat reversed. This was a connection I looked forward to.

Any observation is colored, other than a self-awareness prompted by spirit. I grieve the lack of intimacy and sharing I could have had with my children without the disconnect in their adolescence. Again from higher observation, I am accepting the primacy of my own healing and fulfillment of my purpose.

A Spiritual Practice of Connection along with Meditation

I use a process which anyone can use to express one's highest Intention for another one feels concern for, and especially to family, however unavailable. It follows:

Call forth the person by name, or group of names in a family. I repeat the full name three times and then say, "I send and see within you love and light, peace and joy, and <u>I am with you</u> in love, light, peace and joy for the highest good of all. So be it."

It is a great exercise to send this love/light energy to a person you feel resentment of or critical towards—as well as to one you sense can use the energy of love in that moment. Your ego may say, "no way." Just know that if we want to experience Oneness, we don't have to agree with anyone, but we can acknowledge Oneness in the energy of love, light, peace and joy! As we make a practice of this, we are calling forth Source in each one. This shifts our automatic thoughts of separation to Oneness in Spirit. It softens any pain caused by our egoic interactions or lack of connection.

CHAPTER 37

KIRK'S MEMORIAL, A KARMIC EXPERIENCE

Memorial Day Sunday, 2012

Before dawn on Sunday of Memorial Day weekend, I awoke with a voice in my head that clearly came from Kirk, indicating he wanted to speak to his family at the service. I wrote down the following:

…When the body dies, the veil of forgetfulness drops away. As spirits, we chose to enter into matter and become dense. We are Love. Yet in becoming flesh, we became aware of another voice, the voice of fear. We became flesh in a world ruled by fear and the belief in separation. We forgot who and what we are, all expressions of the One prime creator we call God.

We came to earth to experience being in matter. I, Kirk, chose to experience addiction and to break free of it. When told by a doctor three years ago that I would die if I took another drink, I remembered my commitment to take care of Sue, my partner. I knew I couldn't do that through willpower. Thanks to the teachings of dad and mom, and their love for me, I asked Jesus to help me whenever I felt the craving. It worked.

I also turned my commitment to Sue over to Jesus when my body no longer could hang on. I felt Peace, and was ready to leave pain behind and go home. I didn't have a chance to say goodbye until now, through mom.

Don't grieve for me. There is no death, only an experience of being flesh. Sue has joined me. We are so happy to be free, and to be aware of who we really are. Don't waste your life like I almost did. I don't want to do this lesson over. Remember to love yourself and one another as yourself. Be happy for me.

I love you all,

Kirk

Revisiting a Place of Pain

Most of the family attended Zion Lutheran church together that morning, my first time back since that fateful Sunday almost 30 years ago. Chuck's omission of my announcement of leaving and his words to me to not "hurt his ministry" was part of my dutiful role to be silent. It was easier at the time to slip away. The impression left behind was that it was I who was ending the marriage. It made it natural for the congregation to accept Chuck's new wife eight months later.

After we all enjoyed a meal at the Mongolian Barbecue, we returned to Zion's Memorial Garden for the burial ceremony. We stood in a semi-circle on a large slab of cement with nine-inch squares of the names of the deceased. I saw two squares were engraved with the birth and death dates of Chuck and Kirk, right next to each other. A small hole for the ashes was dug in the grass surrounding the cement base. Cremation eliminated the need for expansive graveyards and big tombstones; there were no symbols or statements of wealth or fame here.

I heard a familiar voice and recognized an old friend and his wife who were close friends to Chuck and me during our marriage. "Foster," the husband, chose to stay in contact with me through email throughout the years. I had asked Jeshua concerning his interest in staying in touch. Foster is in my soul family, and we were women friends in a past life.

I had asked the minister if I could say a few words on behalf of Kirk. He eagerly consented. As I began reading the words I had received that morning, my legs began to shake. I had encountered this before in public speaking, and told myself I had nothing to fear in the presence of family. The shaking became so bad, I feared falling down and asked for support. Shar, Jeff's girlfriend, came first to support me while I finished reading Kirk's words.

Because my body had reacted so intensely, I later inquired of Spirit if there was a past-life issue affecting my body. I learned that I had a life where a priest banished me from a Catholic church and condemned me to hell for being a witch. This was my first time back to Zion in Ann Arbor since my minister husband told me to leave quietly without announcing, explaining, or having any kind of farewell. I also had felt like a witch in my family for trying to get my drug- and alcohol-using teens into treatment. This return to Zion had evoked that cellular memory in my bodymind. This was an opportunity for healing the distant past, as well as the present.

We briefly gathered together with the Minnesota group. When someone said "Grandma," I realized that it was not me they were addressing—it was Sharon, Chuck's widow, who they called "Grandma." I felt a stab of pain, aware I had been displaced as grandmother. As I inwardly processed this, I began to see her as a blessing. She is wholly available to my children, having no children of her own. It frees me to focus on my spiritual family and my mission of Self Healing and identification with our I Am Presence, the true mission of Jesus.

The brief time my daughters and grandchildren spent with us was awkward and disappointing. I felt no compassion towards me, a mother at the funeral of her child. They were focused on a preplanned agenda with Sharon for seeing Chicago on their way back to Minnesota.

Through TaBIA and Ho'oponopono I am clearing whatever negative energy exists between my children and me. Just as Luke and mother Rose are always with me, I expect Kirk to be with me always. Anyone can have this connection to loved ones. Simply ask, and the means will come to you. Ask! Believe! Receive!

Monday, Memorial Day

My boat-ride with Jeff and Shar, ending with a refreshing swim, was a pleasant way to spend Memorial Day. Boating through the chain of lakes was a lovely experience.

Shar, I noticed, is a natural teacher and is patient and assertive with Jeff as he is learning to share feelings rather than avoiding them through offensive comments. My impression of Jeff from his years at home is of a sensitive, intuitive person who isn't comfortable with his loving feelings. With a patient "teacher," that can change.

CHAPTER 38

JOURNEY BACK

Another Missed Flight

Busy at work, Jeff asked Tricia to drive me to the airport. I had been looking forward to time alone with Jeff, which so far hadn't happened. Tricia, pregnant, had her own concerns and was late in picking me up. Going through the Detroit airport was an unexpectedly long trek to get to my gate and it was closed. The airline staff refused to open the door. I was put on the next flight, though it was uncertain if I could get on. Two missed flights and my trip wasn't over yet. The "missed connection/disconnect" theme manifested in unexpected ways. Consciously, I looked forward to some positive connections in Minneapolis as I boarded the next flight.

Minneapolis, Minnesota

In Minneapolis, my brother, Nels, a former Lutheran minister who became a Unitarian minister, met me. I stayed with him and Mary for two nights in a small, separate cabin on their beautiful, wooded piece of property. This was his study and it held a thousand books or more— most about the patriarchal version of Jesus, with few direct words from him.

Nels was a theology scholar who questioned and rejected my metaphysical approach to the Bible and life experiences. The ego and the world of form seemed to be the only reality he accepted.

Friends Closer than Family

I met "Lois" when she was a health-food store manager many years ago, when I worked there part-time. She was especially caring towards me and invited me to stay with "Lee" and herself whenever I needed a place while in Minneapolis. For a time, I lived there and stored many items while in a moving process. A mixed race couple, they have made a bold statement in their long marriage. Two daughters and two grandchildren graced their full and active lives.

My Inquiry about Lois's caring interest in me revealed she was a past-life mother. They have always welcomed me. Younger than me, Lois was still working. Lee, closer to my age, had retired. I had the lower level of their large home to myself. They were fond of entertaining and I was always included—a stark contrast to the fact there was no welcome from my daughters who also lived near Minneapolis.

Lois and Lee held a Greek-themed party on Saturday night, showing the film, *Zorba the Greek*. Though reminded of how badly women were treated, I enjoyed Zorba's dancing, which he did even to express feelings of grief when his three-year-old son died.

Dancing with Life

The next morning, Lois led the small, early service at their church, which encouraged other mixed race couples to attend due to Lois's influence. Another member gave the message. I realize how differently I would have spoken on the text, given my present awareness of Jesus' true intention. It was delightful to sing the old hymn, "Lord of the Dance," especially after the *Zorba* movie. Dancing with life, partnered with Jeshua, was the feeling I experienced.

I had hoped to do a book promotion presentation at their home. Failing to bring phone numbers with me, and unable to find phone numbers of old friends in the city directory, changed that intention.

Chapter 38: Journey Back

Northern Minnesota, "God's Country"

I then focused my attention on Bemidji, a town close to the property I had lived on and sold. My friend Lorrie had created a care home called "Alder Hus" and had five elderly female residents. She was very eager to have me visit and do a book presentation for interested friends. One of those friends was bringing her husband home from a Minneapolis hospital the next day. I seized the opportunity for a ride and enjoyed getting to know this former acquaintance.

Lorrie's efficiency and competence with her five residents impressed me. She called several women for an evening book discussion and I ended up with three participants and book sales. In order to attend Sebastian's graduation, I left the next day for Minneapolis on the Jefferson Bus line. When the second bus driver at my transfer in Wadena restated my name, "Petra, the rock," I knew he had uncommon spiritual awareness, and I gave him my book with only a request to send me a comment on it. I also gave a book to my Jewish seatmate, who seemed to appreciate it. When we stopped for lunch, I bought a wrap to eat and gave him half, as he didn't get off the bus.

Shock and Disappointment

Sebastian's graduation was the next day. If weather permitted, graduation would be outside and I could attend, as seats were reserved inside the auditorium. Even though my daughters knew I was planning to come, I had never received an invitation. Several calls to Kari included directions from Lee for her to pick me up.

The evening of his graduation was beautiful with clear skies. Lois and Lee left for a large concert in some park. All prepared, I waited for Kari. She called, very angry and lost, and said she would miss graduation if she didn't turn around. I told her to go back to the outdoor graduation. I failed to ask her where it was.

Moments after her phone call, my brother Nels showed up with something I had left at his place. Seeing an opportunity for a ride, I called him an angel, but he declined, saying he had other errands.

I was feeling a victim after spending $1500 and coming 6000 miles on a trip organized around the memorial ceremony in Michigan, and Sebastian's graduation in Minnesota. Angry and hurt, I realized I had lots to TaBIA.

A Gift from an Unexpected Source

Sharon called on Saturday, offering to pick me up to go to Kim's church. I was delighted. As I later did an Inquiry, I intuited that Sharon noticed my absence, both at the graduation and at the Saturday party for Sebastian—which I knew nothing about and did what was "pono" (right).

Kim directed the church choir where both of her beautiful daughters participated. Kara, 13, was working with the sound system—she aspires to do more in that area as well as to pursue art and writing, as I later learned across the dinner table. I felt a connection with her. Inquiry revealed a positive past-life connection as relatives.

Sharon was planning to stay around for a 3 p.m. concert until Kim directed everyone to the Rainforest restaurant in the Mall of America. It was a fun choice for a family dinner as this lavishly-decorated restaurant had a ceiling full of leaves and several gorillas moving up and down, along with fish tanks, thunder and lightning—a feast for the senses.

Meeting Another Piece of the Puzzle

New to me were guests, "Faye" and her son, "Seth" from Florida, who were just up for the weekend for Sebastian's graduation. Neighbors to Kari and Jim while they lived in Florida, they had rescued Sebastian at the age of nine when the police showed up—Kari's husband, Jim, had overdosed and died. They called Kim rather than see the county get custody of Sebastian. As I mentioned, Kim went to Florida and took Sebastian back with her while Kari entered treatment. The court gave Kim custody until Sebastian turned 18. According to Kari, the threat of jail got her to stop her heroin habit. She eventually returned to Minnesota to be near Sebastian. Working

Chapter 38: Journey Back

in a fitness organization, Kari is now living with her son. The inner work remains.

After the meal, we split up. While Kim took me to meet Sharon, I asked about the party at Kari's condo. Since Kim made it clear she did not want any kind of relationship or communication with me, my question was answered about not being invited. They controlled the guest list.

First, in recovery, is to forgive everything that has occurred! This is my wish for my talented daughter. In my Intuitive Inquiry process I learned that Kim agreed with me in spirit to play our mother-daughter roles before she came in. Some day we will laugh together at the scripts we acted out.

The process I call "Inquiry" consists of Intuitive questions, and answers, with Muscle Testing (MT) used to confirm. I MT the correctness of my thoughts as I review my experience. At that time, I didn't need to do more TaBIA. Ho'oponopono was the release practice I am to do periodically to shift the energy. Ho'oponopono has changed the energy; after a year, I received an Amazon gift certificate from Kim.

Resolving the Pain

Without a car, and with awareness of nothing left to stay for, I decided to pay the extra $200 to change flights and return to Kauai five days earlier than planned. Paying this much for a ticket change was normally unthinkable for me; staying the scheduled time had become more unthinkable.

Part of resolving this painful experience was the inner prompt to write a letter with Jeshua's guidance. This letter was sent to my three children, and to Jacinta and Sharon. It is really a summary of my present consciousness. I have received no feedback from anyone except Jacinta, who expressed indignation at the way I was treated. Unrelated, yet she represents my real family—another lesson preparing us for this amazing time. As we prepare ourselves for Ascension to a new way of living together on planet earth, many will refuse to change.

Many will experience the pain of leaving those who are not ready to shift out of the 3rd dimension into the 4th dimension of Heart Awakening, and the 5th dimension of Oneness.

Though writing such a letter can feel risky, when done under the guidance of your Higher Self or Holy Spirit, it is truly helpful. It offers resolution and integration of one's experience. I wrote and sent a three-page typed letter detailing my experience and disappointment in unmet expectations. I've chosen not to include it here. I received one response of sympathy. Sharing feelings without judgment is a helpful exercise—it can be done. Disappointment, rather than anger, is a deeper feeling that is more easily heard.

CHAPTER 39

SOUL SPEAK

Perhaps lack of comment can simply mean "There is nothing more to say!" Writing the letter allowed me to return to the present moment. Having fully expressed myself, I was free to focus on the urgency from Jeshua to complete this book. Those of you who attribute guidance to the Higher Self or Holy Spirit are absolutely correct as well. Jeshua became the Holy Spirit. For me, it helps to put a face on my source of guidance. For others it may be Buddha, Krishna, Holy Mother, St. Germaine, or another Master or angel. It is enough to know that the Spiritual heart carries the wisdom of unconditional Love, a vibration many times more powerful than the vibration of *fear*, the voice of our *ego*.

The energy of the heart

First become aware of your feelings; the emotional heart is a portal to the Spiritual heart. Listen and trust your own feelings. Self-doubt can cause you to deny your intuition, as I discovered.

In *The Jeshua Journalings* by Pamela Kribbe, Jeshua has this to say: *Your* **soul speaks** *to you through your feelings.... Trust is essential. To accept the direction where your feelings are taking you and to act upon your intuition is to open yourself up to the guidance of your heart, and to truly make the shift from ego-based consciousness to heart-based consciousness.*

The energy of the heart is quiet and gentle in contrast to the egoic mind which has to control, be right, figure it out, and look good. Bypass these urges. Release any blocks or resistance. Become aware of the desires of the heart for Peace, Joy, Love and Connection, first to Source within, and to others in your life. Become mindful of your breath and the present moment. Allow yourself to enter the deep stillness within.

A mantra like the following can help to quiet ego's chatter. Pause and listen within after each line. One can tap on the third eye with the first line, then breathe and tap on the thymus (the I Am point) on the next line, and simply intuit hand motions for the remainder.

Peace, Be Still and Know I Am God.

Peace, Be Still and Know I Am

Peace, Be Still and Know

Peace, Be Still

Peace, Be

Peace.

The Authentic Self

A term coined by the Integral Enlightenment group who lived communally over 15 years, Authentic Self refers to the same non-judgmental Observer Self who notices all the bodymind patterns and beliefs that obscure the I Am Presence, our pure Eternal Love Being. We tap into this Observer Self simply by embracing change and asking for Spirit's perception, a shift from the head to the Spiritual Heart.

When the wounds of the emotional heart emerge, that is a cue for release or forgiveness. Tapping into the bodymind computer physically is more powerful than simply mouthing affirmations. Our bodies have recorded everything, and tapping into the cellular memory with a release process such as TaBIA will delete it. It then is no longer an automatic-running program.

Devaluing my Work

Another fundamentalist program important to delete is my automatic pattern of devaluing compliments. Though I have been aware of this pattern, at some deep level I valued it. I realized the source of this was the fear of developing pride and self-deception. Devaluing compliments in some way was a safety measure for my ego.

Lisa, my friend on Kauai who does readings, made me more conscious of this habit of devaluing myself, another trait of my early programming which warned me not to think too highly of myself. Over the years it has been difficult to promote my work or attract clients as this block is so pronounced. Others promote many tools and processes in their climb to success—enthusiasm marks their value. I already have powerful tools, which need to be shared. Somehow "enthusiasm" was squelched early in my programming. If I did get enthusiastic, I felt guilty and withdrew. The early imprint of the Bible verse, "…in me dwelleth no good thing," also reinforced the program for devaluing anything I accomplished. Through my committed work using TaBIA, this programming has been nearly deleted; processing may need repeating.

According to the Law of Attraction, it is no surprise that others would also devalue our work if we don't value it ourselves. Feeling devalued by friends, I can only change my own thoughts, beliefs and behaviors to a higher vibration to shift the energy. Resistance to the technical aspects of becoming an internet presence, and the responsibility involved in having a website, blog, newsletter and such, have contributed to marketing failure.

"Too Self-Promoting"

I had written a piece for a magazine of a spiritual college, which usually accepted my articles. In my growing self-awareness, I had started writing more from my heart, and shared tools such as my TaBIA process. I called the office and spoke to the head of the college, whom I knew from my earlier studies there, to ask why a particular article was not accepted. I was told it was "too self-promoting." I was shocked, since I felt lack of promotion was my weakness.

Using my Inquiry process of intuitive questions and confirmation with Muscle Testing, I asked Spirit about my connection to this person. My answer was that we had an antagonistic business connection in a past life. I was confronting an unfinished piece of business that needed correction.

Using Ho'oponopono was my first step, and a letter I was guided to write was delayed for several months. Then, when my words had passed the scrutiny of Spirit and I asked about the wisdom of sending it, I received an affirming YES.

I awaited a response to the letter, perhaps a meeting of the minds or even hearts—but what I received felt very demeaning and dismissive. The response was, "We will pray for you!" This wasn't what I had hoped for. It inferred that I was in the wrong and needed to see it their way. This prompted an awareness of the sanctimonious dismissal of the feelings of another whose perception doesn't match one's own. It did leave me with the feeling of needing to go over the article with a fine-toothed comb and asking what was "self-promoting" and not ok. It did not invite any further dialogue, and felt like a door was closed to me. I had sent them my 2010 book and received no acknowledgment.

Loss of Approval

As I observed their promotion of the works of many students who came after me, I felt a loss. Pursuing their approval as like a child to an authority figure was a pattern I could now let go of. My dollars are required to keep up my license and ordained status. It called for using TaBIA on any resentment attached. Money is never refused! It is the relationships in the spiritual family as well as in our biological family that can undo us. This is my lesson.

Devaluing begins in the family. My child role as assistant mother and caregiver has left me feeling devalued in any other role. It automatically happens in family reunions. My experiences don't fit their reality.

Fundamentalism is an Ego Program

Especially in Western culture, many children such as I had early indoctrinations of distortions coming out of Biblical literalism. The belief in separation comes with our identification with our ego, enabled by our identification with a *body*, rather than *spirit*. Thus we are indeed separate from "God," seen as a male father-figure demanding our perfection. This core teaching of the church required the need for a redemptive savior, one who fulfilled the blood sacrifice (a Jewish practice). This was a natural solution to our separation from God. However, it put Jesus on a pedestal to be worshipped and created more separation.

His teachings could be ignored as possible only to God outside of us, and only doable by this Son of God, also outside of us. The church taught that Jesus didn't marry or have sex, or have children. (That would be too much like us.) Now the truth is coming out, not through Biblical scholars, but through channelers such as Pamela Kribbe in *The Jeshua Channelings,* Claire Heartsong in <u>Anna, Grandmother of Jesus.</u> How is this going to be received by sincere Christians like my former self, who accepted the Bible as without error, so we were taught? The very popular book and movie, *The DaVinci Code*, has caused much re-consideration of traditional beliefs, fed to us as "facts."

My emotional need to prove myself to my father left no room for doubting his teachings. When emotional pain drew me to resources—outside the church—that felt right to me, I began to get a bigger picture of truth. The need for emotional healing could not be met in the platitudes and judgments of my church community.

Patience and Practice are Worth It!

In asking for divine help in my prayer, **Teach me, change me**, I allowed myself to listen to guidance with an open heart. It was a surrender of ego dominance. Ego does not value change.

It took five years of daily use to shift to a more automatic reliance on spirit. I could recognize ego thoughts and release them more easily. Even traumatic changes were easier to accept as part of the plan! The value of practice can't be over emphasized. Choose an easy mantra that speaks to your heart and make it yours. You will be Blessed.

CHAPTER 40

HO'OPONOPONO

Ho'oponopono (ho-o-pono-pono) is a powerful spiritual practice that is about making things right. Historically, it is an ancient Hawaiian practice of reconciliation and forgiveness, and similar forgiveness practices were performed on islands throughout the South Pacific, including Samoa, Tahiti and New Zealand. Traditionally, ho'oponopono is practiced by healing priests among family members of a person who is physically ill. Modern versions are performed within the family by a family elder, or by the individual alone.

One current practitioner is Dr. Hew Len, who has written extensively about it and uses it in his therapy with patients. Len points out that we always need to remember, "Peace begins with me." He says that if there is to be peace on earth; it needs to begin individually with each one of us. As we are willing to be 100% responsible for whatever we experience in our lives, we shift our perception of the world, and that causes the world to change.

Dr. Hew Len says that we all keep looking outside of ourselves for how we can solve the world's problems, but that doesn't work. Working on others is not our job. He was trained as an educator from 1964 to 1982 to help handicapped and developmentally-disabled children, but then, over twenty years later, he learned that that is not his job. Rather, he needed to help himself by letting go of how he perceived handicapped children. He found that as he changed the way that he perceived handicapped children, *they* change. Another time, he changed the way he perceived the criminally insane at the

Hawaii State Hospital in the late 80's and altered (what is typically called) "reality." Len says that the only thing that works is if we look within ourselves and clear up the "stuff" in us. He points out that as he does this, he notices that people get well and are able to start taking responsibility for themselves.

It is a true story: Dr. Hew Len emptied a prison of the criminally insane without ever seeing a single prisoner. He simply took the file of each prisoner and focused on that man's story and said three times each these four phrases: *I am sorry, forgive me, I love you and thank you.*

I embody ho'oponopono by tapping, and highly recommend this to you: begin by tapping the third eye, side eye and under the eye for *I am sorry, forgive me*, three times. Then tap on the thymus while saying, *I love you. I love you. I love you.* Put fingertips together to form an arch and say, *Thank you, Thank you, Thank you!* Repeat this at least three times concerning one you feel separated from.

You may have judgments concerning them, and they have them of you. It may simply be some resistance that makes cooperation difficult. Jeshua spoke to me on this:

Dr. Hew Len accepted the reality of 'all minds are joined,' which you know from ACIM. Dr. Len knew that at the level of mind, he was not separate from these men, and understood that whatever correction he made while focusing on and identifying with a particular prisoner could change the energy in that person. He did not need individual face-to-face contact to do this. Of course this means he saw this person as himself.

The bodymind computer has a lot of programming each person is unaware of. One can be triggered by another person's energy to react. Ho'oponopono erases judgment, reconnects through a request for forgiveness, and calls in the energy of gratitude and love. Gratitude is an expansion and expression of love.

Ho'oponopono connects with the One mind and corrects the energy at that level. This opens the door to change and correction in both parties. The process needs repeating to establish the energy of oneness. It need not involve contact. Dr. Len did not see the men later to determine the end results. Rather, he returned them to a place of choice and responsibility for their lives. He wasn't recognized or thanked by the men for his solitary work. He fulfilled his intention to free them from prison. Ho'oponopono frees us from the prison of resentment and guilt.

Ho'oponopono can restore family relationships in the physical dimension. It is a clearing of energy so that each one can move on to fulfill their heart's desire, untroubled by resentment. A Ho'oponopono practice results in a conscious self. It can be directed to the veiled self by the 'I Am Presence.' When in a state of self-forgiveness, the criticism of others cannot stick or become something we obsess over. This infers that we acknowledge mistakes and seek to correct them or make restitution.

I'm Sorry; Forgive Me; I Love You; Thank You.

I discovered the value of these four phrases in 2013. This mind-cleaning exercise toward anyone I perceived negatively almost always created a shift in energy to a positive receptivity in the other party, as well as myself. When I changed my mind, the mind of the other also changed.

CHAPTER 41

2013: ALOHA PATRIK! THE NEW CHILDREN

A conversation with Jacinta revealed that my grandson Patrik, her 14-year-old son, was apathetic about school, and most everything. My past-life connection with him (our Hawaiian uncle and niece relationship) as well as our connection in this life prompted me to invite him to Kauai to live for a time. I realized it would require a major lifestyle change, adjustment, and move on my part. I wrote the invitational letter, sending it both to Jacinta and Patrik. I was delighted when he accepted and it was fully supported by his mother. Whatever Patrik wanted was okay with his father, my son, Jeff. (Though not together with Jeff, Jacinta kept me filled me in with family news.)

I began my search for a two-bedroom apartment and found one in Kalepa Village near Lihue, where Patrik would be attending high school. I connected with the school and learned orientation day would be in July. I started selling stuff, as one does to pare down before a move. A young Fundamentalist Christian bought my lanai furniture and also offered to move me, and said he had a friend who would help. It sounded like a reasonable solution. I paid him $100 as requested to confirm our agreement.

A Painful Moving Experience

"Jim" with his truck, and his friend "Ben" with his trailer, started loading. Jim apologized for frequent bathroom breaks. After two hours of loading, Ben took a break as Jim disappeared with his fully-loaded truck. I had not given him the new address…where was he going? Ben called Jim on his cell phone and asked where he was. Then I heard, "You have to stop doing that stuff—" and I suspected drug use. Ben acknowledged that he had been in denial of the extent of his friend's meth use. I never saw or heard from Jim again.

My friend John offered to help. Ben said it would take another day and another vehicle to move the remainder my things. Through a neighbor, I was able to hire a man with a large truck for $30 per hour. Ben had to go and remove all the items from the truck at Jim's, who pleaded illness. (Indeed!) Some items were not in the truck but locked inside. Later, I was told to call his wife and she came with some additional boxes, excusing her husband as being ill. I told her he was on meth, and tearfully begged her to get him into treatment. I have discovered I am still missing two boxes, and receive no answer when I call. I have let it go. I wondered if reporting it to the police would have forced him into treatment.

Again, a Christianity that does not acknowledge or work with feelings fosters hypocrisy, hidden darkness, and a phony niceness. Of course I noticed I had attracted a "nice Christian man" who turned out to be a troubled drug addict. The wounding from my own drug-abusing teenage children will magnetize more of the same until I fully process my feelings around that trauma.

Meanwhile, Patrik's mother and sisters worked on getting together the money for his plane flight, and I sent what I could spare after the unexpectedly expensive moving ordeal.

A Traumatic Beginning

Patrik started at the Lihue high school on August 5, and I received a call the second day concerning a teacher's problem with his attitude. His story was that he had his cell phone in his lap and wasn't using it. The teacher demanded it and said he might have to part with it for a year. He said. "no" and she called Security. The security officer came, yelling at Patrik, who calmly asked him, "Why are you yelling at me?" Asking that question was an "attitude issue," according to

Chapter 41: 2013: Aloha Patrik! The New Children

this teacher, who I later heard had a reputation that didn't promote respect.

Patrik was sent to the vice-principal, a woman. I later learned from Guidance that she had been a jealous younger sister in his past life. Patrik repeatedly said, "She has it in for me!" On that occasion, he was ready to go back to Ann Arbor schools where he was treated with far more respect.

I intuited that Patrik was an especially sensitive child, an "Indigo" child. Back in the 70's, the term "Indigo" was used to describe a number of babies born in California who had deep blue in their aura, thus called "Indigos." Claims were made of characteristics different from the average—a kind of specialness. These characteristics include:

- Intelligent, even if learning-disabled; about one-third are geniuses; spatial learners
- Unusually creative, clever, inventive; irreverent quirky ideas
- Very rhythmic, musical; excellent at math
- Intuitive, psychic; many can remember past lives
- Spiritually minded, abstract at very young ages
- Natural healers; humanitarian
- Visionary problem-solvers; knowing
- Ready-to-go entrepreneurs
- Groupies who move as if part of a "collective"

There are more *out there* qualities, too extensive to include here. Any individual Indigo child, of course, will not exhibit every one of the positive or negative characteristics, but the prevalence and similarities are notable.

There are other names besides Indigo which are used in distinguishing these "New Children." These include "Psychic," "Rainbow" and "Crystal" and represent different types of the "new" children. Not really "new," the basic profile can be traced back to

Jesus' time. Every renaissance the world has ever known saw clusters of them.

New Thought and the Oneness movement began with such children. Amma and Bhagavan of India knew they were God, as children. They established the Oneness University. Many westerners, along with myself, have been trained by their trainers to become Deeksha or Blessing Givers.

Children of the Fifth World, A Guide to the Coming Changes in Human Consciousness, by P. M. H. Atwater, L. H. D., is an important book in helping us hold the vision of a New Earth. It helps one understand how this crazy world can become Heaven on Earth by listening to these children. Our task is to be in the role of a mentor, engaging them to help them avoid boredom, steering them away from drugs and destructive forces and into humanitarian projects.

Children of the Fifth World goes on to describe the negative aspects of those called Indigos. These were characteristics which applied to Patrik: impulsive, impatient, feeling entitled, overconfident, "no concept of authority—need mentors, not bosses," and no recognition of boundaries. These "New Children" appear wiser than they are and self-deception can be an issue. Also, Indigos, like Patrik, "expect things to come to them." I was particularly concerned by the attribute "highly sensitive to drugs, processed foods, metals…highly sensitive to electromagnetic fields, toxic and incoherent energy [from computers and cell phones]." Patrik ended up getting into trouble because of these very characteristics and tendencies.

I read to Patrik a description of the Indigo child and he said it described him accurately. Authoritarianism does not work for Indigos or any of the new children. I began looking at alternatives to his current high school, which he was not interested in, as he wanted to connect with the other students, mainly upper-class students, including a senior girlfriend. The freshmen were "too immature!"

I quickly learned not to ask about any of his relationships, especially with girls, as he did not want to share any information.

Chapter 41: 2013: Aloha Patrik! The New Children

His secrecy was quite disturbing as it reminded me of the secrecy in my marriage.

Birthday Present from His Family

To ease his homesickness, Patrik's two older sisters sent him $300 to spend on a new Play Station. I knew little of Play Stations, but felt the money should go toward a computer. Patrik was adamant and needed my permission to purchase his program choice which had a violent scene on the cover. I was horrified. Not wanting to make a scene in the store, I relented. As I struggled to understand my role as guardian to Patrik, I received a message from Jeshua:

Jeshua, 9-26-13

Now we begin. We understand your Intention to provide the highest and best opportunities for Patrik. It is in Allowing that you are being challenged. Indeed you are experiencing a most unexpected opportunity to be the Presence of Love. Hold fast to the vision of completing the karma of interference, with your role as guardian.

Sharing your values and Intention along with acknowledging their generosity and intent will require composing your concerns and needs with the wisdom of your divinity. The ego feels unjustly treated. Beware. You have the power of angels, of your mother, brother, and father, who are very interested in this game you are engaged in. I will help you compose your letter to Jacinta. Know that You have much support from us. Shift from the energy of fear to the energy of love, which holds the vision of your and Patrik's highest good.

Keep the communication open through non-judgment and playful curiosity. Focus on the value he experiences in doing the games. Is there something he is learning from the games that he can apply to the game of life? He has expressed an interest in meditation. Do the games help or distract from this intention?

Address your financial situation with a visioning process. Engage Patrik's participation. Redefine wealth apart from money, which will become obsolete. Let <u>positive connection</u> be an indicator of wealth.

Creative ideas, gifts of service, awareness, time in nature and health become true wealth. Gratitude brings more of what you are grateful for.

Your game will be to find something positive about the Play Station. It is an opportunity to talk about the Game of Life and engage in using the tools to master the game, such as TaBIA, the Inquiry process, The Four Keys, an attitude of gratitude, and the 12 Ps.

Perception, Perception, Perception! Shift your Perception. Let that also be your Intention. There is more to be realized.

Sleep is your need now. We are pau [complete].

I am with you always in all ways, Jeshua

Patrik at Odds with the School System

I sent a letter to Jacinta, sharing my disappointment and concern, but considerably toned down after my message from Jeshua. I was concerned that the Play Station would replace his homework. Patrik continued to deny having homework, in spite of evidence to the contrary.

I had received dire warnings from other adults concerning heavy drug use on the island. Early in October, I was called to the high school to learn that Patrik was being suspended for two weeks for carrying a pot pipe, which he claimed he had just found. It also was regarded as a felony and a court appearance would eventually be required. This made no sense to me. No further information was given.

This incident prompted me to connect him with a counselor at a drug treatment clinic, where he was monitored with urinalysis. Initially his goal was to have a good report in preparation for the court appearance. I also researched community resources and found a man who was to play an important role in our lives, Hale Kipa. Patrik was gifted with this male mentor who took him surfing occasionally, and also to martial arts, specifically jiu-jitsu training, two to three times per week. Hale Kipa picked up the tab. Patrik worked at his martial art and planned to compete at an event in the spring. A

Chapter 41: 2013: Aloha Patrik! The New Children

consistent male mentor was my wish for Patrik and it was provided. The orchestration of our lives continues. We can offer gratitude even for the negative events in our lives.

Contrasts.

Patrik's extroversion surprised me as he was very quiet and non-communicative around me. I tried unsuccessfully to get him to share feelings. At times he was an obstinate 15-year-old and other times a wise, old master. I came to recognize the triggers for my fearful, anxious ego when he didn't show up at expected times. He was a frequent guest in homes of friends and families unknown to me.

My adult friends enjoyed him and remarked on his Presence. He related well with them and attended meetings and potlucks involving my spiritual family, even though he was the only teen. The youth group at St. Michael's church was another connection he enjoyed. I was much more at ease when I knew who he was with. My guardian role was really just a legalized role which allowed a wonderful learning situation that was mutual for us. His teen presence triggered the painful cellular memories with my own teens at the end of my marriage. TaBIA was very useful in neutralizing those feelings and allowing more trust to develop between Patrik and me.

Refraining from judgment and critical commentary became a conscious exercise and spiritual practice for me. He was a gift I treasure in the call for wisdom and patience. We were both teachers and students in our life together.

The contrasts I see in Patrik reminded me of the following reading, titled "Jesus and Judas" in Alan Cohen's book, *A Deep Breath of Life*. In summary, Rembrandt, at the time of his work depicting *The Last Supper* [originally painted by Leonardo da Vinci], walked the streets of Amsterdam looking for a man to portray Jesus. He found a tall, handsome man who held the bearing and purity of the Christ. After he had put all the disciples except Judas in place, he searched Paris for a tortured soul, and found a shabby, homeless man whose eyes held deep sadness. After painting "Judas," he thanked the man, who then asked, "Don't you remember me? I sat for your portrait of Jesus."

Alan Cohen goes on to say that anyone of us can rise to the highest of the high, or sink to the lowest of the low. We cannot judge, and do not know the circumstances that shape what we behold. A quote often attributed to Mother Teresa is, "…there is a bit of Hitler in every one of us." To be the Christ we are meant to become, calls for our compassion. We are not the roles we play. Judas played his role in the crucifixion drama. We cannot begin to fully understand that script, for example, but we can practice compassion for the man. We can never truly know what another is called to do in their lifetimes here.

Past Wound Triggered

Before I recognized that Patrik triggered my cellular memories of the painful past with my own teens and their drug use, I had found myself becoming reactive and critical of him. What an opportunity I was given to undo that programming! TaBIA has released all the fears that have been triggered as I looked for new ways to connect to Patrik. I began to focus on the positive vibrations of the spiritual experiences he was open to. Discerning how to be responsible without being controlling was, is always, my challenge.

The karmic repeat of my past Hawaiian life with Patrik as my uncle has been played out in my role as grandmother sharing Kauai's Aloha. I had a strong sense it would continue for Patrik as he returned to Michigan to reconnect as a loving, wise uncle to his niece and two nephews, the New Children who will help shape the Golden Age.

Jacinta Visits

His mother, no longer working, decided to visit. She missed him so much, but wanted him to finish school. Her four-day visit went very well and, to my surprise, Patrik spent every minute with her. I marveled at their relationship.

Chapter 41: 2013: Aloha Patrik! The New Children

My New Year's Intention

The rapid blasts of fireworks heralded in the New Year. Patrik enjoyed an overnight with a church group. I felt a peacefulness in the thought that 2014 was my fifteenth year on Kauai. I felt gratitude for all my experiences and the Spiritual family I was in. Dispelling the darkness of separation, I could embrace our One Self. The play is not over. Awake and Aware, I intend to be At One with all beings, with nature, and with Source. At the level of the heart, this is possible.

Instead of the usual New Year's Resolutions, I used Jeshua's *Four Keys to the Queendom*. I would identify my Heart's Desire/s. Then I would create an Intention with a clear vision of doing and having the fulfillment of that desire; then Allow the Universe to orchestrate the details, and Surrender the ego to the divine Essence *I Am*.

Embracing our identity and Oneness with all is summed up in the following affirmation: "I am Spirit, a holy Son of God, free of all limits, safe and healed and whole, free to forgive and free to save the world…I am One Self, united with my Creator, at one with every aspect of creation and limitless in Power and in Peace." ACIM; W. 95.

Patrik's Guide has Other Plans

In February, Patrik was caught with leaving the school grounds at 8:30 a.m. and was expelled. His mother wanted him to return to Michigan as soon as possible so he could go to the Ann Arbor school. He was glad to be going home, and confident he could get through school despite the delay. He would miss the Martial Arts event he was scheduled for, achieving his first white band, an accomplishment he was proud of. In spite of his negative school experience, he is very enthused about Kauai, according to his family. Kauai will call him back.

CHAPTER 42

TRANSITION FROM PATRIARCHY TO ASCENSION

Undoing Patriarchal Programming

The Patriarchal system fosters competition, attack, and defense. I have discovered defensive and alibi thinking was automatic in myself, an effect of my fundamentalist programming. The common belief that "I need to be ready to defend myself in order to survive" has led our nation to stock weapons, build up the military, and plan wars for security. Most countries do likewise. We need to look at those countries who don't stock weapons. We will discover they don't magnetize attack. The "belief in separation" permeates everything in our culture, especially religion.

We are told that "nature abhors a vacuum." When a space is emptied, *some*thing moves in as replacement. This is why we need to be aware of, and hold the vision of a new world based on the wisdom and connection of the heart. This begins with ourselves, as we cannot embrace a new way of being without consciously releasing the old ways.

"Defenselessness" needs to become a value, a way of recognizing the other as oneself. This will take practice, a willingness to feel vulnerable, and an intentional sense of connection. It is through feelings, sharing our common desire for peace and happiness.

Non-violent communication is one of several helpful programs, along with 12-step addiction recovery work, and groups focused on *Living from the Heart*. These help us to fill the vacuum while we delete old programming.

Our inner connection to our I Am Presence through *Living in process* and/or *Prayer without ceasing* will become a way of life, magnetizing others to join us. Meditation advice abounds. We can have walking meditations and an ongoing connection to the Holy Spirit, our divine Self, along with formal "sits."

Often guilt is triggered when we don't meditate "properly." Turning inward, sometimes the voice in our head (old programming) gets very loud, before being released. Patriarchal programming limits us spiritually and affects us emotionally and mentally. A particular issue affecting our spirit is the tendency to judge another or our self. It is so automatic in our minds, we don't recognize it. The question is, *how do we distinguish between judgment and discernment?* Practice teaches us these have very different vibrations: Judgments come from the ego; discernment is an awareness of the heart.

The main problem with traditional Christianity is its **judgmentalism,** and its focus on separation from God. According to the Manual for Teachers in *A Course in Miracles,* letting go of judgment is the most difficult task of the spiritual journey. The course teaches that we are **all included** in the term "God's One Son."

ACIM is a radical correction of Christianity. There are many study groups available. It sees all of humanity as guiltless, or innocent. We are in this illusionary world to experience relationships, learn forgiveness, and to accept who we are in truth—all expressions of the ONE.

Religions are imperfect and can change from within as members seek spiritual practices such as *Contemplative Prayer*—groups that invite all to participate. Denominational differences don't matter when the focus is on awakening the heart through an effective spiritual practice.

Example of TaBIA Use

Use of TaBIA here could be, *Even though I may have different ideas than others in the group, about God and who I am,* while tapping on the third eye, side eye and under the eye, (breathe); then move to the heart chakra, and tap the thymus while saying, I *remember I am one with my Source.* Conclude with the gratitude and completion gesture, while giving thanks for our release, and say, *I Am Holy, whole and complete!*

An Ascension Mantra

My Ascension mantra for this time on the planet is: ***I Am Ageless, Awake, Aware and At One.*** The following expands on the physical, mental, emotional and spiritual aspects of ascension.

Ageless: We have been promised in many channelings that our bodies are changing from carbon to crystalline. Fifth-dimensional bodies will be lighter, less dense, which goes with rising frequencies. *Sickness is a defense against the truth,* according to Jeshua. It is a denial of the God Self we are.

When we do our purification work of releasing everything that does not serve us, through forgiveness and spiritual practice, we will notice shifts in our health and energy. Since I started the TaBIA release process in 2006, many different people have told me I look younger. I feel ten years younger than I was in 2006.

Awake, Aware: These naturally go together. When Buddha was asked about his enlightenment, he said, "I am Awake!" Heart Awakening to our true Essence is to be Awake. Our non-judging Observer self is present, activated by our intention to be in the NOW, the only time there is. The feminine way of embracing process, *awareness of feelings in the moment,* helps us stay in the now. It is going inward both for our guidance and for our awareness of thought patterns, and honesty with feelings. This Awareness allows us to direct our *e-motions,* our energy in motion. Alcohol and drugs, including pot, interfere with this awareness.

At One: To be *At One* is the essence of *Atonement,* the "endless chain of forgiveness," as stated in ACIM. At-One-Ment happens when we see another as our self. Embracing the true Self, the *I Am* Presence, is the work of Ascension. We are to Awaken from the dream, the illusion of separation we have been living under. It is

Heart Awakening—the 4th dimension we are moving into after an era of living from our heads for over 5000 years. The Emotional heart needs to be healed through forgiveness of everything that has occurred in order to access our Spiritual heart.

Our Three Hearts

Jesus, in *The Way of the Heart* series of channelings through Jon Marc Hammer, says that we have three hearts: the **Physical**, the **Emotional** and the **Spiritual** heart. Clearing the Emotional heart is clearing the portal to the Spiritual heart—home of our God Self, unconditional Love, I Am Presence, Higher Self, Holy Spirit and Divine Essence—all names for our core identity. The Observer Self is the surrendered and Aware ego, which accepts the wisdom of the heart and is no longer attached to the ego identity.

This **Heart Awakening** makes the 5th dimension oneness, or At-One-ment possible. In Jesus' statement, *A Universal theology is impossible, but a universal experience is not only possible, but necessary*, the "universal experience" is the resonance that comes from connecting heart-to-heart. Theology (ideas about God) is all in the head. The TaBIA process, an ascension tool, is designed to shift our perceptions in the head to the heart, by tapping the I Am point, or thymus (thy muse), in the heart chakra. It is to claim our Love-based identity, and "think" with the heart. Moving from the differences and separation we perceive in our heads, to our hearts, we can see the other as our Self.

Embodiment of Agelessness

A TaBIA practice serves as a tool in the **embodiment** of our divine Spirit Essence, which means the body is meant to reflect the truth of who we are. Entering into the wisdom years, I am encountering health issues that seem to contradict my intention to be Ageless. TaBIA energizes my quest for self-healing in all areas of my life, including symptoms of aging.

Sickness is a defense against the truth (ACIM), is not an invitation to judge those who are sick, or ourselves. We are to reject the idea that sickness is inevitable and the norm. This is one of many limiting

Chapter 42: Transition From Patriarchy To Ascension

beliefs we need to release in order to embrace the *Heaven on Earth,* the 1000 years of peace we are birthing into, as promised.

Our Life Force

In writing this book, I am doing a life review and continue to clarify my life purpose and give it expression, a part of the healing of the many lifetimes of *oppression of expression* in women.

Conception

At 3 AM I awaken with sexual feelings

Longing for the Beloved.

The lover is my muse calling me forth,

To engage in the conception, the creating of this book

In which my soul is expressing fully

her love affair with the Beloved.

The I Am that, I Am,

Thank you Jeshua

We conceive and birth our gifts. This was not the first time Jeshua has used sexual feelings to awaken me to the task of writing and birthing the message he wishes to share with the Beloved, the I Am, the Divine Essence, we all are, the One. As I embrace the truth of becoming fully embodied in my divine essence, I feel an orgasm of spirit. May this energy carry me forth into the full expression of my Purpose on the Planet.

PART III

ASCENSION AWARENESS

CHAPTER 43

WHAT IS ASCENSION?

My Introduction to "Ascension" on Kauai

Until I came to Kauai, "ascension" was only a biblical term I knew, referring to Jesus coming again in the clouds. One of the first speakers I heard was Kay Snow Davis, who had a counseling practice under the umbrella of Global Family Network. She used the word "ascension" in reference to the time we are living in. This was my introduction to Ascension as a change in consciousness. She taught the Emotional Freedom Technique, EFT, a tapping process that would become very familiar. EFT is a rapid and powerful purification process that would later lead me to bringing in TaBIA, a more specific ascension process from Jeshua.

The TaBIA release process is key to my personal healing and work in Purification, which I now identify as the first "P" to the Ascension process of realizing our Higher Self-identity, our Divine Essence. The twelve Ps are identified in my first book: *A Journey of Ps and Cues to Inner Peace and Power: The Embodiment of Our Divine Essence.*

Ascension in the Churches

On Kauai, I visited several churches before settling on Unity, a newly formed *New Thought* church. None of the churches had mentioned ascension in their sermons. I thought "how strange!" I was led to attend a series of special meetings at a Seventh Day Adventist church. These meetings had emotionally-charged sermons emphasizing readiness to "meet Jesus in the clouds." This could only happen through accepting him as Lord and Savior, and his forgiveness of our sins.

Biblical: Rapture and Return of Jesus

I Thessalonians 4:15 says, "According to the Lord's own word, we tell you that we who are still alive, who are left till the coming of the Lord, will certainly not precede those who have fallen asleep." Verses 16 and 17 describe Jesus as saying he will "come down from heaven, and with a loud command, the dead shall rise first…those still alive will be caught up with them in the clouds to meet the Lord in the air…" to be with him forever. These words are taken very literally by fundamentalists. This was once my own belief, and it is the belief of all who take the Bible literally as the accurate and only word of God.

To have Ascension described as *ascension in consciousness* makes it relevant to everyone, including East and West religions, or no religion. This is where the 4th dimension of heart awakening and the 5th dimension of Oneness become meaningful.

Understanding Ascension

Jesus is already here, I have discovered. After *A Course in Miracles* came out, he has used his preferred name, "Jeshua," reflecting his human name on earth. We have forgotten his humanity, which has created separation. I know now he is my inner coach, and he has channeled messages on the Internet, in books, in my spiritual family groups, and in my nocturnal calls to listen and record on my computer.

His coming in the clouds in a body is a manifestation of the idea of separation and bodily identification. We are spirit, he is spirit, and he is embodied within all who recognize his presence. He will recede when we have merged with the I Am Presence, the Oneness of all, including Jesus as one of us. This Oneness is God, the Spirit of unconditional Love.

Chapter 43: What Is Ascension?

As I witness the power and control addiction in governments, the global elite's agenda, and the pervasive distortions in the anxiety-fostering media, the choice becomes obvious: Sharing and holding a vision and awareness of a birthing process—rather than an end to life on earth—can cue the creative process. Many ideas are pouring forth on new ways of living on the planet through our feminine energy. Caring for the earth and caring for each other becomes primary.

Religions Must Change

Most religious teachings are founded on the belief in separation, with ego as our identity. It must be made clear that ego is a false identity, and that listening to the voice of fear blocks the Voice for Love in our spiritual heart, our true identity. This was the shift I had to make to experience transformation. Part of embracing all that is, our Ascension task is to learn the lessons of our faulty identification with ego.

My Definition of Ascension

Ascension is the butterfly process of leaving the cocoon of old forms and ways of being, allowing our wings to unfold in the light of new awareness. When we become Awake, Aware and At One, our vision of a new earth will manifest.

—Petra Rose (Sundheim), *A Journey of Ps and Cues to Inner Peace and Power*

General Unawareness and Denial

When December 12, and December 21, of 2012 came and went and no outward catastrophic event took place, the "believers" felt betrayed. Other observers dismissed the idea of any special happening and declared it was only going to be business as usual. The media also was oblivious and un-Aware. Denial comes in many forms!

Ascension time is a definite change in energy, beginning with Mother Earth's increase in vibration. December 21 marked the **end of an era** of over 5000 years of Patriarchy, and also the end of an age of 26,000 years. Details of this information can now be found on the Internet. The 3rd dimensional consciousness of reality is being replaced by the 4th dimension of heart-awakening, and is moving into the 5th dimension of Oneness. The 3rd dimensional world will shift, ending the old world, as we know it.

The Divine Feminine

Balancing male and female energies is now at hand. **2011** could be called the year of *The Emergence of the Divine Feminine*. Barbara Marx Hubbard models this emergence in her life and her books. Preparation for birthing the New Earth referred to by Eckhart Tolle and many spiritual sources requires the balancing of the male and female energies. The churches and religion in general has been a stronghold for Patriarchal dogma and practice. The work of Ascension is upon us.

The old must pass away to make way for the new. It is a time for everything to come to the light and to allow the collapse of old systems—our money system, our sick care system, our dictatorial governments, the inequity of taxation favoring the rich, and the separation of churches, all controlled by fear and *the belief in separation* from Source within, from nature, and from each other.

Ready Solutions

There are systems such as Nesara, ready to put in place a plan inspired by the spiritual world, when we are ready to let go of the old. Ho'oponopono directed at influential leaders can soften hearts to release power, control, and greed issues to allow these solutions to be implemented. Our own higher vibrational focus on solutions rather than on our collapsing systems will also help to bring the new systems in. It will be grass roots energy of the heart's awakening to the Oneness of all life.

What we resist—persists. Fighting corruption makes it worse. Creating a new system that works will magnetize through heart resonance. This new system can create a following who are ready and willing to abandon the corrupt ways of "dog-eat-dog." Accepting the wisdom of the heart will weaken the egoic thought patterns of greed, power and control. Cooperation will replace competition. These energy shifts to love-based behaviors will be experienced as powerful attractors. It takes the courage of awakened hearts to create new systems.

Reprieve Through a Shift in Consciousness

Mother Earth herself has lost her patience with human greed, abuse of resources, and pollution killing so much life on the planet. The insane shedding of blood would have brought about our self-destruction and end of life on earth, except for a few awakened souls who have cried "enough!"

Many who do not hold the vision of a new earth and a new human through a major shift in consciousness will succumb to fear and leave the planet for places that match their consciousness. We have raped the earth because of patriarchal consciousness and dominance. When men stop exploiting the earth, connect with their authentic self, and partner with the feminine, the ecosystems will recover. It will be a global shift in consciousness.

CHAPTER 44

SMALL GROUP SUPPORT

Finding a Spiritual family in a small group is very important in this time of rapid change. When your heart seeks a focused group, you will be drawn to a group through resonance. It is with much gratitude that I am in four groups, each with a different focus on the spiritual journey.

The **Way of the Heart** group is focused on Jon Marc Hammer's channeled words of Jeshua. Many of us are part of the lineage of those who knew Jesus in his lifetime on earth. That has been a major part of my 3rd transformation. I have come to know my soul as Martha in Jeshua's lifetime. Memories are slowly returning of my connections with others in that lifetime who are present in this lifetime Inquiry and MT confirm my intuitive connections.

Cloverleaf, Ariana's channeling group, which connected me with my father, brother and mother, is a very significant family. Ariana, a Canadian, usually here on Kauai for six months every year, has been channeling for over 24 years and has written several books, mainly recordings of channeled sessions. Celebrities, now in spirit, have come into our gatherings including Elvis Presley, the subject of a book compiling his "visits" from spirit over the years. An Egypt book will soon be out. It has stirred many in our channeling group who remember their lives in Egypt. Ariana prefers to keep a low profile and work with small groups. The media does not know of this amazing work.

Ashtar, one of her main non-physical sources, provides current Ascension information, guidance, and elaboration of the gifts we are to expect and practice as we raise our vibrations. It is "assisted ascension" which means we can be talked through the process of Ascension. We will get our guidance through telepathy and clairvoyance and other abilities. "Love is the message, Ascension is the goal," summarizes Ashtar's message, through Ariana.

A **contemplative prayer group** of persons from different churches has bonded together in a different way. It is not as personal as are the first two groups. It connects me to persons affiliated with different churches. Their experience and perspective is quite different from my other spiritual family groups, who are primarily un-churched and "outside the box." In the non-denominational church group, non-judgment and acceptance is the primary energy I feel as a common Intention. Guidance is not partial to anyone's church connection or role as parishioner or minister. Here, clergy are equal to other participants.

Going within is the way to accesses heart wisdom, and unity can be experienced at this level. I respectfully refrain from sharing my channeling interests and experience, waiting for the right time. The discipline of sitting together in silence for 20 minutes after a short inspirational reading, to inspire a focus word, is meaningful. This quiet time together is a bonding without words.

A discussion afterwards using a well-chosen book on the subject of contemplative prayer as a spiritual practice involves everyone who chooses to share their experience or questions about the spiritual path. Many denominations participate. A bond based on heart connection rather than doctrine occurs. It is a grassroots way of ending separation caused by doctrinal differences.

The **Deeksha** or **Oneness Blessing** group is formed by those who have been trained by Oneness trainers from the Oneness University in India. Deeksha is the creation of Sri Bhagavan and Amma, Hindus who knew from childhood they were "God realized."

Chapter 44: Small Group Support

Two close friends went to India for a 28-day training in an awakening process which involves giving people Deeksha. Jeshua directed me to take the weekend training when it was brought to Kauai. I was reminded that he "laid on hands" when he was on earth. ACIM and Way of the Heart are all about awakening. "Enlightenment" or "Awakening" are terms used by both East and West.

My **Deeksha (Oneness Blessing)** group of three trained women, two local friends and I shared our weekly journeys. All of us have some form of therapy training as well. We gave each other Deeksha, the Oneness Blessing, following the sharing and meditation.

Finding one or more persons who you resonate with that are willing to meet and share thoughts, feelings, and vision/purpose is very therapeutic and grounding in this time of rapid change. "Where two or three are gathered in my name, there I Am in the midst of them." Jesus demonstrated the process of our true being. "I Am the Way, the truth and the life," has a whole new meaning. When we accept our divinity, our I Am Presence as he did, we are accepting him and ALL who have awakened to the I Am within them—both East and West.

Our Core Oneness

My third transformation is my embrace of the call for every human on earth to awaken and accept our Divine Essence, our core Oneness, and live as the new humanity on the new earth. This embrace of a new humanity emerging on earth requires holding a Vision of a New Earth in spite of the fear-based predictions of the global elite establishing a new world order. The numerous channelings from Jeshua, Archangel Michael, St. Germaine, and many more ascended beings, support the Vision of a New Earth.

Directive to Write about Ascension as I Live It

Numerous channelings by others such as Richard Presser, and Carolyn, and Matthew, are available on the Internet. Some are focused on catastrophic events, others on the New Earth including Eckhart

Tolle who wrote *The New Earth*. He doesn't presume to channel, but is keenly attuned to higher wisdom.

My spiritual family and close friends on Kauai are very tuned into Ascension, and some are writing and channeling. My own connections with family in spirit who are very involved in earth's transformation provide further impetus. In my asking for direction concerning the priorities in my life, I sense urgency from Jeshua to complete this book.

This chapter is added to encourage you to seek support for the Ascension journey. Our biological family can sometimes be a hindrance. Let intuition and resonance guide you in choosing your companions. You may need to start your own group. When you are clear on your Heart's Desire, it will magnetize what you need and want—most easily when you feel you have it already.

CHAPTER 45

EFFECTS OF PATRIARCHY

On Christianity and Society

Like substance addiction, Fundamentalism denies feelings. A major feeling fueling Fundamentalism is the *belief in separation* from source. Christian fundamentalism has a rigid recipe for salvation, and a harsh judgment of damnation if you don't accept it. A lot of judgment occurs in its teachings. It views the Bible as the complete and inerrant word of God and uses a literal interpretation. The Bible omits Jesus' marriage to the woman at the well, betrothal to Mary Magdalene, his children, as well as the *Book of Love* by Jesus, and the Gospels of Thomas, Mary Magdalene, Judas, Philip and others.

Denial of the Feminine Principle

This deliberate and systematic portrayal of women as inferior and to blame for mankind's problems is illustrated by the many quotations of the church fathers dating back to the new world after the Fall of Atlantis. A vengeful male energy emerged into the non-physical world after Atlantis fell, which is referred to as "the dark forces." They interfered and deactivated much of the DNA of those reincarnating from Atlantis and Lemuria. Scientists called this deactivated DNA "junk DNA," though it's actually associated with spiritual gifts and ability to access the non-physical world. The domination and distortion of male energy has led to wars, and systems of competition, greed, power and control, sexual and racial inequality, and ego-corrupted religions.

The Beloved One: The Magdalene Mystery, by Karel and Caroline van Huffelen, is very emphatic about the great lengths the church has gone to in denying the feminine principle. It also distorted the masculine principle, causing the "repression of the Sacred Marriage in general, and that of Mary Magdalene (The Beloved One) and Jesus, in particular."

Both Karel and Caroline channeled Jesus and Mary. Karel called Christianity a fraud. Mary Magdalene, a twin soul to Jesus, initiated him through the feminine principle as she spoke these words to Karel: *Jesus was initiated into the Christ Consciousness by me, Mary Magdalene, by the feminine principle, just as all of you are now being initiated through engagement with the feminine. Therein lies your freedom.* Because of the fear of the feminine, Mary's ministry and her disciples who worked with the male disciples of Jesus had to be kept secret and thus left out of the Bible.

Karel and Caroline learned through many conversations with Mary Magdalene that she was black and Ethiopian, saying the original bloodline was from the heart of Africa. She has been called the black Madonna. Karel and Caroline share the following, from Mary: *I possessed the knowledge of the wise women of old, the primordial mothers and the school of Isis. Through our mutual love, we were able to raise each other to the highest level. I initiated Jesus by passing on to him the knowledge of the Mothers; the wisdom that originates from the lineage of Isis.* The church, with a fear-based agenda, elevated Jesus as equal to God, defined him as separate from humans, and denied him his humanity. Also, Mary Magdalene was made out to be a sinner and a whore.

Distortion of the Sexual Drive and Denial of our Feeling Nature

Patriarchy, in its "rational" dogma, ridiculed and put down the wisdom of the heart and the gifts of the feminine. The church fathers blamed women as the temptress and cause of their sexual abuse in rape and violence. They were highly suspicious of women's sexuality. They presented Jesus as a celibate and required celibacy of priests as well. The horrors of this repression have caused bizarre sexual behavior and the pedophile scandal. What is repressed seeks expression and is now coming to light.

Distortion of Jesus and his Ministry

The Book of Love, written by Jesus, was the most sought-after book during the Inquisition and lies buried in a place to be revealed in our time, according to my Intuitive Inquiry Process. The Roman Patriarchy made Jesus and the Bible objects of worship, creating more separation. Jesus did not intend to be worshipped, but rather to demonstrate and point the way to our own divinity and how to express it on earth.

He came as a teacher, not to start a religion. The patriarchal need for control would not allow his radical relationships with women to be known. Current channelings, as in *Anna, the Voice of the Magdalenes,* reveals there were 12 women who worked as equal partners to the male disciples in the ministry of Jesus. His wedding to Myriam of Tyana, the woman he met at the well, took place in Samaria. Jesus, referred to as Yeshua, was only 17 when they met and married. At age 18, his first son was born to Myriam in India. They had two more children before returning to Palestine from India.

The Two Wives of Jesus

Yeshua and his family and two cousins, Martha and Mary of Bethany, along with his disciples, went to Heliopolis and Egypt. Yeshua became betrothed to Mary of Bethany and she became part of his household. Polygamy was not uncommon in that era. However, persecution had begun and secrecy prevailed. Both women were active in his ministry and took turns going with him to India. Later, Yeshua and Mary of Bethany's wedding was celebrated in Cana. This famous wedding is recorded in the Bible with no mention of the identity of the bride and groom! What is recorded is Yeshua's turning water into wine when they ran out of wine.

Mary Magdalene of Bethany was barren until she became pregnant on the night of the Last Supper, just before the crucifixion of Yeshua/

Jesus. The church viewed women as a corrupting risk to any godly spiritual life. Jesus could only be accepted as a celibate Rabbi or teacher. His family had to be kept secret and was eventually forced to flee.

Anna, Grandmother of Jesus, Reveals More

Jesus did not die, but was resuscitated in the tomb. He lived on in his light body, or "ka" body. In the fifth dimension, he could teleport, and would appear at will to his family, who eventually fled to France. The channeled book, *Anna, The Voice of the Magdalenes*, gives a detailed personal telling by many of the characters in the life of Jeshua Ben Joseph (Jesus or Yeshua).

The first book, *Anna, Grandmother of Jesus*, is a fascinating introduction to the human life of Jesus and his message. Anna was an amazing woman who lived 800 years, through the use of many spiritual practices. She is a powerful example of the feminine energy we are now to embrace in bringing in a new era of living from the Heart.

The Later Years of Jesus' Life

Anna reveals that Jesus left his body when he was 89, and his body was buried in India. In his Ka body he separated from his wives and teleported to many places, reappearing unexpectedly at times to Mary Magdalene and his children. Mary had her own ministry and knew this separation was meant to be for their safety. The disciples and close followers had all dispersed to other countries since they were no longer safe in Israel. Mary lived and died in France, reportedly buried in a cave after living there in silence in her final years.

Sananda, the Indian Name for Jesus

Ariana Sheran (a channeler introduced in an earlier chapter of this book) said that Jesus came through to her as Sananda, the Higher Self of Jeshua ben Joseph. "Oversoul" can be defined as a name for the higher Self which may seed several beings of similar vibration. East and West are already merged in the name Sananda, which is revolutionary to those of us who have followed one or the other, feeling they were mutually exclusive. Embracing the direction and wisdom of Sananda from the ninth dimension quickens our journey to Oneness.

A Channeled Message on Effects of Roman Catholic Religion

In Ariana's channeling group, a young woman asked for her father who had passed several months prior the meeting. The father came through Ariana, very joyful and grateful for his passing. "No more rules! No priests and no confessions!"

He said his mission in the Spirit world was to help those who had religion on earth, as their passing was so difficult. Their life in the church was very, very hard on the Emotional body. "It's the dogma… I help them, one by one."

Dogma, beliefs which have been handed down by the church, includes doctrines which must be adhered to. In earlier times, failure to "religiously" follow the church's rules often resulted in punishment by death. The illusion of control was attractive to many, drawing many followers. Karel says that brainwashing is a patriarchal activity, an obsession of the distorted masculine principle.

Male Privilege

Arrogance characterizes "male privilege" and triggers my anger. I am reminded of the male conditioning. The TaBIA Practice has lessened my reactivity. Gratefully, I am meeting more Awake and conscious men. It is a different energy than what I experience with my family.

When I attended the California reunions with my brothers, I often became sick. A nine-hour car trip with two of them involved conversation dominated by them, and any view from me was quickly dismissed. My former spitfire reactivity was gone, and I disappeared into silence. Like many, my brothers tend to believe their ego is their true identity.

As egos go, they compare favorably with other egos, and so why change? Without my reactivity, **awareness** of "male privilege" expressions could allow me to **choose my response** and demonstrate another way to be together. Rather than trying to be right, a practiced sense of humor offers a disarming response. Humor dissipates anger.

In 2013, I became aware that my process is not valued by males who assume spiritual authority. It has become clear to me that the (typical) male way is to value the event and outcome. Failing to understand the male predisposition to external manifestations also triggers my reactivity. It is no wonder women often feel misunderstood or devalued for their inner work.

Early programming (warning me not to think too highly of myself) made it difficult to promote my work or attract clients, as this block is so pronounced. I later discovered that my throat chakra was closed. The thyroid cancer was a direct outcome of that.

The Law of Attraction has helped me understand the effects of my own devaluing. As I express the value of the gifts of others, my own are coming through. Enthusiasm is the emotional energy needed to follow through. Desire, Intend, and Allow! I see myself speaking my truth in Love, prompted by the I Am Presence within.

CHAPTER 46

THE PATRIARCHAL WOUND

Our Wounding

Male arrogance in many men came out of the idea of a male God as King and ruler over women by divine decree. St. Paul in the New Testament is blamed for much of this. Women were seen as existing to serve the needs of men. Women became property instead of partners, and their role was limited to birthing, nurturing the children and the men who "owned" them. Women became the spoils of war, with mass rape of women by the conquerors who considered them the property of the enemy.

In some cultures (even today!), girl babies are not welcome and often are aborted or killed upon birth. Excision of the clitoris is also performed on girls, to prevent them (as they mature into women) from having pleasure from sex. Sexual pleasure is regarded as evil, especially for women.

The mind was/is considered the male domain. In my early experience, the term "ego" generally referred to men and was to be protected, according to my husband, who cautioned me not to say anything to contradict a man's opinion because it would hurt his ego. After growing up with six brothers, I had very little respect for male opinions or their egos.

Male Dominance and Female Oppression

As I shared previously, Rene, my childhood friend who married a fundamentalist missionary, chided me for stepping out of line to seek a Master's degree. Other women come to mind who felt their major spiritual calling was to be subject to their husband. This was/is a primary teaching in many churches.

A major event in my past as a Lutheran was the first ordination of a woman to be a Lutheran minister. It still is unaccepted in Catholic churches. Priest celibacy has fostered homosexuality and sexual abuse of both male and female children under a priest's influence. I happen to know and admire one rebel activist priest who did marry and refused to bow to the church authorities.

Male dominance in politics, in vocations, and in every system is further demonstrated in unequal pay and advancement, even when women have surpassed the men in their field. Slowly, this is changing.

A Fear-Based Consciousness Promotes Guns

Men have sacrificed their feeling nature to serve in war. Suicides have become epidemic among US soldiers in recent and present conflicts. As they reclaim their feeling nature and listen to their hearts, war will cease. They can no longer kill their brothers or accept the dehumanization thrust upon them.

The whole military system is based on fear and a focus on physical defense and domination. The system is based on the "belief in separation." The power of love over fear is the power of the heart, which is the power we need to awaken now. It has been demonstrated many times but ignored. The clinging to "the right to bear arms" (now in the forefront of the news) reveals the insanity of fear.

Mass shootings in schools, random drive-bys by unfit minds, and increases in inner-city murder rates have not affected change in the climate of gun proliferation. A new local sporting goods store has a prominent display of guns and assault rifles. What is the message they are giving? That killing people is a sport?

A Radical Shift in Consciousness

In defenselessness, my safety lies (ACIM). This alternative is difficult to grasp without examples. Peace Pilgrim comes to mind. As she slept in the car of a "would-be rapist," an energy surrounding her kept the man from following through with his intention. Upon awakening, she told him how safe she felt with him. For a time he became her devoted protector. When we see the other as our self, and choose love over fear, defending won't be necessary.

Christian Religion

Fundamentalism teaches separation as a reality, "sinner" as our identity, and judgment as a fundamental characteristic of God. We are asked to implore God to forgive us. ACIM says God doesn't [need to] forgive, because Love doesn't condemn. We have projected a fictitious God in our image. Only the false/ego self we invented from fear condemns and needs to forgive. We need to forgive ourselves as well as others. The church says little about forgiving ourselves. If, in reality we are One, there is nothing outside of us.

The masculine energy has run amuck in all fundamentalist religions by using fear to control the beliefs of the people, dominate, and use women as property. Rigidity and fear, judgmentalism, and rules characterize many of its followers—until the heart awakens.

Christian fundamentalism proclaims (with Apostle Paul) that we are born sinners, and that is our identity until we accept Jesus as Lord and Savior—then we are "sinners saved by grace." All those who do not ascribe to this are lost and forever damned to hell, an invention of the church. Fearful images and pictures abound. Paul's message and Jesus' message are not the same. Paul emphasized separation as truth, along with the rules for women to be subservient to men. Denial of feelings goes with male domination. Strict and separate roles for men and women are specified.

The Original Sin

In the Bible story, Eve tempted Adam to eat the fruit of the forbidden tree of good and evil. The Patriarchy regarded sex as the fruit which man could not resist due to the seduction by women. Therefore, Jesus, being God, could not be portrayed as being contaminated by relations with a woman. They demanded celibacy of priests and nuns who, in service to God, could not partake of this fruit. This doctrine was so strong they denied evidence to the contrary. Misogyny results from this distortion of sexuality, which is based on seeing women as inferior and to blame for the fall into separation from God. Patriarchy also denied one's feelings and intuition, considering these inferior to the rationality of the mind (ego). This is the masculine rape of the feminine.

The protesters, or Protestants, changed the celibacy requirement by accepting marriage among the clergy. How else can the sanctity of marriage be demonstrated? When the sexual drive can be satisfied in a committed relationship, it frees one to focus on a form of service or ministry. As I've mentioned, the Bible does not acknowledge Jesus having twelve women disciples, who worked with the twelve male disciples. In *Anna, Grandmother of Jesus*, Anna describes the disciples' expansion to 144, or 72 couples.

Sex orgies among priests and nuns have been known about, yet denied. Sex abuse of children has (finally) been brought to light as those children became adults who, in their recovery and healing process, have exposed it.

Isis and her priestesses regarded sex as sacred during the time of Atlantis. The Essenes regarded sex as the Life force to be used wisely and consciously. This was the lesson, Martha the cousin of Jesus, had to learn.

Mentalization

Perhaps the greatest evil of Western culture is "...*mentalization*—getting lost in mental fabrications and concoctions..." says Karel van Huffelen in *The Beloved One*. The masculine mind centers on doctrines, authority, theological concepts and rational interpretations. When feelings are dismissed, philosophy and science dominated by men can be "heartless." Wisdom from the heart that conflicted with the rules was dismissed. "Women's intuition" was not taken seriously as a message from Spirit.

Augustine's doctrine of original sin was a translation error according to Hans Kung. This primary doctrine of original sin was

Chapter 46: The Patriarchal Wound

one I held for many years. It simply means we were born in sin and "sinner" was therefore my identity.

Channeling Raises Questions

The Patriarchal persecution of the true Christians who followed Jesus is coming to light in the historical novels, such as *The Expected One,* by Kathy McGowan. There is a proliferation of channeled books where Jesus speaks as Jeshua and corrects the distortions and omissions.

Up until these writings came out, I accepted the teaching that Jesus was a celibate, with no marriage or children, until I learned he had two marriages and children from each, plus another child they adopted. There was also another relationship with Marietta in Egypt.

Jeshua also said, "Embrace the heresies, for which the martyrs died." They were his true followers. The martyrs followed the truth that threatened male domination, and needed to be destroyed.

A Contemporary Martyr

Now in 2013, another martyr has been revealed. Karel van Huffelen, co-author of *The Beloved One: The Magdalene Mystery,* was mysteriously killed in a bus "accident" shortly after his book came out in 2010. Information from an acquaintance who knew Caroline (Karel's wife and co-author, and a channel of Mary Magdalene) shared that Karel had been warned not to speak and publish his findings on the Patriarchal distortion of the Bible and the omission of the feminine. In their book, Karel courageously and thoroughly details all the distortions of Jesus by the Roman Catholic Church.

Perhaps it was Karel's statements about the Vatican that called for his death. He wrote of the collusion between Hitler and the Vatican, and said a pope referred to Hitler in his prayer, "Our dear Lord has blessed Germany with a leader [Fuhrer] in this time of deep need."

Karel was one of the persons we were to contact in our Rescue Circle. Channelers present went into meditation with the intention of connecting with Karel. One person in the group felt his energy.

He was angry and said, "They finally got me." After further dialogue, his spirit left the astral plane and went into the light.

The Church Fathers' Deep Hatred of Women

The Beloved One was shocking for me to read. Karel describes how in the fourth century the Church Fathers projected their own fear of the feminine, of intimacy, and sexual lust unto the women. One scholar referred to "woman" as "the failed man…a deficiency."

Tertullian, a clerical scholar in 200 AD, declared the "daughters of Eve" to be the gateway to the devil. He blames women for the death of Jesus and destruction of God's image. Karel notes that the Bible has thousands of alterations by the "Father cult."

The Old Testament is full of violent sexual behavior, incest and adultery. Having concubines was the norm for royalty. To use women as spoils of war was, and is, justified as "God's punishment."

Medieval popes and bishops held sex orgies. Current violence and pornography finds its origin there, according to Karel, who finds it hard to believe that the Bible was inspired by the Holy Spirit. The patriarchal theologians identified the female with Satan, which prompted targeting women sorcerers and witches as having a diabolical plot involving copulation with the devil. The pope proclaimed an Inquisition and witch-hunts were declared. Even nuns and virgins were not exempt. "The Inquisition boasted of having burned at least 30,000 women in a period of 150 years." Karel writes that both Catholics and Protestants executed five to eight million "witches" in the 15th to 17th centuries. My Inquiry confirmed this astronomical number.

According to Karel, the repression of sexuality and the feminine resulted in nunneries becoming brothels visited by priests. Resulting babies were sometimes killed. Asceticism brought in contempt for the body, and self-flogging became a virtue and a practice for punishing perceived sins of the flesh.

Chapter 46: The Patriarchal Wound

Uncovering the Lies

"Uncovering the Lies and Feeling the Truth in our Hearts" is an article by Aniana, and is her response to Karel and Caroline van Huffelen's book. Aniana, a member of Ariana's channeling group, noted the vibrational correction of these revelations was experienced in a channeling, and said, "The uncovering of the lies and feeling the truth in our hearts IS the hope of the future."

Karel describes the Cathars as "a peaceful group, a highly-evolved culture…which was rigorously destroyed by Rome…. the first genocide in Europe, in which more than a million people were killed." A murderous crusade was initiated by Pope Innocent III, directed against the Cathars, a Christian sect originating from a reform movement calling for a return to earlier (less political) Christian messages. The Vatican still denies the genocide of the Cathars, according to Karel. He reminds us that "history is falsified daily." He notes that the church's constant reminder of sin keeps mankind in suffering, and thus easier to manipulate. Those with excessive guilt give away their power and freedom "to a Church, which pretends to have a monopoly on God. That's how brainwashing works."

The Patriarchy views Jesus's mission as being our Savior from our sins, and instructs us to venerate his suffering on the cross. In current channelings, Jesus basically asks us to take him off the cross—the time of suffering is over.

Karel describes The Father, Son and Holy Ghost Trinity as a construct by St. Augustine. This is so ingrained into our consciousness that it becomes an automatic utterance. As Karel deconstructs this dogma, he offers an alternative Trinity that resonates with his heart:

"Holy Ghost, Mother and Father"—Printed in columns in his book, this offers a corrective balance of the Feminine and Masculine Principle. He includes what is meant by each term:

Holy Ghost—Source of All-That-Is, Divine Principle, Creator, Brahma, Christ Consciousness, Soul, Oneness (God).

Mother—Eternal Mother, Feminine Principle, Creation, Shakti, Earth Consciousness, Body, Truth.

Father—Eternal Father, Masculine Principle, Creative Force, Shiva, Stellar Consciousness, Mind, Love.

Karel offers this to open up dialogue about a concept, which is not reality. He is showing how strongly our minds have been programmed with "a one-sided Father cult." This separates us from Unity Consciousness.

"Soul," our individual expression created by Source to have a will of its own, does not seem to belong on the list. Created by Source, souls are extensions of Source. Soul represents the various psychological/emotional expressions of Spirit. In *The Way of Mastery*, The Holy Spirit is said to be our identity and is One. In the body, we have been both male and female throughout our many lifetimes. However, we tend towards one or the other.

The Vatican and Hitler

Karel describes in detail the Vatican's approval of the second world war and support of Hitler and Mussolini's leadership that left "two million dead, twenty million wounded and mutilated, seven million dead of starvation and an armaments industry that flourished and grew." War justification hasn't changed much today and weapons have become more deadly.

Instead of all the Memorial days in various countries honoring the dead and the (needless) sacrifices, Karel and others suggest an International Day of Reconciliation. Heart opening would be in preparation for healing these deep wounds.

The Holy Bible

The Bible is worshipped as the Divine and only Word of an external male God/being, above and separate from us. This was my programming I followed for many years. Metaphysics (or New Thought) and ACIM has changed that. Jesus is crucified anew through the distortions, omissions, and falsehoods by the Patriarchy. Coming

Chapter 46: The Patriarchal Wound

to know that Jesus is as we are, as I Am, (but awake) has removed the Bible from its pedestal of inerrancy. There is truth and inspiration in the Bible, but it is not the whole truth, and it has been altered and slanted—by the Patriarchy, to serve the Patriarchy.

Besides the omission of a number of books which are more representative of Jesus teachings and the feminine equality that Jesus affirmed, Karel points out the numerous errors in translation. The appalling stories about wars, murder, rape and humiliation of women, genocide, extermination of tribes and villages, are said to stem from instructions of a vengeful God, particularly in the Old Testament. Karel's anger can be felt as he reveals the many distortions thrust upon the masses by the church's insistence on the inerrancy of scripture.

My father echoed these teachings as a Lutheran minister and tortured himself with guilt over his failures as a Christian. Guilt was the goal of his preaching. If we weren't feeling guilty, we weren't worthy of communion, the partaking of the Eucharist.

It wasn't until I could separate Jesus from the church's teachings about him that I could feel close to him. Now, experience and connection with Jesus as Jeshua through my own process takes the place of any Biblical foundation I once depended on.

Misquoting Jesus

Misquoting Jesus, the name of a 2005 bestseller written by Bart Ehrman, describes his discovery of the many discrepancies through his extensive experience as a Bible scholar. A "born-again" Christian in high school, he went on to attend the ultra-conservative Moody Bible Institute and Wheaten College, and later, Princeton, which revealed more contradictions.

He concluded that the Bible is a very human book and using it to prove anything, as in "the Bible says so," puts us on shaky ground. The Bible has become a false idol for many Christians.

Changing the Patriarchal Mindset Necessary for Heaven on Earth.

The prevailing conviction of humanity is one of scarcity/not enough for everyone. Some billionaires addicted to money, power, and control are among the global elite who have declared the earth is overpopulated and 95% of the population needs to be eradicated. This is already being put in motion through the endorsement of guns (made to kill), wars, control of food supply, control of availability and cost of medications, poisoning land, air, water through GMOs, chemtrails and discouragement of organic farming. The medical system is paid for and dominated by pharmaceuticals, which are a leading cause of death. It takes conscious effort to change *poverty-consciousness* into *abundance-consciousness*, our spiritual heritage.

CHAPTER 47

HEALING OUR WOUNDING

Healing the Patriarchy's Distortion of Jesus

We have been deeply programmed in our Western society by the distortions of Jesus message. Therefore, the correction of this distortion is one of the keys to healing this wound.

Many are channeling Jeshua. With an Intention of knowing who Jesus really is and what his message is, you will magnetize the channelings most helpful to you. Exercise discernment. It is impossible to acknowledge all the channelings I have come across and benefited from. One that offered new revelations to me is from Pamela Kribbe, referred to earlier. Some key points bear repeating.

The Jeshua Channelings by Pamela Kribbe

Pamela Kribbe has a doctorate in philosophy and works as an independent spiritual counselor in the Netherlands. With her husband, she gives readings and workshops, working closely with the energy of Jeshua. This book can be ordered at www.jeshua.net/book

"Christ consciousness in a new era" is the subtitle and the intent of these channelings. It is a very clear and helpful book in words from Jeshua ben Joseph, his preferred name. Jeshua begins the book by clarifying his mission on earth 2000 years ago. He states he came "too soon" and was misunderstood. Through Kribbe, he wants us to know: *I am **not** the Jesus of your church tradition or the Jesus of your religious writings… Misguided interpretations rose to meet and fight each other in my name. It has taken a long time for Christ consciousness to set foot on earth… Now the time has come.*

The main characteristic of Christ consciousness is the **absence of struggle, resistance, or judgment.** In Christ consciousness, we experience duality, and in the acceptance of both light and dark, we find unity.

Jeshua, Jesus, Christ

In describing his three identities—Jeshua, Jesus, and Christ—he says, *Jesus was an emissary from the spheres of light, incarnated in me… From my perspective as the man Jeshua living on earth, Jesus was my future self, who had become one with the Christ energy.*

The Christ, clearly present in Jesus, appeared as "divine" to his listeners, beyond their own selves, thus perceived as separate. Jeshua states his enlightenment was unnatural in that it was an infusion of the Christ energy from the future. He agreed to play that role before he incarnated. His mission was to show choices beyond the limited ones humans were engaged in.

Jeshua says the force of the Jesus presence within him challenged him physically to hold the *intense energies of Light. . . As the human being I was, I sometimes became desperate and doubted the value of the journey I undertook. I felt the world was not ready for the Christ energy. Light is confrontive. It wants to break structures of power and set the imprisoned energies free.*

The dark reacts and much violence is the result. The spheres of light were much concerned with the direction humans were heading, and as an emergency measure, sent Jesus.

My message was that the Christ energy is present in all human beings as a seed. …

I wish to invite you to believe in yourself, to find the truth in your own heart and not to believe in any authority outside of you…the official Christian religion has placed me outside of your reality as an authority figure to worship and obey, the <u>opposite</u> of what I intended, which is to be a living Christ yourself. Recognize the Christ within, and return my humanness to me.

Chapter 47: Healing Our Wounding

The Observer Self is actually a partial surrender of the ego to the wisdom of the heart and the awakening of the third eye, our spiritual vision. The I Am Presence is our identity we chose to veil when we incarnated. Jeshua's true mission was to show and demonstrate our true Essence, which we are to claim and embody. .

Embrace the Truth; Allow the Grief Process

The light of truth can leave us *numb* and in *shock*. Many who worship the Bible as literal and without error will have great difficulty hearing Karel's findings. *Denial* comes up as an automatic response, at least initially. If the heart has truly been opened and accepting of new revelations from Jesus himself, especially those who follow ACIM, the distortions by the Patriarchy are less of a surprise. For those who have invested their whole lives in preaching the gospel, *anger,* the second step of the grief process, will be major. The third stage of *bargaining* may increase any addictive tendencies, as well increasing denial. Compromising and discrediting the whistle-blowers may be ego's attempt to save face.

The fourth stage of *sadness or depression* is a normal part of the grief process. What we believed in, and depended on, is collapsing. Some greatly benefited from the old system which is no longer working. Allow all these natural stages of grief. It is problematic only if we get stuck in a stage. The fifth stage of *acceptance* comes naturally when we have allowed the feelings of the first four stages to be felt and acknowledged. TaBIA helps us do this very quickly.

Acceptance of Jesus, as the revelation of the Christ we are, can bring such a gift that makes forgiveness easier. Embracing our Oneness with the energy of unconditional love, God is no longer a being who is separate from us. It is only the embrace of Love as our identity that will make peace possible. Awareness that individuals will be naturally be in different stages of grief will help us accept people as and where they are. The task of changing the programming remains. The Heart's desire to do the release work can serve as a uniting force for small group support.

Purification Comes First

The 7th Principle of Miracles from ACIM states, *Miracles are everyone's right but **purification** is necessary first.* This purification takes different forms for individuals, from gradual, through intention, to a crises or wake up call. It is now happening on a global level as Mother Earth has said "enough!" and is shifting and changing from within. Literally, the earth's crust is re-arranging itself through volcanic activity.

Global warming is a global <u>warning</u> about our polluting practices. Awareness is rising amid much resistance to our need to change our relationship to nature. Our "belief in separation from nature" needs to be released. Partnership will restore the earth.

To survive, the profit motive cannot be primary. When committed to a purpose which works for nature and everyone, corporations will find it profitable, as do individuals. Money is a neutral energy. Our use of it determines its true value.

Some prophecies speak of a world without money—a system of exchange of services, credits, etc. Love of life and the gifts that support it will bring forth the creativity to restore paradise on earth. Nature is very resilient if we learn to cooperate with her, as demonstrated by Perelandra asking nature where to plant and how to take care of her.

Awareness Precedes Profound Change

The facts of history have come to light in Huffelen's book, *The Beloved One*. Learning these facts has made it difficult for me to give credence to the dogmas handed down to me and others as accurate divine inspiration. Learning that the Vatican supported Hitler, and the Roman church carried out the genocide of the Cathars, a genuine and beautiful group of Jesus-followers, plus the Serbian slaughter, left me in shock. Yet, out of this hierarchal religion have come the mystics—Mother Teresa, Hildegard of Bingen, and the many modern writers, Cynthia Bourgeault, Thomas Keating, Thomas Merton, and Richard Rohr. Rohr has come close to the truth of Jesus without the channeled information coming through many current Jeshua followers.

Vibrational Awareness

Power Vs. Force, by David Hawkins, needs to be taken seriously. He has measured the vibrational power of feeling states, resulting in his Map of Consciousness. When I learned to Muscle Test, my measure of the vibrational levels was identical to his, which he predicted for anyone who learned to Muscle Test. It was the denial of my request to insert his Map of Consciousness into my *Ps and Cues* book that prompted the creation of The Feeling Frequency Guide. This guide uses and revises his work to include Jeshua's Four Keys, forgiveness, gratitude, the TaBIA process, Ho'oponopono, and more. "Love" measured 500 frequency units, in contrast to "Fear," measuring 100. Vibrations are changing with the earth's increasing frequency. In my Muscle Testing, "Love" now measures 550.

Mahatma Gandhi demonstrated the power of love over fear on his journey over mountains in India. He was accosted by bandits and he simply said, "Don't be afraid; I won't hurt you." They let him pass. His lack of fear and his simple recognition of their feeling state struck an inner chord. Boys learn early the mistaken idea that aggression proves their manhood. Implying that fighting and inflicting hurt comes from fear was a profound unmasking by Gandhi.

Intervention

There is a distinction between trying to control another person, and stepping in to affect change, present to Christ consciousness. Deeply spiritual people often suggest non-interference with someone we deeply love. They justify doing nothing by saying something like "we don't know another's soul path." No, we cannot and do not need to know all there is to know, but the deep-seated belief in separateness, displacing the possibility of Oneness, often causes missed opportunities for healing. I have seen intervention work with addictions, and have seen amazing turnarounds. When we listen to guidance and see clearly, we need to act. But we need to be very sure of our guidance before taking any action. With substance abuse, drugs give false feelings and a false release from pain. Drugs alter the brain and interfere with judgment. Our feelings are part of our guidance system, and without awareness of them, our thinking is distorted and destructive. Drugs cause a disconnect with our soul.

Insight is so damaged in the drug user that our words of caution fall on deaf ears. However, noted changes in behavior and other results of their drug use, plus sharing one's own feelings of hurt and disappointment, can be heard. With professional wisdom on intervention, the drug user can choose a recovery program known to work.

A wake-up call also can come in the form of a trauma, which demands attention. Inner work becomes a must for survival. This often results in a change of direction in one's path.

Jesus and the Heart

When the Emotional heart is filled with resentment, guilt, and feelings of separation, the Spiritual heart or Voice for Love is not being heard. The physical heart is also affected. My father, Peter, in a channeled message, said his heart condition reflected his unhealed emotional issues, namely his inability to love and forgive himself. It was after his physical death when he learned that the denial of feelings and matters of the emotional heart brought on his heart condition. In the channeling session, he encouraged us to take care of our feelings. Jeshua's *Let the Heart be the master, and mind becomes a very useful servant,* applies. The mind is masculine in energy. When ego is given the power to rule, it can block intuition, the inner voice of our Spirit identity.

In other words, internal direction from the I Am Presence, the God presence in the heart, comes first. The is-ness of Spirit, the now, the "I Am that I Am," is our true reality. This Voice for Love informs the mind, which tends to be controlled by the ego, the Voice of fear. Love casts out fear and corrects the mind's perception. Our immediate perception is always conditioned by our belief in separation, the core

Chapter 47: Healing Our Wounding

belief taught by most religions, including Christianity. Our task is to ask the Holy Spirit or Higher Self for a love based perception. Peace results.

Jesus's mission is to awaken the heart, the Voice for Love within. "Teach only Love, for that is who you are." (ACIM) Love is our identity! Accepting this at the level of the mind is not enough. Knowing this experientially is the work of opening and clearing the emotional heart. This is what he spoke to. This is not possible through mental resolve, but only through Love's Presence revealed through forgiveness of self and others. ACIM focuses on making a shift in perception which requires a surrender of the mind to the Voice of Love within the Spiritual heart.

In putting Jesus on a pedestal, separation is created. The Patriarchy couldn't allow Jesus to be "defiled" by relations with a woman, so they made him into a celibate and set up a priesthood limited to men and based on celibacy. This is so firmly entrenched in our consciousness after 2000 years of indoctrination that shock can be expected in the revelations of *The DaVinci Code*, the *Anna* books and *The Beloved One*.

It is incredible how they have made the Bible into the inerrant Word of God and so many of us bought it. Much of it is inspired. There are many passages from Jesus that have been very empowering and comforting to the reader, even though some of them have been altered to change their meaning. Leaving out the Feminine Principle greatly distorts them. As Karel points out in *The Beloved One*, there were many changes and omissions of the original text and whole chapters which were written later. The true authorship of the material is also in question. Listening to the Voice for Love, the Holy Spirit within unites us, regardless of different beliefs in the mind. This listening to Source provides the universal experience of connection, essential for Oneness and Heaven on Earth.

Dealing with Dogma

The Nicene creed is considered dogma. It was the truth as we understood it. When it becomes dogma is when it is not to be questioned, according to the church. In my conversations with Jesus regarding who introduced Christianity, Jesus has this to say:

…Christianity was not invented or established either by the apostles or by me. My name was not Christ, but Jesus, and I came into the Christ Consciousness at a certain point, as will you. You and I are following the same path. What has been made of me, what the Church has created out of me, never existed. That was a grave distortion of the truth.

The original rituals and ceremonies that powered Christ Consciousness have been taken away. The Church has usurped these powers as a control mechanism, and presented their version as the only truth. The worst part is that the Church has expunged and eliminated from the story those who originally introduced the rituals and ceremonies, namely the women. A prime example is the "rule" about making confession to a Priest rather than using the inner processing of feelings and thoughts with the Holy Spirit and finding resolution in a feeling of peace.

You are all Christed ones… I was and am only an example for the process you are all currently moving through…

Head to Heart, Dogma to Experience

Rome continues to venerate priests as the only way to approach God. Many protestant churches which accept married clergy still advocate Apostle Paul's admonition for wives to obey their husbands. It reminded me of Rene's disapproval of my getting a Master's Degree as it implied an interference with my husband's headship. For me, Jesus has the last word as he speaks to both sexes: "Let the heart be the master. Then the head becomes a useful servant."

In ACIM, the term "Christ" is the face of God, or its expression. How can we define God other than the one self we all are? Would there be such a thing as an atheist if God were correctly defined?

Chapter 47: Healing Our Wounding

The gifts of music, art, and creativity come from a higher source called inspiration, and can measure above 700 frequencies in vibration. The individual usually operates at a much lower vibration than inner peace, which is 600. Listening to the Spiritual heart can inspire high vibrational music and art. This can be confirmed through Muscle Testing, as I have discovered.

Process, the Female Way of the Heart

Some men have embraced the way of the heart as a process for awakening. It is embracing their feminine principle, the capacity to receive and love the I Am Presence seeded within all of us. Ascension is both a process and an event. To balance over 5000 years of imbalance, it is the feminine way which must lead us into the 5th dimension via the Queendom within. The inner work of purification is necessary for the ascension of consciousness. Clarifying this for myself and understanding the male conditioning can help me articulate this from a place of love and authority.

The omission of women's accomplishments in history still persists in the church and male-controlled religions. Theology is being rejected because of its male-mind orientation as conscious people in professions are focusing on the heart, the yin energy within. The move from head to heart is long overdue in the churches.

A universal theology is impossible, but a universal experience is not only possible but necessary. This refers to a universal Heart *experience* of God within. It is experienced in meditation, trusting and honoring intuition—the Holy Spirit. *Prayer without ceasing* refers to living in a state of connection, a receptivity to Source which results when we release our belief in separation.

The churches focus on niceness, looking good without dealing with the pain within through its denial of feelings. The masculine emphasis is on correct beliefs established by the church. Processing feelings and listening to our Intuition will bring us wisdom from Source. Living in Process helps us avoid attachment to beliefs that remove us from our direct communication with Source.

Trust Brings Abundance

Abundance is not found in the hoarding of money, but in the consciousness of connection to the Source of all supply. Then we trust that our needs will be supplied. It is trusting that a Presence is always there, that it has never gone. Love, Joy and Gratitude create a sense of abundance and vibrationally attract more of what we are grateful for. Clarity of Purpose and trust in guidance to provide the details brings a feeling of abundance.

The 2013 experience of inviting my teenaged grandson to come to Kauai to live with me was a leap of faith. Faith is freeing. Homeless-by-choice friends of mine trust in Source to connect them with opportunities to pet- and house-sit, many times in quite fabulous places. They feel prosperous, despite all the uncertainty from ego's standpoint. Certainty of being cared for, regardless of circumstance, is a quality of true abundance. The Universe works in many ways to support our gratitude for being taken care of. We begin with that knowing, which comes from our relationship with Source, our connection to the heart.

My experience of this transition did not leave me with abundance in terms of money. A contribution towards Patrik's airfare, a mover on drugs, plus a high deposit for the apartment depleted much of my resources. Getting an apartment so quickly in an ideal location for access to school and friends was truly a miracle. In this I realized abundance.

Abundance can come from an Intention to discover and acknowledge it, no matter what the circumstance. A friend took Patrik paddle-boarding and said Patrik was a natural. Enthused, I found a moving sale the next Saturday which had paddleboards. The woman wanted close to a thousand dollars, emphasizing their value. I gave her $100 to hold one while we went to another sale. I ran into a friend, a water athlete, who informed me the one I'd seen was way too expensive and new ones at Costco were cheaper. I went back an hour later to retrieve my $100 and the woman refused to give my check back. I resolved to go early to the bank on Monday morning to cancel it. When I got there, she had already cashed it. I didn't know this bank opened at 7:30 AM.

Inquiry revealed we had a past life relationship in which she (then a man) and I (a woman) were engaged to be married. I changed my mind, called off the marriage, and kept the ring. Guidance directed me to tell her this—I never did, and I lost her contact information. I have tapped on it and consider it a karmic completion. The sting of losing $100 gradually left.

How could this be abundance? Perhaps it is the gratitude for the lessons I am learning.

It is also clarifying my purpose on several levels regarding the connection between fundamentalism and addiction. I could have called the police and pressed charges against the mover. I chose not to. My abundance awareness comes from knowing that I am serving a divine plan.

The Science of the Heart

In an aside, Karel describes how he tests Biblical statements, news accounts, and every dogma. Simply ask whether the words resonate with your heart. You will have a sense of peace, a *yes, it feels right*. You can also use kinesiology. The heart—the body—knows. The deep knowing of the heart surpasses "the linear, intellectual habits of thought, of established science, religion and theology. The science of the heart transcends the limitations of time and space."

I use Muscle Testing to ask, "Are my thoughts correct about this?" I continue with more intuitive questions as needed for clarification and expansion of the thought. My intuition has become sharper as I verify its accuracy with MT.

When one is ready, and seeking spiritual tools and resources, the good news is that many are established and accessible (more easily today with the Internet). For example, Heart Math was founded by Doc Childre in 1991 to help individuals, organizations and the global community incorporate the heart's intelligence into their day-to-day experience of life. They say they "do this by connecting heart and science in ways that empower people to greatly reduce stress, build resilience, and unlock their natural intuitive guidance for making better choices."

Heart Math has studied in depth the gifts of living from the heart. It offers many tools such as "freeze frame" to monitor one's thoughts and live in harmony with our inner knowing. It offers research on the effectiveness of their approach.

<u>Gnosis, Denied Knowledge of the Heart</u> .

The Greek word *gnosis* refers to knowledge and insight, and has evolved "to occult knowledge, then to inner experience or inner knowing." It is also called the knowledge of the heart. Mental or linear knowledge is always limited. Intuition, our inner knowing, is our natural connection to our Higher Self.

Gnosis is the practice of perceiving with our heart rather than with the judgments of our ego in our head. We notice and retain only what resonates with our heart. This is Self- knowing. We can choose the higher vibrations of love over judgment.

The true church is within, as we discover the I Am in our spiritual heart. Cultivating the *observer self* is easier when we recognize our innocence. We have all been programmed to trust external authority. The going inward is the awakening of Sleeping Beauty, the feminine principle. This activation is the hope of Heaven on Earth. Gnosis is our Self-knowledge through insight, experience, and the acceptance and digestion of emotions.

The hierarchal church cannot control the people if they acknowledged the heart as the core source of truth rather than the mental constructs we call dogma or doctrine. Scholars ignore channeled work, resisting gnosis, and accepting only the rational (egoic) approach, or what can be understood in the mind. Inner knowledge or intuition is suspect.

Chapter 47: Healing Our Wounding

Accept Doctrines or Face Death

In the Middle Ages you had to believe the clerical doctrines or risk torture and being killed.

Now we can question. Yet, those whose faith depends on the Bible as being without error will react when the foundations for their life has depended on outer rules and belief systems. This is where contemplative prayer can prepare people for the uncovering of the lies. They can discover an inner foundation for their life that respects the I Am within and respects the truth that resonates in their heart.

The contemporary understanding of gnosis is the knowing of oneness, that everything is connected with everything else, in ultimate harmony. This realization will bring *heaven on earth*. The doctrines of separation taught to us, called "Christianity," have nothing to do with the real message of Jesus who came to help us claim our Christ identity.

Hell vs. Self-knowledge

Karel questions the doctrines of sin and atonement as designed to produce guilt along with fear of a fictitious hell. Hell, we have managed to make on planet earth. We have been brainwashed to give our power away. Our true power is in "self-knowledge through insight, experience and the acceptance and digestion of emotions."

The Apocryphal gospels were rejected because their core message was self-knowledge. Who knows himself knows the All and needs no priestly intermediary. Our increasing consciousness becomes our awakening, which we can accelerate through Intention, Allowing and Surrender. Perceive with the heart and let any idea pass through, retaining only what resonates. Resonance is the language of the heart.

In his discussion of belief, an activity of the mind, Karel says in conclusion, "The Heart <u>believes</u> nothing. The Heart knows!"

Impact of Karel's Exposé

Perhaps a verification of the truth of Karel's research and conclusions about the immense brainwashing perpetrated by the church, foundational to the Patriarchy, is in the desperate means used to still his voice. Sharing it with highly respected leaders in the church would shake up the system, as it would be hard to refute Karel's findings.

Karel's book is the most provocative work I have come across that so bluntly challenges our assumptions about the foundation for the Christian church. It is a time for everything to come into the light for healing. Love IS being expressed in words and service along with the salvation message of Jesus as Savior. Love can embrace a shift in consciousness and gratitude for undoing our belief in separation. Jesus then becomes our teacher and helps us to identify with him. He makes it all possible, not as an insurance policy against hell, but as a partner who empowers us to be the Christ as he is.

Focus on a *Universal experience*

Though *a universal theology is impossible,* we can share *a universal experience* of awakening to our true Christ Self. This has helped me to focus on the Intention of bringing this to light. It calls for listening deeply for guidance from Jeshua himself for the steps most helpful for sharing the truth. Pointing to the obvious omission of the apocryphal material can open up discussion, as we begin to read for ourselves what we have been denied.

Change

Change starts when the victim stands up and says, "Enough! I won't take it anymore!" Change calls for "the rebirth of the male energy." When the male energy reshapes itself and values the feminine, cooperation is possible.

Rampant terrorism on our planet is an expression of the death throes of the power and control energies, which realize their time is up. Jeshua encourages us not to become victimized but to stay conscious. Do not react in anger or helplessness, which vibrates at the level of the perpetrator. Jeshua assures us we will be safe and protected by our own light. When we stay or quickly return to the higher vibrations, we will not draw the lower energies to us.

Chapter 47: Healing Our Wounding

Everything that happens collectively mirrors processes at the individual level, Jeshua reminds us. Our inner release work is the one thing we can do to effect change in the collective.

Greatest Wounding

Chakras are part of our body, each a center where energy flows through (if not blocked). Jeshua emphasizes that most emotional pain occurs in the lower three chakras in both past and present lifetimes. This unprocessed emotional pain causes blocks in the upper chakras as well.

The tailbone chakra is our primary earth connection and calls for being grounded in the present. Our reluctance in being seen as different (and being rejected for it) has caused an avoidance of grounding. Clearing emotional blocks, grounding, and a third focus on chakra healing brings balance. Here the ego is accepted as possibly useful in a surrendered state. Yes, it can be insane, as he states in ACIM. The proper function of the ego is to lend focus to our consciousness in the expression of our individuality. When the ego is in the service of the Heart as the Master, it serves a useful function.

CHAPTER 48

TRUE MASCULINITY AND TRUE FEMININITY

Meaning of Masculine, Feminine

Our Yang energy is our "doing" nature. It is meant to be the outward expression of an inner process, which is our Yin energy. We incarnated as human *beings*, not human *doings*. The Yin (or feminine) is receptive energy. To be whole beings, we need both, despite our external expression of gender. This inner energy involves our feelings and our heart energy.

All humans have both Yin and Yang energies. Patriarchy has greatly distorted this by beginning to wean boys from their mothers at an early age with *be tough* messages, discouraging any connection to feelings, imprinting "big boys don't cry." Also, boys are conditioned for war at an early age.

The rational mind is promoted, and the feeling nature is not to be acknowledged, according to the Patriarchy. The message includes—women can't be trusted. Feminine is considered soft by nature, and male energy, firm and decisive.

I had developed a hardness from my conditioning which shifted when I started to do my inner work and feel my feelings. Positive feedback regarding my softer energy as a result of my process was instructive to me. The highly defensive stance I developed growing up with six brothers and a dominating father had to be dismantled.

Yin energy can, in some cases, be stronger in a male than in some females. The opposite is true for some females who have a strong Yang energy. Intuition is considered a female quality that is attributed to greater connections between the right and left hemispheres of the female brain. Growing up in my highly analytical male family, I had to learn to discover, develop, and respect my intuition. Moving from the analytical brain to trusting the wisdom of one's heart is a journey we all must take to bring in Heaven on Earth. This is what is meant by *bringing in the feminine.*

Karel refers to these energies as the Masculine Principle and the Feminine Principle. In the history of Christian religion, he contends that it is based on the masculine principle, denying altogether the feminine principle. This denied principle has resulted in the emasculation of the masculine principle. Denial of the feminine principle in both men and women brings imbalance, a disregard for the whole, and a loss of connection with Source and with one another. Karel describes the resulting repression "of the Sacred Marriage in general, and that of Mary Magdalene and Jesus in particular."

Masculine/Feminine Imbalance and the Church

The Sacred Marriage did occur, but all accounts were omitted from the Bible. The beautiful example of harmony and unity that Jesus and Mary's relationship offers was denied us. It is needed today to demonstrate how the male and female can relate for ultimate happiness and fulfillment of purpose. Just the one act of truth of bringing forth their relationship would transform the church—and the world. It is their union which informs the nature of Ascension and Heaven on Earth.

Women are rising up and becoming heard, yet suffer with less pay, and still have a minor presence in government and church leadership. Women still are the primary victims of rape and domestic violence. Within religious institutions this is often justified or overlooked because of the belief that male domination is God-ordained. God is referred to as a Supreme Being, even though the Bible acknowledges, "God is Spirit." We have difficulty comprehending the reality of Spirit—Love, without form. Spirit creates from its love, energy, which is both masculine and feminine. Soul awareness is feminine;

the manifestation is its masculine energy. There is no separation between these energies.

The Sacred Marriage; The Union of the Masculine and Feminine Principles

When this Sacred Marriage occurs, "our polluted planet will undergo a metamorphosis, and the Garden of Eden will flourish again." Karel's words describe this marriage as demonstrated by Jesus and Mary Magdalene in their relationship to each other. He states that they were twin souls and Mary actually initiated Jesus into the feminine principle.

Mary says, *…through our mutual love, we were able to raise each other to the highest level. I initiated Jesus by passing on to him the knowledge of the Mothers; the wisdom that originates from the lineage of Isis.*

Wife and twin soul of Jesus, Mary Magdalene is also referred to as the black Madonna. She refers to herself as Ethiopian, originating from Africa. The Patriarchy made Mary Magdalene out to be a whore and a sinner, while elevating Jesus to a supernatural status. Instead, she represents the divine feminine, which the church maligned and suppressed.

The true followers of Jesus, the Cathars, were destroyed in the Inquisition in March of 1244. Two hundred remaining Cathars walked singing into the fire, with the promise to return in seven hundred years as the seed of Jesus and Mary. That refers to our present time, as the souls of their children have re-incarnated at this time, along with the numerous descendants of the children of Jesus and Mary.

The *Magdalene* is the embodiment of the Feminine Principle and is coming into recognition and awareness. In summary, Karel says, "Jesus and Mary Magdalene had a planetary assignment and an archetypal function. Two thousand years ago they prepared the Great Awakening that is currently taking place." Initiations were done by the feminine. Magdalene says the initiation into Christ Consciousness will be through the Feminine Principle.

True Masculinity and True Femininity

Jeshua, in *The Jeshua Channelings*, describes male energy as outwardly focused. It is highly focused and goal-oriented, and is driven toward manifestation of some form. This creates individuality. Male energy projects and protects. It wants to be of service.

Female energy, the energy of Home, is the energy of the Primal Source, pure Being and flowing light. It is oceanic and does not individualize. It receives and nurtures. The two energies are aspects of the One and belong together in cooperation and joining.

The mystical mantra of I AM, our identity, is the joining of male and female energies. The "I" is the male energy and the "AM" is the female energy. I AM expresses the Oneness that we are. Jeshua says this unity has been forgotten and a black and white opposition has resulted in victim and perpetrator roles. A result is the Patriarchal condition of the distorted masculine energy becoming ruthlessly violent, and the feminine weakened through devaluation. The feminine has lost her sense of Being.

Chakras

Jeshua emphasizes balance between the feminine and masculine energies within us through awareness of the chakras, the energy centers in every human. He discusses seven chakras beginning with the root chakra located in the perineum, which is predominantly male in energy. The second, or sacral chakra, below the navel, is the receptive and emotional chakra, predominantly feminine in energy. (My complete hysterectomy is a significant comment on my history of the denial of the feminine.)

The third chakra is located in the solar plexus and is called the chakra of empowerment, primarily male in energy. Jeshua refers to it as a center of action and creation, involved with manifestation. A chakra test indicated mine was closed which suggests my resistance to manifesting wealth and external recognition. My awareness has opened it through the TaBIA process. For it to become strong will require focus on manifesting and release of resistance!

The fourth chakra of the heart can be closed or open, weak or strong. The heart is the bridge between head and belly, or mind and emotion. It connects the three lower earth chakras to the three upper or cosmic chakras. From the heart we can transcend the ego and experience our oneness with all life. The heart allows us to connect and relate. The Heart chakra is the gateway to Home and clearly a center of connection, thus primarily feminine in energy.

The inner life of ideas, emotions, and communication is experienced through the outward use of the voice in the throat, or fifth chakra. It is primarily male. This rather surprised me, until I realized that in general the words of males are given more credibility than those of females. On the chakra test, my throat chakra was "closed." No wonder I had thyroid cancer, the result of the "oppression of expression." Just when I think I have finished working on myself, there is yet much to do. The first step is awareness and willingness to step out of old patterns of expression and to value what I have to say. If we don't value our words, others won't either.

The sixth chakra, the third eye, is located mid-forehead. It is largely feminine. It is your spiritual vision and is connected with the heart, which I call the fourth eye. It is extra sensory, intuitive, and connects with energies of other individuals. Where it is strong one can see auras, a gift common in the new children, both male and female. Ego is transcended. Along with my heart chakra my third eye was strong. Clearly, balance of my male and female energy centers is needed.

The crown chakra on top of the head is neither male nor female, according to Jeshua.

When balanced, there is an equal reaching-out and receiving. Reaching upward to other dimensions, the crown chakra seeks support and meaning for the deeper layers of the Self. The peace of knowing that answers will come at the right time balances the seeking. I am grateful for its opening, a result of my choice to do my inner work.

Jeshua asks us to focus on the lower three chakras, which are earth related, to heal the inner child and bring forth its joy and playfulness in the body. These are the chakras involved in our early childhood experiences, a necessary focus for healing the past. It is here that most traumas occur. Clearing the wounds is our road to divine compassion and enlightenment. It is also necessary for attracting and sustaining healthy relationships.

The female energies of intuition, sensitivity, and connectedness are being recognized and appreciated. Because of the male stereotypes, the male energy is seen as primarily about power and aggression. The service qualities of protection, and support of a strong Presence, are not so clear. When fear is replaced by love, then power and control disappear. With a rebirth of the true male energy, a joyful and equal partnership is possible.

The Sacred Marriage; Conversations with Jesus and Mary Magdalene

By Karel and Caroline van Huffelen

Jesus speaks to the men and asks, *Are you honest and prepared to live from the heart?*

Are you prepared to face the truth that you no longer support the feminine principle? That you have lost contact with the feminine within yourself, so that you are dominating as a man and as a father?

That was not the truth that I proclaimed. It was not the truth that I witnessed. I testified for an integrated truth in which the masculine and the feminine principle are of equal value and are indeed one. I accepted women in their strength and wisdom. And I let myself be guided by women so that I could do my work in the outside world. My beloved Mary Magdalene was the embodiment of the feminine principle. I brought the mutual equality and the fusion of the masculine and feminine aspect

Chapter 48: True Masculinity And True Femininity

to the attention of the public. Later on, something quite different was made of this in your holy scriptures.

It was my mission to represent Christ Consciousness as a man. You have no idea of what true manhood and true femininity really entail.

It was my beloved Mary Magdalene who bestowed upon me the knowledge of the feminine that liberated me, so that the Christ living within me could come fully to bloom.

The divine feminine is in everyone, but cannot come into its fullness if the masculine fails to respect the feminine within.

Jeshua continues, *The divine masculine is the protector of beingness. The true divine masculine protects every life form, does not condemn, and does not misuse situations. Therefore, I speak of mindfulness, presence, and being in the here and now, so that whatever unfolds and develops can literally, be protected through alertness and awareness. In this state of consciousness we can discern, use our intuition, and be in integrity.*

When the male embraces his divine masculine, he will no longer exploit the earth or kill his brother in war. An inner voice from my ancient sister, Mary Magdalene prompted me to listen to her words.

Mary Magdalene 6-5-13

Indeed I wish to speak. All those who honor the Christ in themselves are Magdalenes as well as Christs. Embrace both the Divine Masculine and the Divine Feminine within you.

Recognize the energies and bring them into balance through your spiritual practice and use of the Four Keys to the Queendom within. Feel your Heart's Desire. Express your Intention to allow the divine Feminine to be expressed, knowing the Divine Masculine protects and supports that Intention. Your openness will Allow that Divine energy to be expressed in the right time at the right place.

Your ongoing Surrender to your I Am Love Presence empowers the Divine Feminine and corrects the distorted masculine energies that appear to dominate the planet. You are noting the gathering of the feminine energy in India to protest and correct the abuses of the male energies there. Coming together and declaring an end to the victim role is part of bringing balance. It is also appreciating the emergence of the Divine Masculine. Know that you are supported by those in the spirit world who have sacrificed their lives to the Patriarchy.

Focus on your purpose and the value of what you have to share. The more you share, the easier it becomes to express your wisdom from the heart. Simply allow the Voice to express.

You are empowered by all the Magdalenes that have gone before you.

As One, Mary Magdalene.

Farewell to Duality

Mary Magdalene says the greatest loss in her life was the rape of the feminine. When we consciously choose balance and harmony we are saying farewell to duality. She tells us to embrace our pain and embrace our rage. Mother earth is ready for bloodletting to end in our reconciliation and forgiveness. The masculine and feminine are meant to complement each other, not compete. The repression of the feminine is the root cause of all war, conflict, and imbalance on earth.

Heaven on Earth calls for surrender to All-That-Is, which means to embrace matter with gratitude, seeing the divine in everything. Duality dissolves. Hearing the sounds of love and creation, we are tuning into Source and the heart language of resonance becomes primary. When the heart is open, Mary Magdalene can speak to us. There is no more need for cathedrals of fear; the cathedral of love is founded in our hearts.

Sexual Energy, the Life Force

"The phallus cannot be tamed by repression." Karel details the scandals of sexual abuse of children by priests. The Vatican resists. The coming to light of other abuses is part of the catharsis needed.

Karel continues, "When you renounce something, you're stuck to it forever." He quotes an India guru, "Every time a prostitute comes to me, she talks about nothing but God. She says, 'I am sick of this life I am living; I want God! But every time a priest comes to me, he talks about nothing but sex."

Activism

As long as we are fighting it, we are giving it power—whatever "it" is. This gives me pause. There is a fine line we hold in the area of activism. I asked Jeshua to speak to this.

…It is this. If your vibrations are focused on resistance, you are in fear. Notice the martial arts teaching is to feel and focus on your position and simply step aside when the aggressor lunges. Staying centered in your own truth and demonstrating a better way to work with this sexual energy, such as channeling it into creativity, i. e. music or that which fulfills the heart's desire, i. e. poetry to the beloved, is a wise use of your life force. Few can accomplish this, so seeking a compatible partner is appropriate.

An imposed vow of celibacy is a set up for failure. When it comes from a heart's desire to express your passion totally on your purpose, and an intimate relationship would hinder it, celibacy is your choice. It is the Patriarchy's view of the feminine, not only as inferior but as a hindrance to the ministry, that creates the sexual abuse. I did not find my relationships with women a hindrance, but rather a very necessary part of my emergence as a Christ. My women teachers gifted me with the profound wisdom of the heart as our connection to Source.

They understood best the role I chose, and grasped my message more quickly than my male disciples who tended to focus on external power, such as overthrowing Roman rule. When the male and female energies are in balance within an individual, you have wholeness.

It is a stressful life to live under the rule of ego and the push to control. To accept the feminine principle is to accept flow and trust in the process of life; feel the feelings and trust the higher wisdom of the spiritual heart.

Jesus' use of "Father"

I have wondered about the ongoing use of "Father" in the messages from Jesus. This is what he has to say about this:

Indeed, you can question this in light of ending the rule of the Patriarchy. Creator energy is male, not in gender but in its outward manifestation. At the time of my incarnation, only "Father" had any authority. The image in the Old Testament of God as judge and avenger and separate from his creations was an unquestioned belief of the church. I felt it was a big step just to shift the image of God to a loving father. This invited a relationship of love between father and 'son' (a term inclusive of women). This was to serve my primary intention of imaging a God of love rather than of fear.

'The Kingdom of God is within you' is a radical and transformative statement that miraculously remained in the accepted scriptures. It is only through Jon Marc Hammer that I revised it to say the 'Queendom of God is within you!' It has taken over 2000 years for that to be acceptable.

They would have totally dismissed what I had to say if I was egalitarian in my words, acknowledging female equality. My relationships with women included having them as partners, teachers, and disciples. Here, I needed to be discreet for their safety as well.

God, as some of you have begun to accept, is the energy of LOVE—all powerful, everywhere present, and all-knowing. It is the wisdom of the Spiritual heart within every human being, the greatest untapped resource on your planet. Unconditional Love is the Voice of Spirit, your Divinity.

The Invention of Hell

The Church uses the invention of Hell to better control people, through fear. This is not a new practice, admittedly, as men with religious power have been doing that for many thousands of years. At least, now, the veil is lifted enough for us to see through this manipulation, and even men in power have begun to acknowledge it. Bishop John Shelby Spong is quoted as saying, "Hell is an invention of the Church to control people with fear."

Both heaven and hell are states of mind. There are places that can certainly be described as "hell" because of the dominant energy present—the energy of the belief in separation, attack and defense, and the power and control aspects of the ego. The "right to bear arms," which is so hotly defended, is nothing but the voice of fear. Weapons promote the illusion of safety, based on the identification with the body.

The use of firearms to save anyone is far outweighed by its use to destroy life. Only a massive shift in consciousness can change this insanity. Our true protection comes from within. Peace Pilgrim's inner love power kept her safe on her well-over 25,000 mile walk for peace. (She didn't carry a weapon.) Her love energy was also her key to health. Ironically, a car accident took her life, when she was 76.

Recognition of Error

With the recognition of error in the omission of the feminine influence in Jesus' life, and his schooling in India and Egypt, the truth will come out. It can be devastating to those whose lives were fully invested in what they understood to be the truth about Jesus' life and mission. Compassion and forgiveness of the Church's distortion of the truth will be difficult and challenging for many who have devoted their lives to its teachings. When practices such as contemplative prayer bridge differing churches, the people themselves experience a shift that is inclusive and affirming of their common Love identity. This will allow them to recognize the ego's distortion of the truth from a place of Love, Compassion, and Gratitude for the awareness brought by the Light of Truth, which resonates with the Heart.

There is no condemnation, as the Love Essence is the core identity in all beings, only to be activated by an awakened heart. Even though an experience of the heart may have initiated a following, the *belief in separation* by the ego dominated the established religion. This has occurred because the feminine, or inner being, has been devalued by the Patriarchy. This is now changing through meditation, a practice recognized in the West primarily for its health benefits.

The recognition of the spiritual aspect of human nature has yet to be widely accepted. And yet, the natural attraction we feel for Spirit sometimes falls prey to exploitation. Product promotion often uses spiritual terminology to sell: *Bliss* can be achieved by relaxing and imbibing their brand of drink or food. *Peace of mind* can be attained by investing in their product. *Intuition* is also used by some planning departments to create more business. Beware the distortions of the ego! Poisons are being sold, appealing to the fear or ego aspect of our human experience.

Martha's Voice and Vision

Martha spoke of Yeshua's mission as for us to not only serve God, but to BE God. When we feel separate, we are trying to *make a god in our image. In truth, God is an unnamable, unborn, undying Presence, whose essence is both emptiness and bare intrinsic awareness, expressing as pure Being and Love. This Great Presence manifests in all forms and walks in earthly bodies, as one family of humanity…It is time to establish Heaven right here on earth,,, our hearts… our lives, moment by moment.*

Martha says her vision is for us to forgive and allow healing as individuals, families, and society. We need to take far better care of our mother, the Earth. In her vision, women will experience *true sisterhood, nurture and support each other. Men no longer compete, use women in lust, or go to war to prove themselves.* Men will allow and develop their feminine traits and women will use their masculine energy for the good of all.

When we are aware…our Divine Soul is given space to live and act. The compassionate heart of the Soul guides the human mind to listen and obey its quiet, inner voice… In the New Day, the lamb and the lion shall peacefully lie together, and Earth Mother shall thrive as a fertile garden.

A Model of Mature Male Energy

In May of 2014, I met "Gary" at a Way of the Heart meeting. I felt a resonant energy. As he was visiting the island, I offered opportunities for connection. I soon learned he was a gifted, capable creator of tools for meditation and healing. He knew his purpose and was aware of a past life with Jesus, as well as with Moses in building the Egyptian pyramids. He offered an engaging presence, attracting many who wanted to experience his healing techniques and tools. I held a meeting in my living room that attracted 21 people who came to hear of his healing work. This resulted in many appointments for him in the remaining two weeks of his stay.

He indicated that I was his mother in Jesus's lifetime. My Intuitive Inquiry indicated I was his mother in India where Jesus came to learn from spiritual teachers, and Gary was one of his teachers. This was a lifetime my soul was incarnated in two different bodies, as I was also Martha.

I also did a healing exchange and experienced his gifts. He encountered young women who he was partnered with in past lives who also recognized him as a former partner. Though very caring and interested in these women, he was very circumspect in his behavior and show of affection, so as not to create an attachment. He knew what other aspects of his purpose he needed to do and kept from getting emotionally involved. I was very impressed by his personal discipline and his keeping integrity a priority. He frequently stated his role was to be of service. I knew he did at least a half hour of yoga practice each morning. He was the most open and self-disclosing male I had ever met.

My Intuition indicated he is an Ascended Master who, like many others, is back on the planet to help us bring heaven to earth. I felt privileged in being able to share his energy and facilitate his stay. It also gave me a glimpse of what can be experienced in a cooperative venture without attachment.

CHAPTER 49

THE RESTORATION OF THE FEMININE

Everything Scattered Will Be Gathered is more than a title—it is the promise of the hidden coming to light. Truth will be unveiled. The power and control motives behind our government, economic, scientific, commercial, agricultural, religious and educational systems will be exposed and overturned. Money will NOT be the bottom line. Everyone's needs will be met in a spirit of cooperation rather than competition. Abundance will replace scarcity and fear of *not enough*. What is *pono* (right) will rule as a cherished quality of the Spiritual heart.

The *belief in separation* will be undone. Our Oneness will become realized. Unveiling of the soul's purpose in coming to earth will manifest. Lessons will be expected. Our multiple expressions of God in form will be accepted and realized in the equal opportunity for the variety in gifts to be expressed.

Our relationship to the unseen will be accepted, and inner Source guidance will prevail in co-creative endeavors. Consensus will be a common goal. Forgiveness will be cherished as a given for restoring harmony in a mutual approach to correction of misperception. In my vision, defensiveness is unnecessary and judgment is avoided; clarity and discernment are valued.

The restoration of the feminine comes through healing the emotional heart through the acknowledgment of feelings. Tenderness and compassion will prevail. Access to the wisdom of the Spiritual heart, the Voice for Love, will prevail over the egoic voice of fear in the head. Truth will be welcomed and true transparency will be the prevailing order in the safety of the nurturing energy of the feminine.

The Vision of a New Earth can offset the immense negative energy on the planet now. Despair can so easily overcome us without the vision. The Bible states, "Where there is no vision, the people perish." *Change or Die* is an imperative for now. It is no longer the 11th hour—it is the hour. The change called for is *Heart Awakening to who we are*—At One with the earth, each other and Source. Our language is **resonance**. Love is the means and the goal. *Teach only love for that is who you are*—words from *A Course in Miracles*.

Featured at the 2013 Kauai Expo, one speaker talked about Project Heaven on Earth. His focus was on the idea of heaven on earth, and talking to others about it, accomplishing it through the mind. Nothing was said about the necessary process of Heart Awakening—forgiveness, and heart-to-heart connection through resonance. Until we value the Inner Queendom, the divine feminine, Heaven on Earth cannot happen.

Athena , 2-12-13

Athena is an angel, twin soul to Ashtar, a primary channel to Ariana. Now one of my guides, Athena has asked to come in and speak to us about **Heaven on Earth.**

Thank you. Now we begin. I asked to come in because you have a strong feminine energy, which has been suppressed and devalued in many lifetimes up to now. This is the energy that is coming onto the planet to cleanse the imbalance of male domination, and bring Heaven to Earth. Your Purpose up until now has been Purification and Self-Healing, an important preparation for Heaven on Earth.

Heaven on Earth begins with Heart Awakening through the healing of the emotional heart. It is allowing the painful feelings of lifetimes to come up and be healed. Confession and self-forgiveness will be primary. This is trusting the process, the process of allowing feelings to be felt, accepted, and released so one's nurturing nature can be the guide, instead of external power and control.

Chapter 49: The Restoration Of The Feminine

As a disciple of Jesus, you have come to understand his feminine nature and embraced the truth of his relationships with women as his teachers and his lovers, who described the amazing energy of love they felt in him. This energy never took away from his manhood. The Patriarchy didn't get it, as their idea of manhood was power over others, over women and over nature. The 'belief in separation' then put Source outside of them as a separate, dominating power instead of a power within. Men regarded their feelings as unmanly. Many like your father succumbed to heart disease, a dis-ease of the feelings.

This is part of the correction now needed and women will lead the way. Also your awareness of one's inner process was absent in the lecture on Sunday of Heaven on Earth. The focus on the outer talking about Heaven on Earth is a typical male focus. He asked people to accept the idea in their minds, which is controlled by the ego This approach invites figuring it out, engaging the ego's perceptions rather than the intuitive wisdom of the Spiritual heart. The shift from body identification to Spirit identification is only possible through engaging the Queendom within. When the Heart becomes the master, the mind will be a very useful servant.

Eckhart Tolle [author, The New Earth] recognizes this and identifies the need for awareness of the pain-body and its release. He has embraced the inner process as key to Heaven on Earth. Jeshua Ben Joseph, who has brought his true teachings back to the planet through <u>A Course in Miracles</u> and <u>Way of the Heart</u>, plus many other channels you are familiar with, provides everything needed for Heaven on Earth to take place. There are others from the East who echo Jesus' teachings more so than the Western patriarchal churches.

Jeshua's Four Keys to the Queendom within, an expanded Law of Attraction, emphasizes the <u>Heart's Desire</u> as the starting place. This is engaging the feminine. <u>Intention</u> calls in the will and the Visioning of the third eye, the spiritual part of the mind. <u>Allowing</u>, the 3rd Key, is Process, inviting the Universe, Source or God, to orchestrate the 'how' the Heart's Desire will manifest. 'Allowing' is a trust process, which avoids ego interference. <u>Surrender,</u> *the 4th Key, is a surrender of ego identity to the I Am Presence in the Spiritual heart.*

When the Higher Self (or God Self) is in charge, you will have Heaven on Earth. The I Am Presence is the energy of unconditional love. Forgiving everything the 'belief in separation' has prompted, is necessary first. Listening to the Voice of Love in the heart instead of the voice of fear in the ego mind is the shift humanity must make to manifest Heaven on Earth. Peace and Joy are Love's fruits.

A Woman's Worth

There is more awareness now about how girls, even in these modern times, are brainwashed by Patriarchy messages which instill self-doubt and in some cases, self-loathing (many times leading to hating one's body, anorexia, depression, bulimia, obesity and other serious health problems.)

A Woman's Worth, by Marianne Williamson, is a must-read book for women to understand and help themselves, their sisters and daughters. This requires Intention—as for centuries the programming has been to devalue women. Physical results of devaluation can include breast cancer, fibroids, endometriosis, cervical and ovarian cancer. The body expresses through the malfunction of female organs. Indeed, I have had endometriosis, a complete hysterectomy, pre-cancerous fibroid breast tissue, and thyroid cancer as the body's expression of repression.

"We cry in shame, because we feel no right to cry," Williamson writes. "We cry for the world. We cry for our children. Our sons are sacrificed in war under the guise of patriotism, when we know there is a better way… Like every woman, I know what I know… New things lie in store for the earth, and one of them is us… we're pregnant, en masse, giving birth to our own redemption."

Our Three-Headed Jailor from Within

"A woman makes a choice between the state of the queen and the state of the slave-girl," Williamson continues. "In the world of illusion, we are lost and imprisoned, slaves to our appetites and our will to false power. Our jailor is a three-headed monster; one our past, one our insecurity, and one our popular culture… Our past is a story existing only in our minds. Look, analyze, understand and forgive."

TaBIA is a simple, practical and effective way to approach this necessary healing. Notice, process feelings, understand the lesson, shift perception, forgive and release with TaBIA. This process of correction becomes a spiritual practice. We are free to empower ourselves and celebrate our process of self-healing. Sharing our process affirms our power to speak our truth and encourages others to shed their limitations as well, in acknowledgment and without shame. It is embracing what is, and our power to change it. That is easier said than done. Our first task is becoming aware of "what is."

A Woman's Worth According to the Patriarchal Culture

The values of our culture focus on looking good according to the commercialization of the feminine body. Though totally unreal, these cultural values have filled the coffers of the many corporations who exploit this.

I felt inadequate because I hadn't sought or learned to paste on eyelashes, noticeably absent. The ideal female shape plastered in every fashion magazine is a pure fantasy for most women who identify with their bodies. That these ideal bodies are sexually appealing to men has not escaped our notice. The media emphasis on the female body as the key to attracting a man (who could then own us) comes from the Biblical and pre-Biblical valuing of women as property rather than partners.

One of our compensations for a less-than-perfect body is to become a superwoman with expectations involving multitasking, and serving the male system. Indeed, "We are tyrannized by a belief we are inadequate," the second monster head of **insecurity**.

The belief, *I am nothing without a man,* and the question, *who am I without a man?* was typical of my generation. We depended on a male breadwinner for security and also our identity. My self-esteem soared when I was on the arm of an esteemed man, my source of value. Otherwise I felt invisible, and unworthy.

When we embrace our spirit identity, the divine feminine, these monsters begin to disappear. Until we go within, valuing and nourishing the wisdom of the heart and our inner process, we will be subject to the feelings of *not enough* and cultural expectations. Identifying our purpose—first, to accept our spirit identity and intuitive guidance and then to claim and express our gifts—will banish the emptiness we tried to fill with food, fashion, and fantasies.

Fear Made "Witch" the Bad Name for the Mystical Power of Women

Men, identifying with their mind, are compelled to *know*. When they encounter something they do not know nor understand, such as the magical and mystical power of women, they experience extreme anxiety. For relief, they use their ability to exert control through force, brainwashing, or any means necessary. Williamson speaks of the magical and mystical power of women and how her knowledge is needed to heal the world. Her research on Friday the 13th, considered a bad luck omen, indicates it was a day women gathered to share energy, pray, and heal. This frightened the power and control nature of the Patriarchy. These gathered women were called witches, especially if they showed up and expressed themselves.

The witch hunts are considered distant history—the banning, burnings and beheadings. Yet, there are still cultures that kill those that are out of line with the male program. Recently in Australia, a young woman was labeled a witch, tortured, and burned on a trash heap in front of a crowd of onlookers. In America, yes, America, in 2011 an Arizona man was convicted of murdering his 20-year old daughter (running over her with his car). He had been extremely upset with her for becoming "too Westernized." She was guilty of rejecting an arranged marriage and choosing to go to college.

Male fear of feminine power is still in the consciousness of many on the planet. It is their own inner power of Love they are afraid

Chapter 49: The Restoration Of The Feminine

of. The programming and conditioning of young boys has to be extreme to allow this to occur. Unfortunately, this is not an isolated case of dehumanization that is still present on the planet. My body remembered, on Memorial Sunday of 2012, the penalties of being a witch in the eyes of the male clergy. It is time to heal these cellular memories that many women carry.

Woman as Goddess

A key message in Williamson's book is for a woman to own her beauty, honor her courage, and allow the rule of the Goddess within her heart. Not all women will change. When a critical mass is reached, the whole will shift. The uncomfortable feelings I have about the term "Goddess" bears witness to the church's demonizing the feminine. How programmed we are to devalue ourselves. She says "all that separates the queens from the slave-girls is a shift in consciousness from denial to acceptance of personal power." The "miracle of feminine transformation …begins with a decision to change, and a willingness to accept God's help."

Marianne Williamson received more criticism when she became more committed, enthusiastic, and more public with her message. She tells aspiring women that feeling guilty invites attack. When we no longer care about societies' criticism of ecstatic women, we have liberated ourselves.

She reminds us that the thought and treatment of women as inferior is in the mental kingdom of the Patriarchy. It has "no power in the face of a woman who knows she is a queen… The real beauty secret is finding your inner light…When we remember our royal inheritance, men will become our true partners."

Atlantis and Isis

Equality between men and women has existed before in history, according to archaeological evidence showing "the existence of a twenty-thousand-year period of history when men and women lived as equals, with neither sex dominating the other. The earth flourished. The so-called feminine qualities of compassion, nurturing and nonviolence were shared by men and women alike, and were the most vital elements of social structure. Women were revered as priestesses and healers… We healed one another through our compassionate connection to spirit and earth."

This was true of Atlantis. The male priest takeover preceded the collapse of this civilization, referred to as "The Fall." Thus the great civilization of Atlantis sank beneath the sea.

In a reading, I was told I was a priestess of Isis during this time. My traumatic cellular memories dating to this period have been cleared. In July of 2013, I received the following information regarding Isis, from Jeshua:

Isis is a Goddess of great wisdom, known as a great teacher who was revered by the Magdalenes and other followers in Jesus' day. Isis fell out of favor with the priests during Atlantis and a male god was invented, you know today as 'God.' Atlantis preceded the Old Testament. The souls that lived as males and followed the rebellious Priests who destroyed Atlantis went back to spirit. Their lust for external power and control followed them and they invented a male God capable of wrath, as depicted in the Old Testament. That is the God concept dominating the Patriarchy and the Old Testament recordings.

Buddha's wisdom softened the conceptual framework and he did not speak at all of a God who was other than one's Self. Women were still devalued, however.

Male domination was a given right to those born male. A Jewish Rabbi declared, 'Thank God, I was not born a woman!' God was a male, external being, who judged and punished those who didn't worship him. Sex was a man's right. It didn't matter if the woman wanted it or not, so rape could be justified, since she was naturally a temptress and therefore caused it.

I, as Jeshua, tried to change that, and said God is Love and God is Spirit, as are all beings.

Chapter 49: The Restoration Of The Feminine

The concept of separation began with the fall of Atlantis. This 'belief in separation' is the sole cause of misery on planet earth. As Jeshua Ben Joseph, I was aware of my purpose but needed to grow in wisdom that comes from the earth experience, so I wasn't as clear about that as I am now. I was hormonally male and subject to temptations like others in physical form, but I did not feel superior to women, and deeply respected them as my teachers, beginning with my famous mother.

There is no God outside of you. When you are free of ego, you are in your God Self, your natural state of Being Love, which is One. This state of being is the fifth dimension. Earth's vibrational ascension allows this state to be experienced now in the body. That is why your bodies are changing from carbon to crystalline, even though most are not aware of it. It is a challenge for the body to go through these changes, so you have symptoms of illness, like dizziness, indigestion, or headaches, which may be only the body's attempt to integrate the new energy.

I felt these challenges in the body, as my earth assignment was to embody the fifth dimension 'Jesus' and release the ego. It was a process that began at birth. I was not veiled as other souls were in their incarnations. Because I ascended in consciousness while on earth, I Am in charge of the Ascension. Those who are blocked by the church's distortion of me and reject me are not in any way condemned. They simply are supported in their ascension process by other beings, the ascended masters they are drawn to.

Because of your lifetime in the church with the clergy, and your relationship with me, you are one of many who can speak to the church through your writing and your ascension into an ageless body. You are aware of our orchestrating your life to facilitate this. Painful severance from your family and former friends is all a part of this mission you have accepted. Many of us are with you to empower you in this important mission. We need your voice and others like yourself.

As you already know, all systems are going through collapse and re-creation. We need clear voices, those who have done their inner work of releasing all the blocks to Love's Presence. This is why I gave you the TaBIA process, a spiritual practice, not only to embody forgiveness, but to identify with the I Am Presence in the Spiritual heart. With the completion of your book, you will be ready to share this process easily and effortlessly, as we will orchestrate all manner of opportunities.

Resistance is to be expected. Do not take it personally. The patriarchal fundamentalists of the world are lashing out in their power and control fury, which simply adds to their karma. The many whose lives have been sacrificed agreed in spirit to experience this. They are not caught or stuck in the astral plane. Others whose experience brought sudden death may be stuck and are released through your rescue circles. Prayers of family and friends can also release them. It is Love which releases. Teach only Love for that is what you are. You are surrounded with Love.

I am with you always in all ways, Jeshua

CHAPTER 50

RELATIONSHIPS

A Lesson from Marilyn Monroe

After watching clips of the last days of Marilyn's life through the eyes of those who worked with her on her last movie, I received the following message from Jeshua:

JESHUA 7-26-14

Now we begin. You have concerns about Marilyn Monroe, after watching clips from the last days of her life.

Indeed she regretted her actions while in the astral plane. There were prayers on her behalf which brought her through after about seven months in human time. She is in your soul family and so is aware of your thoughts. She would like you to know what she has learned. To be valued only for your body is a very painful experience. Despite all the adulation, she never felt loved for herself.

She has reincarnated as a nun in the Catholic Church. She chose a life of penance as a very plain woman for a contrasting experience, and is working with children in an orphanage. Her service in the spirit world is with the "new" children who are less veiled and who are drawn into movie roles, helping them act with feeling and touch the hearts of audiences.

She is grateful to you for connecting with the spirit world and writing about it, which encourages others to connect. Marilyn would like to have you share a message from her:

'The glitzy glamor that many women aspire to is very hollow. Even with all the male attention, the real you is not loved or recognized. Physical beauty got in the way. That is why I couldn't sleep and relied on sleeping pills, as I couldn't let go of the feeling of emptiness. Identifying with your body, no matter how beautiful, will not give you love and happiness. Thank you for letting me share.'

Follow-up Information

A new person came to a spiritual family group event and after I shared this experience, s/he told me Marilyn was murdered by two public figures that had made promises or lies for her "favors." This took place after she planned to expose them. This information MT as *true*. Their similar fate brings a kind of justice to this script.

In my Intuitive Inquiry, I learned that when beings return to the spirit world, they reconnect with their perpetrators and victims for additional healing and an increase in consciousness.

Relationships and the Women who Want Them

We have done all sorts of things to win the favor of the man we want, except to be ourselves. Marianne Williamson shared her own pain of being dumped for a woman she felt was less than herself. It was in claiming her masculine power to act which gained her fame and recognition.

That masculine energy didn't work in the area of intimacy with men. At the podium, she could express the masculine energy, as the audience became the receptive energy. If we want a masculine man, we need to value both energies within us. She explains the contrast of male and female energy, active to passive, dynamic and magnetic where "the masculine *does* while the feminine *is*".

American women have used *liberation* to mean that pursuit of "the man" would get them what they wanted. In the area of romance, that usually doesn't work. Many men today are afraid of making the first move. It is a confusing time for relationships. Marianne devalued her mother's work as homemaker, and like many American women wanted to grow up and be just like daddy who had won the world's applause. She denied her tender feelings, opting for toughness, she now calls "the Amazon neurosis: the woman who achieves at the expense of her tender places" which puts achievements before emotions.

Equal Power to Express

Whether male or female, our relationship will depend on our definition of power, whether we regard it in worldly terms as external, as in having money, or whether we define it as internal.

David Hawkins, author of *Power vs. Force*, clearly defines power as the vibrations we carry at the emotional level. He does not distinguish between masculine and feminine. Measuring our vibrational power by the Feeling Frequency Guide reveals our energy level. To accomplish my purpose of getting my message out, I am aware of the need for recognition at the worldly level of public accomplishment, along with money as a tool. The inner work comes first. Then our *joy* attracts—rather than our neediness.

A woman will not be free until she can express herself as freely as a man, and not be censored or devalued. Marianne says, "…outside the bedroom, we are still not equal partners, and until we are, the world will not be healed. Women are still in emotional bondage as long as we need to worry that we might have to make a choice between being heard and being loved."

A secure man can handle a woman's passion. It is looking within for the beloved that attracts the partner we want. When I accept my goddess Self and find my purpose, I will attract one who resonates to that purpose with a compatible purpose of his own. Two, committed to being Love, can multiply the expression of a common vision to bring heaven to earth. The energy and substance of love has no gender.

The Rebirth of the Male Energy

In *The Jeshua Channelings* by Pamela Kribbe, Jeshua states: *The female energy has arisen…the most urgent matter in this time and age* is the transformation of the male energy. It is only in reunion with a matured and balanced male energy that the female energy can flourish again.

Jeshua explains that the current conflict between male and female energy needs to change to cooperation to bring forth the New Earth. *A new wave of energy is dawning within the collective male energy that honors and respects the female energy.*

I see this in public places where the male is holding and interacting with their children. There are couples who work together with a common vision, one of the markers for an enduring relationship.

Sensing their power is no longer valued or respected, the old order of the *heartless aggressor* male is coming out in terrorist attacks and genocide. These aggressors are driven by an inner powerlessness. How will we respond to these horrors? If we allow anger and powerlessness into our own energy field, we are giving them power. The good news is that the old male energy has served its time and will end. As males honor their feminine energy, they feel its power from within. The collective mirror processes at the individual level. Therefore we can be the change that can bring this about.

Two Aspects of the One

In *The Jeshua Channelings*, by Pamela Kribbe, Jeshua describes the ancient male and female energies as two expressions of the One. The male energy is outwardly focused, the part of God that creates. Goal orientated, it is highly focused and creates individuality.

The energy of Home and Primal Source describes the female energy, which Jeshua describes as flowing Light, all-encompassing, like the ocean. We each have both energies within us and need both for balance.

He suggests using **I Am** as a mystical mantra to remind us of our wholeness. Breathe in 'I' as the male energy, and breathe out '**Am**' as the female energy. In this practice you experience the joining of the male and female energies.

Chapter 50: Relationships

Law of Emergence

"Pain pushes until vision pulls." Words from Derek Rydall, best-selling author and Life Coach, define the *Law of Emergence.* This summarizes my process through several transformations. Pain got my attention and prompted me to shift, to embrace inner change, and release the obstacles to my expression of who I am. Pushed by pain to connect more consistently to Source, I became aware of a purpose to the experiences I was having. *Teach me, change me*, was a prayer that brought answers, and a vision I couldn't quite accept but was willing to be guided in that direction. This has been and still is an *emergence* process for me.

The pain lessens as the vision unfolds. A new way of being becomes easier. "When we remember our royal inheritance, men will become our true partners." Indeed!

Emergence: The Shift from Ego to Essence, by Barbara Marx Hubbard, is an inspired book that details (in her unique languaging) a personal process for becoming one's divine Self on earth. Rather than waiting for crises and wake up calls to make a conscious shift, we can embrace the Vision of Heaven on Earth and accelerate our personal experience of becoming the "new human." Barbara offers tools and exercises to guide us into increasing and sustaining higher vibrations.

She defines a Universal Human as one "who is connected through the whole of life… and has shifted identity from the separated egoic self to the deepest self that is a direct expression of Source… Emergence is a way for those of us who feel called to enter into the co-creation of a new world through the fulfillment of our own life purpose, creativity, and love." The emergence process "involves a *fundamental definitive shift in identity…* This is a shift from the egoic, self-conscious, personality self—the local self—to the universal, non-egoic co-creative divine self—*The Essential Self.*"

It is important to note Barbara differs from Jeshua's teaching in ACIM, which describes the ego self as a false self, created by the belief in separation, and is recognized as the Voice of fear. His clarity simplifies and empowers my choice to listen fully to Holy Spirit.

Barbara's statement, "The **desire** to bring essence into form is vital to our full emergence as Universal Humans," uses Jeshua's 1st Key (*Hearts Desire*) of the Four Keys to the Queendom within. She describes her first step as "Entering the Inner Sanctuary" and receiving Guidance from the Higher Self she calls the Beloved. In the process of life, it is unlikely that we would experience her steps in the orderly way given, as several may occur at random. Jeshua, as Jesus, came early into my life (in contrast to Barbara's growing up with no religion or knowledge of metaphysics). Her journey, then, is very helpful to one raised outside the church, and her work validates my process as a woman, which is not recognized in the churches.

Awareness, so prevalent now, of "feeling driven, separated, anxious, as if something is missing" is a cue . you are ready to be born. "Crises is our birth!" Barbara describes the confusion all over the world about how to emerge from a world we know as a polluting and warring world, to a new, sustainable world of peace and prosperity. It is a journey of an awakened heart inspiring the mind with new possibilities. The guidance must always come through the Spiritual heart.

Jeshua's 2nd Key of **Intention** can be enriched by her *ten steps to the universal human*. Visualize the Inner Rose Sanctuary as a space to be with the Beloved (our Essence or Higher Self). When we back up our intention with spiritual practice and holding the Vision of being the beloved we all are, we undo the control of the ego. This calls for forgiveness and release of all the blocks to our intention. Doubt and resistance can be tapped on to release these energies from the bodymind computer (refer to TaBIA process).

Identify resentments and their source. Subject all perceptions that are not peaceful or loving to the vision of the Holy Spirit. Simply asking for another way of seeing an experience changes it into a lesson and a blessing. This means to see with the vision of the third eye. The third eye is activated by the contemplation in the heart.

The 3rd Key of **Allowing** is letting go control, and allowing help from the unseen world. All manner of miracles and synchronicities occur. In Allowing, we are not trying to figure it out. We are open and receptive, trusting the resonance from our heart to cue our steps. A simple awareness of our preference without further feelings of *must have* can bring instant manifestation. Allowing is an exercise in trust. The energy of neediness works against us.

Believing and feeling you already have the desired objective is a completely different energy. Then you can avoid obsessing about making it happen. It is all about being ready to receive. We take an inspired action without asking if it is practical, sensible or done before.

Surrender, the 4th Key, is our full emersion into our true essence, Essential Self, I Am Presence, Beloved, Holy Spirit, Christ, Source, Higher Self—use a name you prefer, one you resonate with. The *belief in separation* resulted from identification with the body. In our Essential Self, we no longer feel separate.

When we accept our identity as *Spirit having a human experience*, we are ready to focus on our purpose in choosing to incarnate. The bodymind becomes a tool for experiencing and using our internal guidance system. Our feelings get our attention. Our emotional heart processes these feelings according to our beliefs. Those feelings shift when we go to our Spiritual heart or I Am Presence for a new perception. When we surrender to our divine Self, this can become automatic.

The true work of Jesus in the world was to teach and demonstrate what we are meant to be—Christ, the face of God/dess. S/He is very present in each as the Voice for Love. Barbara Marx Hubbard, and others, simply call it by another name. We are One in Essence, regardless of the way we have chosen to facilitate our journey.

The Peace of Christ

"Let the Peace of Christ rule in your hearts, since as members of one body you were called to peace. And be thankful." (Colossians 3:15)

My expanded awareness of this verse now knows the "Christ" is the Higher Self in my Spiritual heart, and the "one body" is the Oneness of the 5th dimension that is Heaven on Earth. "Be thankful" is a high vibration practice that makes this peace possible. You may find other verses in the Bible which you feel resonate with the Intention of Oneness and Heaven on Earth. Attending a traditional Christian church service can still be comforting and uplifting, as we practice listening for the seeds of truth which lie in many, but not all, of the messages.

CHAPTER 51

BRIDGES

Bridging Two Worlds

The challenge in this transitional period is to forgive and accept the old as an obsolete experience. You begin to hone new skills and awareness. At times you may feel crazy. We are developing new norms, new ways of being, new ways of knowing. Note the way energy flows in response to thought and emotion. It will be much harder to "fake it." It is a time of contrast between old and new.

Our emotional state is key to our health, which is determined by the vibrations we carry. Rapid change calls for a flexibility that can ease the bodymind. Tuning into what energizes, uplifts, and restores your energy becomes increasingly important. Note people and circumstances that deplete your energy, without judgment, and choose accordingly.

Prioritize spending time in nature and appreciation of sensual delights. Feel yourself one with the many life forms. Unceasing gratitude for the beach and the healing salt water, and the presence of the sun's light and warmth have brought me a huge boost in vibrational and physical health. Another may find it in tending a garden or swinging in a park. Use what is available to you. Also, sound therapies are coming into recognition for the power to change vibrations. Seek uplifting music.

Centering Prayer

It is not in mental agreement that truth dawns on us but in an experience of coming together. Such is the practice of *centering prayer*. Members of different churches, or no church, gather weekly in a quiet setting, usually a church. One enters in silence and sits in an empty pew if possible. A brief, inspiring quotation is read by a trained leader. A bell tone signals the beginning of a silent meditation of twenty to thirty minutes. Prior instructions include choosing a focus word to stop wandering thoughts and bring one back to silence. Oneness in Source may be experienced. The leader tones bell to signal the end of the "sit." Participants leave in silence, often to a social hall where a chosen book on contemplation is read and discussed. Continuing a regular practice on one's own is encouraged. An altar at home is helpful.

A Home Altar

A visual reminder and place to meditate can be a personal altar upon which you have placed physical matter which resonates with Spirit—crystals, reminders of departed loved ones (ashes, urns, photos), incense, candles, and other objects for spiritual reminders. Living near the ocean I have shells, special stones, and small pieces of driftwood. A meditation book is useful. Whatever sized area works for you is perfect—I've seen large areas in a living room, a coffee table on a lanai, a corner table in a bedroom. A small covered luggage stand serves me well in my space.

Helpful Readings

<u>The Naked Now</u>, by Richard Rohr, a former Catholic priest who is now a global leader in spiritual awakening, helps us recognize ego resistance and dualistic thinking. He reveals mystical Christianity, a lost tradition. Rohr refers to Jesus as the mystical leader in the West.

My introduction to contemplative prayer began with a book by Cynthia Bourgeault, *The Wisdom Way of Knowing: Reclaiming an Ancient Tradition to Awaken the Heart*. It appeals to whoever begins to look for a deeper meaning to their life, whether they have grown up in the church or not. She identifies Jesus as a wisdom teacher recognized as such by the East, particularly Sufism, but lost in the West. Here I see the West making him a Savior to save us from

Chapter 51: Bridges

a fictitious hell, an insurance policy, so to speak, rather than the feminine *going within* and seeing from our core essence of love in the Spiritual heart.

Saint Augustine, who believed humanity was hopelessly corrupt, gave us the Original Sin doctrine, declaring we were born in sin and therefore separate from our Source.

From Belief to Experience

Presence is being in the now with body, heart and mind. Intuition from the heart takes precedence, and informs the mind. Through the practice of Centering Prayer, we wake up to who we truly are. Even though none of the current channelings by Jesus were part of Bourgeault's experience, she arrives at many of the same tenets of the Way of the Heart. In the process of surrendering to this life force of the divine presence realized in periods of silence, we can experience a life of synchronicity, which feels miraculous.

The books I have experienced so far have been very thoughtful, full of wisdom, inviting inner awareness and self-knowledge. A couple of paragraphs may inspire an hour's discussion. Personal sharing is welcome. Discovery is affirmed, and controversy is avoided.

Some books can help us be a bridge—in contrast to *The Beloved One*, which could antagonize and invite resistance. Rohr helps to "awaken desire for God, connect to Joy within, free self from crippling fears, see as mystics see, and live in awareness of the Naked Now."

Jesus found God in "disorder and imperfection." Rohr sees the church teachings that require a <u>belief</u> in God as ineffective, in contrast to our <u>experience</u> of God.

Rohr calls himself "a values conservative and process liberal." He sees **both/and**, as in the following quote: "All saying must be balanced by unsaying. Knowing must be humbled by unknowing. Without this balance, religion invariably becomes arrogant, exclusionary, and even violent. All light must be informed by darkness, and all success by suffering…"

Contemplation "is a non-dualistic way of seeing the moment... the 'sacrament of the present moment' will teach us how to be in our experiences, whether good, bad, or ugly, and how to let them transform us." Words alone will divide us. Pure Presence lets it be what it is. This is process, the feminine principle as an experience of the present, which includes the feelings of the heart.

"Our hope is not deceptive. The love of God has been poured into our hearts by the Holy Spirit that has been given us." (Romans 5:5)

"You already know, 'the Spirit is with you, and the Spirit is you'" (John 14:17)

In contrast to religion, Rohr says, "True spirituality is not a search for perfection or control or the door to the next world; it is a search for divine union now…Union and perfection are two different journeys with very different strategies… Union is a shared knowing; hope and union are the same thing."

Rohr contends that the center of our religious problem today is our failure to understand Jesus' core message. We lack a concrete program to discover this for ourselves within the church, as I found out. Al-Anon (a program founded on the principles of Alcoholics Anonymous) was a beginning. The surrender, called for in the 12 steps, is a surrender to process and purification through self-awareness and correction. Union is discovered in the group setting, which allows safety, in order to look at our experience of imperfection, which unites us! Heart resonance occurs.

"Created in the image of God" tells us of our birthright. Trusting the existence of the *I Am Presence* within invites *prayer without ceasing*, our union with the divine, which contemplative prayer affirms. This will change the church from the inside out through a focus on a direct connection with Source. Attacking the falsehoods will not be necessary. Truth will emerge from within.

Chapter 51: Bridges

Ways of Seeing

Rohr talks about three ways of seeing, as for example, when one gazes upon a beautiful sunset. The first is simply seeing with the senses. The second way analyzes and sees the sunset in the context of his knowledge of the Universe; he sees and explains through reason, his "second eye." Seeing with the third eye (mid-forehead) involves the first and second way plus the imagination and intuition of the third eye. Jeshua/Sananda/Magdalene would add that the third eye connects with the heart, which, when awakened, becomes the fourth eye, seeing from the perspective of Spirit, the I Am of the Spiritual heart. The fourth eye in the spiritual heart is the Feminine Principle that has been denied by the Patriarchy.

Accepting the words of our governments and religions without fully seeing how they are egoic and self-serving, we remain short-sighted and in a state of separation and conflict. We thus remain *blind* to the truth, when we need to be *seeing* in every way possible, so we can be discerning.

Rohr sees the mystic as one who sees with the three ways of seeing, and defines the mystic as "one who has moved from mere belief or belonging systems to actual inner experience."

Organized religion has a vested interest in the first two ways of seeing, which keeps people coming to church and the clergy in business. "Theological training without spiritual experience is deadly… Observing our inner dramas without judgment is foundational to spiritual seeing, to egoless seeing," Rohr writes. "Without a higher level of seeing, we have the dualism of atheism, rationalism, and secularism on the left, and fundamentalism, tribal thinking, and cognitive rigidity on the right"

To see properly requires both a change of heart and a change of mind. The *Change me, teach me* prayer accomplished that, for me.

Rohr says we cannot understand Jesus with a dualistic mind. "We see what we are ready to see." Contemplation is a radical perceptual shift—away from judging and away from the belief in separation.

Practicing it brings us into our inner knowing and releases our attachment to our beliefs.

The rational mind, which has been the home of the ego, can become a servant, Rohr concluded. This echoes Jesus/Jeshua ben Joseph's words, *Let the Heart be the Master and the mind becomes a useful servant.*

Jesus said to *pray without ceasing.* This is not referring to formal prayer, but to an ongoing awareness of the divine within. It is surrender to the God Self with the desire to give this God Self primacy in our thoughts, intentions, and behaviors. This practice becomes a dialogue.

A Different Day

I awoke after six hours of sleep, still feeling tired, with thoughts of finding an editor, without having funds to pay for one. My writing project was to create a flyer briefly describing my book, offering my services for barter to a qualified person interested and willing to use my services in exchange. After completing the flyer and eating breakfast, I was feeling sleepy and asked if I could go back to sleep. I MT *no*, and got a *yes* to meditating. Sitting upright before my altar, I fell sleep. I awoke from a dream where I was in a church aisle, walking towards the back and feeling I needed to help a person ahead of me who was walking out of the church. It was a church of my childhood with a balcony in back. Just as I caught up to the person going under the balcony, I felt a spirit lift me up to the level of the balcony, and I woke up. My immediate feeling was of awe of what seemed to be an experience of levitation.

I asked Jeshua about the lesson. *You don't have to ask permission to go to sleep when your body is asking for it.* He didn't explain the dream at that point. I did lie down and slept for an hour, waking up at noon, still with a headache. My swimming buddy called and I decided to go swimming instead of starting any Saturday project on my list. It was a delightful experience of immersion in the ocean, plus we saw a large pregnant monk seal lying at the water's edge.

Later, I felt the headache returning and asked Jeshua if this had anything to do with re-experiencing early menopause symptoms,

Chapter 51: Bridges

and MT *yes*. I took a headache-relief tablet and lay down for a brief rest. Two hours later I awakened and intuited there was more to the dream which Jeshua wished to relate to me.

About your dream... *The 'church of your childhood' represents the theology and beliefs you took in. Your going after someone leaving the church describes your target audience now. Those happy in the church are not going to listen to you. Your feeling of levitation, as you intuited later, was my spirit leaving your body. It is true I am with you always, but there are times I will enter a body. My spirit leaving your body is what you felt. No more explanation is necessary now.*

I Am with you always in all ways. Jeshua

I had other questions, which he declined to answer. Indeed it is a way of trust in a mystery. My experience reflects numerous channelings I have read that say we are not able to fully understand it from here. We will get what we need in the moment. This is what makes our participation in the play genuine, according to our current consciousness. Knowing too much can spoil the experience and we miss the lesson we need to learn through process.

Power of Belief Beyond Death.

In a recent Rescue Circle, one of the names given was that of a Seventh Day Adventist woman who had died suddenly in a fall, hitting her head. Often in calling forth the spirit, someone in the group feels that spirit and takes on their thoughts and feelings. Ariana felt a tremendous headache as she felt the woman's spirit (and her head injury).

Ariana told us how to block the pain which she had forgotten to do. It is to simply affirm three times, "The energy in my aura is my own!" Because of the woman's literal belief that she was confined to the bones in the ground until the day of Jesus' coming in the clouds, she was stuck in what is called the *astral plane* or 4th dimension. As we talked her through this belief to go to the light, she was free to join her family in "the heaven world." The Rescue Circle offers another bridge!

CHAPTER 52

CALIBRATION OF ENERGY VIBRATIONS

The following *FEELING FREQUENCY GUIDE* illustrates the energy power of feelings. Feelings are vibratory and have varying strength. Even though feelings come and go, we tend towards particular feeling states or levels. These have been measured through the science of kinesiology by Dr. David Hawkins. Through many experiments in Muscle Testing, he has come up with consistent units of energy we will call vibrations. His Map of Consciousness can be found in his book, *Power vs. Force*. A laminated map can be ordered from his website. I am referring to his map as the alphabet of feeling vibrations, and will use some of the key feeling states where my muscle testing has identical results.

There are some energy states he does not include, which I have muscle tested and place in their relationship to his basic map. I have indicated where my word choices differ as well, especially in the accompanying emotion and Process, as it relates to my work and purpose here.

Hawkins included a God-View and Life-View, which I am incorporating under Perspective/Perception, a basic attitude or system of thought that determines the feeling vibration we carry. *Energy flows where attention goes.* Think of a horizontal figure-eight where energy flows from thought to feeling and back again, intersecting in a state of reinforcement where they cross, and if flowing freely can shift to higher vibrations, unless stuck in the middle.

Perception, power and process sum up this flow.

Perception has to do with our thinking mind, largely controlled by the ego through our identification with the body. Thoughts and interpretations of what we perceive are colored by past experiences, with our interpretation forming our beliefs and attitudes.

We give everything the meaning it has for us. (ACIM)

Power here refers to the vibration of the feeling state, calibrated in energy units.

Process includes the emotion as energy in motion as well as the intent behind the feeling state.

Perceptions are not addressed in the chart below.

Feeling levels and calibrations from Hawkins are noted with an asterisk. The Four Keys for Manifesting from *The Jeshua Letters* are preceded by a + symbol. I added the unmarked power levels.

FEELING FREQUENCY GUIDE
© Petra Sundheim

Power Level	Vibration	Emotion	Process
* SELF is Enlightenment	700-1000	Bliss	Being
Ho'oponopono	850	At One	Cleaning
© TaBIA (I AM)	800	Empowerment	Embodiment
+ Surrender	650	Freedom	Transformation
* Peace	625	Serene	Illumination
* Joy	600	Delight	Happiness
Gratitude	575	Expansion	Thanksgiving
* LOVE	550	Oneness	Being Love
Compassion	525	True Empathy	Heart opening
+ Allowing	500	Trust	Letting go
Knowing	450	Certainty	Truth
* Reason	375	Understanding	Abstraction
FORGIVENESS	350	Acceptance	Healing
+ Intention	325	Willingness	Focused attention
+ Heart's Desire	310	Passion	To be, do or have
* Neutrality	225	Impartial	Openness
* Courage	200	Affirmation	Empowerment

Chapter 52: Calibration Of Energy Vibrations

EGO, THE FALSE self

Power Level	Vibration	Emotion	Process
* Pride	175	Grandiosity	Self deception
* Anger	150	Judgment	Projection
Depression	130	Despondency	Anger at self
Hurt	125	Pain	Seeking relief
Craving	110	Compulsion	Addiction
* FEAR	100	Anxious	Fight flight freeze
* Grief	75	Sadness	Loss
* Apathy	50	Indifference	Numbness
* Guilt	30	Self blame	Defensive
* Shame	20	Worthless	Avoidance

Credits:
*Power VS Force, **D. Hawkins MD**
+The Four Keys by Jeshua

How To Use The Feeling Frequency Guide

The Power Level refers to feeling states. Notice your thoughts. Where do they fit in most of the time? Whenever you are reacting, check out the thoughts and resulting feelings. Our *Perceptions* are ego-based—in our heads. Note the vibrations. Pause and ask for a different perception from your heart wisdom. Think of an alternative positive experience. Try gratitude. When the intention is to feel peaceful in spite of disappointment, hurt, or attack, another perception is born.

The TaBIA process acknowledges the feeling before it is released. This is not about denial, but about shifting the energy to a higher level of perceiving. Allow yourself to experience a higher vibration through noting the process you are in and choosing new thoughts and behaviors (process) which the desired feeling state suggests.

All the levels named under the ego stem from fear. The Power Levels support and reveal the innate divine self of love. The heart is the home for our essence. The choice, then, is between fear and love, listening to the head or the heart.

Power and Control

As earth's frequency rises and light is increasing, the dark forces of fear are reacting. Those who are energized by greed, power, and control at the frequency level of craving are desperate. Under the guise of religion and use of fear as a force, terrorism is their way of life. It becomes an insatiable addiction.

We have not yet discovered how to contain or stop it. The power level of government and of war has the same frequency level of response. As we should have learned from 5000 years of Patriarchy, this does not work.

Fear is behind acts as sad as child-bullying as well as acts as horrific as senseless murders. In January of 2015, masked gunmen armed with AK-47s and shouting "Allahu Akbar" stormed the offices of a French satirical news magazine in a terror attack that left 12 people dead, including the editor and two police officers. The magazine had included the Prophet Muhammed in its list of many characters to make fun of. If the magazine could have unmasked the fear behind the terrorism, a different outcome might have occurred. If we knew there was no death and that real power was power over ourselves, we would have a different world.

It is important to recognize that someone who would read this is not likely to be a terrorist (except to oneself). Power and control can accompany the best of intentions. We can notice this and allow flow and embrace unexpected detours and delays as simply part of the obstacle course called life. It calls us to invite in the highest vibrations to respond and reshape the playdoh of our journey.

Head to Heart

Let the heart be the master and the mind becomes a very useful servant. (ACIM)

Rapid shifting, as with mood swings, is not desirable. Fluctuation is normal. A feeling state is one that dominates and we tend to return. Marcia Shimoff, in *Happy for No Reason*, refers to the happiness set point we each have. This point can be influenced by inherited factors, and we can change it through awareness, release work, and choosing a higher vibration. In changing our thoughts we can change our life.

Once we accept responsibility for our moods and state of mind and remember Peace is a choice, we will discover freedom and a measure of serenity that can't be bought or affected by the chaos around us. We can still feel a full range of emotions, even profound sadness, when we have learned to be "happy for no reason." Our core is rooted in the love essence that we are. The roles and the events on the stage of life need not diminish who we are, once we own that our true identity is not the body or the ego, but a spiritual Presence having a human experience.

CHAPTER 53

THE CONTROLLERS—THE DARK FORCES

The Dark Forces

Jeshua has often referred to the dark forces as those who have exerted mind control of humans on the planet. Financial tyranny, recently exposed by New Age authors David Wilcock and Drunvalo Milchizadek, and many other happenings across the planet have pointed to the collusion of banking and the dark in hoarding the gold. The dark forces that have been controlling the earth for thousands of years are coming to light. Mass arrests will take place. Many bankers have quietly retired.

These dark forces include a religious order and very wealthy controllers in the Illuminati, estimated at close to 2000 people. Some will be imprisoned. "The Cabal" is a term referring to them.

"The fall," spoken of in Genesis in the Bible, happened when rebellious priests wanted power and control, causing the breakup of Atlantis, a 20,000 year civilization of peace and gender equality. Back in spirit, these priests initiated the 5000 years of Patriarchy. Identified as Reptilians, they occupy prominent places in government and banking. Naming them here is not my purpose. It is the energy of power, control and greed of those committed to the goals of the *global elite and the world order* that identifies them. This control includes: government, religion, medical and mental health systems, the media, science, education, entertainment, nature, air, land, water, money, the economy, control of the food sources and supply affecting the animal kingdom as well.

This is currently demonstrated by large GMO companies pushing for legislation giving them absolute control with government cooperation. A GMO (genetically modified organism) is the result of a laboratory process where genes from the DNA of one species are extracted and artificially forced into the genes of an unrelated plant or animal. The foreign genes may come from bacteria, viruses, insects, animals or even humans.

Some reports say that many thousands of farmers in India committed suicide following a restriction to use only costly GMO seeds. These companies were kicked out of India by a conscious government, respecting the feminine principle as demonstrated through Dr. Vandana Shiva. She was a speaker in a rally of over 1500 attendees on Kauai concerned about the GMO presence. Dr. Shiva, though loving Kauai, said she would not return until the GMO companies were booted out.

One of the core intentions voiced by names associated with the one percent global elite who control the wealth is to depopulate the earth by 95 percent. The evidence is becoming more and more obvious. It is being accomplished through wars, control of food supply, medical practice controlled by Big Pharma, compulsory vaccination with its toxic components, poisoning of land (GMOs/pesticides), water (fluoridation), and air through chemtrails and factory emissions. America's government no longer is *by and for the people*. When the feminine is respected and informed, the number of offspring will be limited. Poisoning the earth and killing each other is not the answer.

Control of food is becoming very obvious, when those who attempt to garden organically, produce raw milk or heal through natural means are threatened with arrest and a shut-down of their business. Mass starvation could be prevented. It is not only allowed, but promoted. The earth has enough to provide for her inhabitants, but governments and corporate control prevent distribution.

Chapter 53: The Controllers—The Dark Forces

Disease Encouraged

Disease is big business. Natural cures can't be patented, so drug companies suppress any discoveries of mother earth's power to heal.

Cancer can be cured along with other so called terminal illnesses, but talking about these cures has to be accompanied by disclaimers, to make the established medical system the top authority. The fact that the fourth largest cause of death is the legal use of pharmaceutical drugs was my response to my former doctor who was trying to convince me of the superiority of Western medicine over any alternatives I was using or seeking. She had no answer to that.

Cut Poison Burn is a documentary film about cancer treatment, chemotherapy, alternative cancer treatment and natural cancer treatment in the U. S. Many doctors do know that the official "Cut, Poison and Burn" system is not the road to health, but are censored by the American Medical Association (AMA). To continue to practice, some caring doctors have learned to say to a health-conscious patient who doesn't exhibit the progression of deterioration they are conditioned to expect, "Keep doing what you are doing." They don't ask what you are doing. How can you expect otherwise when the drug companies help finance the training of doctors, not to mention other ways they support doctors' profit centers (free samples, etc.)?

GMO Deception

Some GMO companies are wooing the children in schools with money grants and prizes. They want to look like benefactors, even though five GMO companies are poisoning the land, water, and the air all over the world, including on the tiny island of Kauai. Their pesticide and herbicide sprays, including ones equivalent to Agent Orange, are sickening nearby school children, staff, and neighbors. Windows can't be opened near their experimental "farming." Organic gardens are contaminated.

According to a patent lawyer, nature can't be patented so there is no profit in natural cures and remedies. The GMO companies alter the seeds through their experimentation, so they can patent them.

They forbid reuse of the seeds. Independent scientific studies show the stunting of growth and the hormones affecting reproduction in rats. This causes abortions and inability to reproduce. When informed patients stop eating GMO foods, their symptoms may disappear.

"Just a Conspiracy Theory" Label Promotes Denial

There are many who simply can't accept that we have been controlled by "the 1%" and that this is not a theory, but a fact. Fear is always part of the controller's tools. The ego is the *voice of fear*, according to the Jeshua teachings, beginning with *A Course in Miracles*. The ego can wear a mask of niceness. Charm is a common characteristic of the alcoholic and some other drug-users. It is characteristic of any addiction, including addiction to money, power and control. Fear and the belief in separation and scarcity fuel the global elite's agenda.

To downplay the reality of this control, the idea of a "conspiracy theory" is made fun of and it is quite unpopular to call attention to it. I've seen it first-hand. A respected colleague effectively squelched my comments regarding a possible world order agenda, referring to it as "just a conspiracy theory." The signs are becoming increasingly obvious. Perhaps a better term is to call it the "power and control" agenda of the global elite. It is time to understand the Intentions of those serving this agenda.

"Pot is Harmless"

A discussion with a teenager suspended by school authorities for having a pot pipe has given me some incentive to observe its effects. This teen, along with many adults, sees nothing wrong with smoking pot.

I have noted the following effects of habitual use of marijuana on the Physical, Emotional Mental and Spiritual (PEMS) areas of our being. Confirmed with MT, the following is observed:

- Pot interferes with learning
- Lying about pot use and lying to oneself (self-deception)

Chapter 53: The Controllers—The Dark Forces

- Don't-care attitude
- Dishonesty with feelings; denial of pain
- False euphoria; false cover for depression
- Lack of insight and good judgment
- Trouble in school or work; blames authorities
- Triggers co-dependency, and distrust by others
- Pot-user associates with those who use
- Limits brain development (teen brain not fully developed)

Global Elite Vibrations

Pot also serves the global elite's Intention to anesthetize humanity, so like the frog in water slowly coming to a boil, it is too far-gone to jump out before it is cooked.

The weapon of the global elite is fear. Rather than labeling them evil and separate, it is an opportunity to look at our own vibrations and note whether we are vibrating at the level of fear or of love. Know that love can act tough when called on. When we begin to live from our Higher Self, the Voice for Love, and join together, we can be inspired to act in a way that reaches the hearts of the unaware. It is from the Spiritual heart that the fundamental change in our society can take place.

There are many who are a part of this power/control agenda without realizing it. Money has been the bottom line for determining value and success. This is but one of the effects of *the belief in separation*. When the *way of the heart* and *oneness* values are embraced, a major transformation of society will occur. When we recognize that the *belief in separation* is the common factor in every one of the systems mentioned, it simplifies our objectives. Recognizing our Oneness raises our vibrations. Fear energizes "power, control and greed." Love energizes a sense of Oneness and cooperation.

Power Cut on 12-12-12

Nothing happened, according to most observers. We have been assured by numerous messages from the unseen world that the power of the dark forces was cut on that date. Yes, atrocities continue, political insanity seems to be increasing, and power grabs dominate the media. When we connect with Source within and join with like minds focusing on the energy of love, we are empowered. The Love bug is catchy and we can trust this inner *I Am Love Presence* to create a resonance of resistance to fear-based propaganda. It magnetizes the God-seed in others. Oneness awareness is a whole new way of being in the body.

Now that the power of the dark forces has been cut, they will be exposed. The resignation of the last Pope, reportedly because of age (85), may have greater significance. The pope is a symbol of power and authority to a large portion of the church. Expect a domino effect of exposure of a whole history of the abuse of power by the church. A new and more informal, "one of the people" pope has been appointed who may bring in a new consciousness and soften the impending exposure. I hold the belief that change will come from within, as well as without.

It is more important than ever to practice a new way of being on earth. The 5000 year age of the Patriarchy is over. A new age of Love and Light has begun. It may not look that way as threat of war increases with incidents of gunmen on a rampage. The controllers are desperate and are showing their fear. The deaths of children, in particular, evoke compassion and a desire to end violence. One recent channeling stated that the children will save humanity. They touch our hearts—from where the solutions must come.

What is the truth about 9/11 as an inside job? The truth is long overdue and will come to the light. Unpatriotic? True patriotism or love of our country does not deny the truth, but seeks the healing of this great nation and its responsibility of leadership in the world. "Pride goeth before a fall." We will not heal without massive confessions and humility. America has much to answer for. When all is revealed, it behooves us to remember, 'There, but for the grace of God, go I." We are a part of all the systems now operating, which are facing a "Change or Die" ultimatum—or maybe it is "Dying in order to live."

Birthing Contractions

Transformation is to be welcomed. Know it is not an occasion for lament, but rather the necessary contractions for birthing a new world of Love, Light, Peace and Joy. It is time to practice these qualities now in our relationships, and to forgive everything that has occurred in our own lives.

This is not about denial—it is to be accountable and corrective by choosing again, prompted by Love rather than fear. Self-forgiveness is primary. Holding a Vision of what is possible empowers our willingness to change.

Stories of exposure and drama dominate the media. When we recognize it is a birthing, we will look for the Heaven on Earth baby coming forth from awakened hearts, and a rise in feminine power. Mother Earth has the last word. She will nurture us and supply our needs, when we stop polluting and respect her power. There are quiet experiments now in communal living and organic farming, which is under attack by our government. As we withdraw our support of corrupted practices and cleanse ourselves, we create space for the new energy to manifest.

A Helpful Mantra

Affirm daily the Ascension mantra, *I am Ageless, Awake, Aware and At One.*

Agelessness is an attitude that is more positive than "anti-aging," a term so popular now in the supplement world. Our Spirit identity is ageless. Identifying with Spirit and its qualities will slow down the physical deterioration of the body (which is not you!). **Awake**

and **Aware** go together. When asked, "Who are you?" Buddha said, "I am awake!"

When we recognize and live from our spirit identity, we are Awake. We are One with Source and all life. Awareness of our feelings, patterns, and behaviors as correctible and forgivable opportunities for lessons, empowers us to fulfill our purpose on the planet—to experience our Oneness or At-One-Ment. It is to fully embody our Spirit identity.

CHAPTER 54

ONENESS

Ascension Awareness

Oneness is encouraged by the following awareness:

- The non-physical world is co-creating this with us.
- Earth's energy is shifting into higher vibrations, requiring our own vibrational alignment.
- Spirit becomes embodied and can experience the 4th Dimension here without physical death. This is the Heart Awakening to the One Self.
- Our goal is the Oneness of the 5th Dimension, which includes telepathy, teleportation, and unconditional love.
- Channeling is accepted as a normal process for humans.
- Our Purification comes first. Dark forces of power, control, greed, fear, addiction, and ignorance are disempowered and released.
- All systems will change when the heart awakens, leads—and the mind follows.
- Jeshua/Mary Magdalene, now Sananda/Magdalene (one entity) leads the Ascension process into Christ consciousness.
- The feminine is restored to full equality bringing balance to the earth.

- The distorted masculine principle is corrected to embrace its function to protect and support the feminine, both within and without.

Patience is required as many of the predictions have not occurred in outward manifestation as expected. It is occurring on the inner plane first as a process of shifting from the masculine focus outside of us, into a focus on the inner change of the heart. This requires true forgiveness and a shift in consciousness. Focus on our inner work of Purification will raise our vibrations.

Choosing our responses to life with the Voice for Love rather than reacting from our wounded ego, takes awareness and practice. This is empowered by our surrender of ego to the Holy Spirit.

Oneness, End of Duality

We embrace and accept All that Is by forgiving from the heart, shifting our perception, and embracing our lessons as part of the script we are playing. This unlearning, or Purification, is part of the Awakening process that brings us into a state of Oneness.

The Awakened One responds to circumstances and lives in humility rather than trying to cultivate it. Release of all judgment does not mean ignoring what needs correction. One notices and answers the call for love by being a non-judgmental Presence, a mirror of the true Essence of those out of alignment. This alone can shift the energy

Not afraid of truth, the Awakened One allows destiny to be created, and experiences freedom from one's own self-limiting beliefs. Allowance brings forth the highest good.

Up to this point, we have merely entertained the idea of *ONENESS*. The focus has been on Heart opening or *Awakening*. Becoming fully present (releasing thoughts and patterns of separation) involves both our Intention and Attention. Allowance by trusting the process has become a practice. Surrender still brings up resistance. As shared in earlier stories in this book, a threatened ego can resort to

Chapter 54: Oneness

pretense, as in "I love you" or "I will pray for you." Becoming trite, words can be used to ignore issues of harmful and hurtful behaviors. Tolerating injustice is not a virtue.

Bhagavan says that Awakening is not a given and requires an awareness of helplessness and a Surrender to Source. Referring to God as Light, he says we must talk to this Light within us as mother, father, friend or whomever. Jeshua has referred to this God within as *The Beloved*, *I Am Presence*, and *Holy Spirit*. Both would say God has no form.

The awakening process will be experienced in all religions according to the programming a person has been subjected to. It involves transcending the patriarchal aspects of that programming.

You will not have a peak experience all the time. It will come and go, but your basic state will come from out of one of the upper chakras; heart, throat, third eye, or crown, depending on your culture, background, past lives, and conditions. No one of these is superior to another; it just fits the way you are designed.

For the Kundalini to move you into Awakening, it has to move a certain way and this is not within your control. All you can do is to Surrender. Awakening is a spiritual shift affecting our biology—the neurons or electrical wiring in the brain, and also the DNA. Bhagavan says, "It is a very complicated process; some wirings are deleted. Other new ones are formed. This you cannot do on your own. For this to happen, you need to connect to the Divine inside." Your part is to be a passionate seeker, ask for the Divine, and surrender and allow the seed of God (in each of us) to take over.

Bhagavan distinguishes between Awakening and God Realization where you and the Divine are One, and suggests that people go for God Realization first, and Awakening becomes easier.

Jeshua Speaks on the Face of God

There is little difference between what I would say and what Bhagavan is quoted saying. As I do not identify myself as Christian, but as the Christ or Face of God, it is this I wish to Awaken in those who hear my voice. To Awaken the Christ in each being, one indeed has to Surrender, the fourth step in realizing the queendom within. The Four Keys: Heart's Desire, Intention, Allowing and Surrender are essentially the same as what Bhagavan has said.

The 'belief in separation' is not as strong in the East as in the West. My emphasis is for the veiled to release the 'belief in separation.' The head to heart focus is also necessary to correct the denial of the feminine principle.

Self-Honesty

What it means to become ONE with all that is, takes practice and a willingness to be completely honest with oneself. Our automatic judgments are the last to go. Notice them without judging the judgments, and surrender them to Source. Look for the light and the lesson in the experience.

Accept the need for boundaries and set them accordingly. We each have different personal requirements for staying in peace and wellbeing. Feelings and Resonance become our cues for guidance. As we abide in the Awareness of our *I Am Presence*, the most loving response occurs and surprises us. We don't know what another needs to hear or experience, but Source does. When we relax and trust that Voice of Love to prompt us from a higher wisdom than our present awareness, we are in the service of the Divine.

"The key to all you would accomplish in this lifetime hinges upon your willingness to embrace all that you are, for the chance that you may come to experience—in Oneness—all that you truly Are." These words are from Rasha, in her book *Oneness*. "Oneness" is her word for God. Her dialogue with Oneness fills 400 pages with belief-shattering insights, amazing metaphysical concepts, ascension signs and symptoms and tools for the inner path to enlightenment. What I am discovering in reading her book is that it echoes so much of my experience and enlarges it. Indeed, we have mighty companions that go with us when we commit to this inner journey.

Chapter 54: Oneness

It is very important to note that no two journeys are alike. Some experience and sustain an initial experience of Enlightenment. Others like myself, a heavily-programmed self-doubter, needs many experiences. To "Know Thyself" requires much patience and Self-love. When committed to the journey, Source gives us all the experience we need!

It will take patience for the changes needed for this promised heaven on earth. Yet with holding and sharing the vision of Oneness based on heart wakening to its Love identity, it will explode when a certain number of people hold the vision.

Simplicity will replace complexity. Remember ACIM telling us that the ego loves complexity. Holding the vision, forgiving everything that has occurred, and following the Voice for Love will hasten the emergence of the new human.

Vibratory Health.

Our form reflects our inner vibrational levels of beliefs, thoughts and emotion. "Your form is a direct reflection of your vibratory levels at any given time, for the human body is merely the manifestation of energy as form (*Oneness*, chapter 15). The wisdom needed for our health in this ascension time must come from spirit. In *cellular memory* (vibrationally-based encoding) lies the key to physical and metaphysical transformation or healing. Thoughts and emotions have vibrations, as explained in *The Feeling Frequency Guide*.

I believe most cancers occur at moments of low vibration where the immune system may be compromised by stress that hasn't been fully processed. Often a death of a family member or friend has occurred. A traumatic divorce or trauma of any kind weakens the immune system. Any incident, that we haven't made peace with, triggers cancer cell growth. It is said we all have cancer cells in our system, which merely wait to be activated, and only an honest process in the release of feelings can avoid this activation. This is true for any dis-ease.

The accelerated energy we are experiencing brings increased stress on the bodymind. Learning to forgive an experience and ourselves needs to happen more quickly to restore our equilibrium. This calls for our re-story of the event to gratitude for the lesson.

A Tool for Vibrational Awareness

The Feeling Frequency Guide is a tool described earlier as being inspired by David Hawkin's Map of Consciousness. There are many ways to use this Guide. When we realize that the lower vibrations involved with stress trigger dis-ease, our goal becomes the maintenance of the state of inner peace. It isn't done by denial, but seeing clearly our perception and letting the Spirit of love change that perception to a higher vibrational way of seeing. Use this guide to increase your awareness and TaBIA what you are willing to release.

Heart Awakening Invites Oneness

Spirituality has become a conscious desire for many. Ken Wilber, writer and philosopher, reminds us that, "Spirituality must shift from belief to direct experience of the Divine." Experience involves feelings and thus the Emotional heart is the portal to the divine. This portal involves conscious awareness of feelings. Anger and resentment block our peace. Here, our lower vibration feelings need to be processed with the help of the Holy Spirit/Higher Self. This involves our willingness to forgive, and to see our negative experience differently. When we are open to this release work we are receptive to the Voice for Love and receive the guidance we need. Our awareness expands. We become awake to the experience of the divine. Oneness at this level is then possible.

How we get there varies from person to person, but it is an experience which calls for Heart Awakening, which is universal and connects us to each other as One. Our connection to the Divine *I Am Presence* within becomes that universal experience which makes us One.

The process of Heart Awakening is our 4th dimensional portal to Oneness, the 5th dimensional state of Embodiment of our Divine

Chapter 54: Oneness

Essence. Though even higher dimensions are realized by some, it is the 5th dimension of Oneness that is necessary for Heaven on Earth to be manifested. It is especially important to hold that vision now in the midst of chaos and fear.

Perfect Love casts out fear needs to become an automatic response to our thoughts of fear and separation. What that perfect Love entails will be different for each person. Asking and trusting Source within for direction in every decisive moment also happens with Intention and practice of the Four Keys.

The Way of the Heart

Many are listening to their awakened hearts and can unify with others under the umbrella of love. Yet they suffer needless doubt and judgments because of the distortions in theology based on masculine interpretations by the Partriarchy. Jesus's direct words to us through the natural connection we have in our hearts, as well as the channeling of his words to many seekers of the truth, will correct these distortions. Ask and you will receive. This direct relationship needs no priest or go-between. Jesus is the Holy Spirit, our Higher Self. "You are as I am. I am as you are" are his words in *The Way of the Heart*, channeled by Jon Marc Hammer.

Buddhists, Hindus, Muslims and Sufis have the same Love Presence within. The power and control of the Patriarchy has affected the theologies they follow, especially in regard to women. There is less distortion of the truth about God spoken by the initial originators of Eastern thought than in Western thought. Though cultural observances may differ greatly, some Eastern mystics are more aligned with the thinking of Jesus than is the West.

CHAPTER 55

HEAVEN ON EARTH, A NEW HUMANITY

The Light Has Come

The function of Light is primarily to bring clarity, awareness, and transparency to the invisible structures of thought and feeling that shape your life. Opposite of mind-control, it breaks the bonds that have bound us, and the systems that misuse power to take away self- determination. Jeshua

Heaven on Earth is the prophesied outcome of these times. It is the vision we must hold in the midst of chaos. As with any major shift, multiple reactions to our present collapse of systems are occurring. Dire predictions, increased government controls, internment camps, and gun proliferation are but few results of mounting fears. GMOs and corporate food control with increased toxins "for profit" are poured into our environment. This is illustrating the truth of the one percent's effort to reduce the population by 95%, saving 4% for slave labor, the not-so-secret plan which no one wants to address. The global elite, or Illumanati, are orchestrating this and include names holding the wealth. It has been revealed that we have been controlled and programmed for some time to fit into their overall plan. The dark forces are being exposed. Yet a greater power is at work. We mobilize this power by our inner work.

Most all the channelings through other sources on the internet tell us the power of the global elite has been cut. Regardless of the outer signs, our focus on the promise is what will hasten the arrival of Heaven on Earth. It is not about denial of these negative energies, but holding the focus on correction through listening to the heart and becoming the change.

Prophetic voices on the Internet include Drunvalo Melchizadek, David Wilcock, Richard and Carolyn Presser, and many others. Numerous speakers on our evolutionary journey include Barbara Marx Hubbard, Craig Hamilton, Ken Wilber, Deepak Chopra, Marianne Williamson, and Eckhart Tolle. *Healing with the Masters* program hosted by Jennifer McLean, and many other trainings, workshops and books are now available, just as more of us seek this knowledge.

It has been my privilege to be in a group with Ariana Sheran and be in direct contact with the many entities speaking through her. Besides the Mayan prophecies and the ending of the Mayan calendar in 2012, we have the Biblical prophecies.

The following **Biblical Quotations** from the New International Version, Applicable <u>Ready Reference,</u> compiled by Bob Phillips, are used here.

Lake of Fire and Second Death

Revelation 20:11-15. Rev 20:14 "…then death and Hades were thrown into the lake of fire. The lake of fire is the second death." I asked Jeshua if he would comment on this.

This refers to the idea of everlasting hell as a lake of fire, which is false. Some souls do not return to the heaven world, but anxiously cling to the earth and remain in density, unaware of the light. They find a certain solace in that. It is a very limited consciousness. Clinging to family still in form is their focus. Indeed they are ghosts. They do not know where home truly is, nor what they are missing.

Others may intentionally join dark forces addicted to power and control. They caused the long period of unawareness and density on the planet. Their power has been cut as of 12-12-12. It may not appear so, as it is an energetic shift on the inner plane. Many are awakening, including some of these souls as well.

Chapter 55: Heaven On Earth, A New Humanity

Kingdom Age :

Isaiah 25: 8-9 ". . . he will swallow up death forever. The sovereign Lord will wipe away the tears from all faces; he will remove the disgrace of his people from all the earth. The Lord has spoken. V. 9. In that day they will say, "Surely this is our God: we trusted in him and he saved us. This is the Lord, we trusted in him; let us rejoice and be glad in his salvation."

Jeshua's comment on this verse follows: *Death of the body need not be experienced in the fifth dimension. As you know through your son's words, 'There is no death,' meaning that the body is simply let go of like a suit of old clothes. It is the awareness of your God Self, the I Am, that wipes away the tears. Oneness is the 'sovereign Lord'—this passage assumes separation, which is simply an illusion.*

Mark of the Beast:

In Revelation:13, according to Jeshua, the "beast out of the sea" refers to the ego, the *rational* mind.

Revelation 12:1 "A great and wondrous sign appeared in heaven: a woman clothed with the sun." This is the light of truth, the feminine birthing Jesus. Indeed the divine feminine is what Jesus and Mary Magdalene intend to bring forth. Now Sananda/Magdalene is the new energy which will heal the distorted masculine and bring in the Goddess energy.

It will not be a matriarchy, but simply an opening up of the unconditional love or heart energy in every person. Women, conscious of our feeling nature, will lead the men to recognize their own feeling nature. The nurturing, cooperative and process orientation in women will make them natural teachers. War, power and control, and domination to get needs met will become obsolete.

New Heaven and Earth

Isaiah 65:17-25: "Behold I will create new heavens and a new earth. The former things will not be remembered, nor will they come to mind". This refers to living in the Now.

The new Jerusalem will be a delight and its people a joy. Verse 22-b: "My chosen ones will long enjoy the works of their hands." In my mind, I hear Jeshua saying, *You did the choosing.*

V 24-25: "Before they call, I will answer... the wolf and the lamb will feed together...They will neither harm nor destroy, in all my holy mountain."

Revelation 21-22—21:1 "Then I saw a new heaven and a new earth, for the first heaven and the first earth had passed away. I saw the Holy City, the new Jerusalem coming down out of heaven from God, prepared as a bride, beautifully dressed for her husband...God will live with them [mankind embodied with Spirit] ...no more death or mourning, crying or pain, for the old order of things has passed away... I am making everything new."

Chapter 22: The river of Life, v. 1-6: Jesus is coming. 7-20, Jeshua comments:

Indeed, your I Am is making everything new Since I became the comforter or Holy Spirit in every heart, whether or not I am recognized, I have never left. I don't intend to return in a body. As I am embraced as a teacher, when your consciousness matches mine, you will no longer be conscious of my presence—for we are all One. Many with other guides are in that same consciousness when they know they are divine love and accept their Oneness with all life.

A New Earth, Awakening to Your Life's Purpose by Eckhart Tolle is based on Revelation 21. He states, "'A new heaven' is the emergence of a transformed state of consciousness. 'A new earth' is its reflection in the physical realm."

Our egos get in the way. Tolle, along with Jeshua, defines the ego as our false personality which misperceives and takes everything personally. Even when we are correct in understanding truth, it gets contaminated by the ego's need to be recognized as right and another as wrong. The ego emphasizes separation. Know what is true for you in your heart. The mind can distort with its neediness to be right. Love will guide us in the expression of our truth. When love is shared from the heart and connects with the heart of another it can bypass the ego's need to be right.

Our egos confuse opinions and viewpoints with facts. Our egos are masters of selective perception and distorted interpretation. Differentiating between fact and opinion comes through awareness—not through thinking. This awareness can be accelerated by Jeshua's advice to simply ask our Higher Self (Holy Spirit) for a new perspective that gives us peace.

Tolle defines grievance as "the baggage of old thought and emotion." Forgiveness has to bypass the ego and let the wisdom of the heart recognize other ways of seeing the situation. Many churches have identified "relativism, the belief that there is no absolute truth to guide human behavior" as a dangerous belief. Tolle agrees, but says the error is in expecting absolute truth to "be found in doctrines, ideologies, sets of rules, or stories," because these all come from thoughts in the mind, which can at best point to the truth, but never *is* the truth. As Buddhists say, "The finger pointing to the moon is not the moon."

Religions profess to be in the service of Truth, but have looked to external authority for that Truth when actually it is to be found within. The patriarchal or male pattern is the focus on the outer or external expression of truth. This needs to be preceded and balanced by the inner feminine principle.

I am the Way, the Truth and the Life

Jesus pointed to the absolute Truth when he said, "I am the way, the truth and the life." I thought that those words pointed to Jesus as the only way. It can be misunderstood, as Tolle explains. "Jesus speaks of the innermost *I Am*, the essence identity of every man and woman, every life-form, in fact. Some Christian mystics have called it 'the Christ within'; Buddhists call it your Buddha nature; for Hindus, it is Atman, the indwelling God." The core *I Am* in every human being is the Truth! Tolle says that being in touch with that dimension is "your natural state, not some miraculous achievement." Actions and relationships will reflect that deep sense of oneness within. This is Love. (Laws and regulations are necessary for those who are cut off from the truth of who they are.)

The Collective Ego

Tolle describes the *collective ego* with the *I am right, you are wrong* mentality, which Jesus simply describes as the *belief in separation*. Regarding oneself as victim and the *other* as evil dehumanizes the *other*—conflict and the insanity of war continues. "By far, the greater part of violence that humans have inflicted on each other is not the work of criminals or the mentally deranged, but of normal, respectable citizens in the service of the collective ego…on this planet, 'normal' equals insanity," Tolle writes. Jesus flatly states in ACIM, "The ego is insane." Jesus also says that the ego is the "devil" that humans have projected outside themselves.

The Pain-Body, a Major Block

Tolle's extensive description of the pain-body refers to the insanity of the ego. Tolle calls the accumulated, un-dealt-with cellular memories "the pain-body." Emotions result from the thoughts in our head. Our mind tells a story that the pain-body believes. Emotions arise from the thoughts generated. A cycle happens with the feedback energy to the thoughts, "giving rise to emotional thinking and emotional story-making." Past experience creates assumptions or beliefs that, when unexamined, perpetuate negative experiences. The *Law of Attraction* manifests more quickly as earth vibrations increase.

Tolle's generic term for all negative emotions is "unhappiness." Addiction to unhappiness is behind the entertainment's profitable use of violent movies. Perhaps almost all promotion and advertising exploits the chronic condition of "unhappiness" as it fuels the need for "more."

Emotional States of Being

Deeper emotions which come from your natural state of Higher Self such as Love, Joy, and Peace are really a state of being that has no opposite. This is illustrated in the *Feeling Frequency Guide*. These emotions/states of being don't depend on story. **You can be happy for no reason.**

Accepting the I Am Presence as our true identity will help us stay present in the context of total awareness and forgiveness of the past. My experience of cellular memories affecting bodily reactions can occur in the present. My shaking legs while speaking at Kirk's Memorial Service carried the cellular memories of past life experiences of standing in my truth at great risk to my life. Forgiveness of a past trauma usually requires a connection to the emotions of that experience and a conscious release.

Born with the Emotional Pain- Body

"Every newborn coming into this world already carries an emotional pain-body," says Tolle. Some babies are happy most of the time and some cry a lot for no apparent reason, even if attention and love are equally present. Babies also reflect the energy of their parents. The density or lightness of the pain-body does not determine their spiritual awareness and growth, according to Tolle.

For many, the suffering image of Jesus on the cross strikes a chord of recognition of one's inner pain-body. Jesus demonstrated the Christ we are meant to be. Yes, he could feel pain and was able to transmute it.

According to Tolle, in most people, the pain-body has a dormant and an active stage. It can lie dormant until something triggers it. Tolle speaks of it as having a life of its own. It is another aspect of the ego and can manifest a number of different ways. Someone with a dense pain-body can cover it up by "being nice" no matter what is occurring. It may be from their childhood experiences, or they may have incarnated with it. With the Intention of awakening, present and past life issues come into one's awareness to be healed. The pain-body is unprocessed karma.

Working with the Pain-Body

Acceptance of our unhappy feelings from an observer standpoint lessens their power over us. Cultivating this observer self is simply getting in touch with the compassionate *I Am Presence* and looking at the thought patterns and emotions we get stuck in. The ego resists giving up its victim-perpetrator-rescuer cycle. In a world that values drama, it feels like "…something is wrong with me; I am not fitting in!" We are at choice from a place of awareness.

Tolle's description of the release of a dense pain-body in a client resembled the kind of "spirits" Jesus cast out. The energy needs to be cleared from the area, as it is a negative energy that can attach to a matching frequency in another person, as Tolle discovered. The pain-body carries a vibration that magnetizes another pain-body's matching frequency. High drama or over-reaction is characteristic of a pain-body's activity.

When encountering another's similar pain-body, staying fully present and accepting will allow the other to observe their own behavior. The egoic (or thinking) mind cannot understand the wisdom of the Spiritual heart, and so will often misinterpret it. Intuition feels alien to the ego mind and it will distrust it at first. Yet, a true joining comes from the heart, not the head. Accepting and knowing the oneness of yourself and the other is true compassion. Ego's experience of love is conditional. Only unconditional love works.

The Awakened Consciousness: A New Heaven

Recognizing our pain-body, without identifying with it, empowers us to stay in our *I Am Presence*. This actually diminishes the pain-body every time we choose Presence over reacting. When a pain-body becomes disruptive, it can become a wake-up call. Then we can take responsibility for its existence and for releasing it.

When we seek guidance and self-awareness, help shows up and the journey has begun. "Awakening is the realization of Presence."

Chapter 55: Heaven On Earth, A New Humanity

This is a process, a process involving the Four Keys; Heart's Desire, Intention, Allowing and Surrender.

Tolle, through his own process, uses these Four Keys without specifying them as such.

Tolle concludes with, "The foundation for a new earth is a new heaven—the awakened consciousness. The earth—external reality—is only its outer reflection…"

Awakened to our essential true nature as consciousness, we recognize that essence in all other life forms. When we live in the surrendered state, we feel our Oneness with the whole and with Source.

Signs of the Times are Birth Pains

Some physical signs are foretold in the Bible. Matthew 24:6-8 "You will hear of wars and rumors of wars, but see to it that you are not alarmed. Such things must happen, but the end is still to come." V. 7: "Nation will rise against nation, and kingdom against kingdom. There will be famines and earthquakes in various places." V. 8: "All these are the beginning of birth pains." In verse 4, Jesus also warns against self-deception. Deception has become a very blatant factor in all our systems—religion, government, media, medicine, finance, education, marketing, science and food production.

A New Humanity

The Jeshua Channelings: *Christ consciousness in a new era,* by Pamila Kribbe, offers me a clear understanding of who Jesus is. The mission of Jesus includes The New Earth, Light workers, and the ego-to-heart process. I strongly urge individuals to study Kribbe's book together in groups. It is easy enough to read and rings true, clearing up much confusion and misunderstanding. I honor Pamela and her husband Gerrit with much gratitude for bringing forth these words of Jeshua. It will take several readings for me to fully digest it. In a gentle and loving way, it lifts the veil.

Duality Provides Experience

The experience of duality is the substance for *spiritual alchemy,* which is Christ consciousness, a third energy. This alchemy produces a pearl—YOU, transformed. The illusions have served a purpose to provide experience; now we are to shed the illusions and the game of duality. An emotional life see-sawing between happy and sad that sees the outer world as real, stems from our illusions. Judgments, strong opinions, and beliefs feed this game.

We release duality by listening to the language of our soul through our feelings,. Follow the cues from the soul for actions to take. Value quiet time and hear the soul. Question, as you become aware of limiting thought patterns or rules.

The Event

After this quote came to me, I opened up a forwarded email titled, "The Plan for 'The Event.'" The article was written by Therese Zumi Sumner, March 2, 2013. I am directed to at least alert readers of this information. Change is so rapid now, it could be obsolete by the time this book is published and read. Jeshua assured me of the truth in this 40 page article.

An organization called The Light Resistance Movement (LRM) has been working towards the manifestation of "The Event." The LRM knew there was a way to "hack the matrix" (the computer program that keeps us prisoners in an artificial reality). This matrix is disintegrating. Light is increasing daily. An Event Flash refers to a flash of divine energy from Source that will cue the lightworkers who will contact "the dark forces" to invite cooperation.

The Matrix and the Light Resistance Movement

The Event was planned to happen on 12-21-12, and was delayed. When the matrix has finally collapsed, the Light Resistance Movement (now waiting for the right time) will stage The Event. Ask for the protection of the *White Light* when bombarded by negative things, as we are now experiencing. I would add, use *The Feeling Frequency*

Chapter 55: Heaven On Earth, A New Humanity

Guide to move out of egoic fear, and hold the vision of the Birthing of the New Earth, which will be heralded by The Event.

Some 300 "Operatives" in LRM are prepared to ask the *dark forces* if they are willing to cooperate. If not, they will be excluded. The article states that the Flash may take only 15 minutes before the Event. There will be NO announcement, but it will simply happen, coming as a surprise. Rely on Intuition, stay calm, and give people the information now coming through on the Internet. Your Intention will help bring this information to you.

Possible Scenarios

"Cobra" is the name of an information source in the non-physical world which has summarized the following possible scenarios: Extra-terrestrials will land and join many aware people in the LRM to set up new systems to replace the collapsed and bankrupt systems. "In the first few hours of The Event, the Galactic forces will take over the satellites and communication stations." Intelligence will be received. The elite-controlled financial system will be shut down. Credit cards won't work and banks will close. This shutdown will be over in a week, according to this article. Have some cash, as well as food and water on hand. Many scenarios are possible.

Monsanto will be bankrupt along with similar companies. A new and better financial system will be put in place, which will redistribute the wealth. No more homeless, as homes will be available to whoever needs one.

The medical system will change to natural health and holistic practice. Harmful vaccines and drugging will stop. Cooperation will replace competition. A shorter work day allows for creativity to flourish. Transparency in government will truly be possible. A positive "military" will be in place that does not use weapons.

Many people are mind-controlled and will be de-programmed and invited to heal, including some of the Light who are not free to express according to the wisdom of the heart. 50% of the Illuminati born into that system will be freed also from mind-control to become what their heart desires.

Factories developing new technologies using Free Energy will spring up and replace nuclear power sites. Nature will be restored and depleted resources renewed. There will be no more horror movies. A total change in the education system will take place. Animal abuse will not be tolerated.

These are possible scenarios for us to envision. They are <u>not fact</u>. What is fact is the following: The Light Resistance Movement on earth is connected to a large confederation of spiritually-advanced galactic beings assisting us. Underground bases for the cabal almost destroyed the Light Resistance Movement in their underground chambers. The Ashtar command has taken over.

An enormous spiritual awakening will take place. Cities of Light will spring up! As we raise our vibrations and hold a positive vision of a New Earth, we are in co-partnership with a great company of non-physical beings, including family members on the other side. These include Sananda/Magdalene, the lineage, Archangel Michael, many angels, and all the nature spirits of mother earth.

Hold the Vision

The above paragraphs are incomprehensible to my ego. Yet holding this vision allows the Law of Attraction to bring us Heaven on Earth. As we do our inner work and see another as ourselves, we bring forth the New Humanity. It is our choice!

The resistance of the Power and Control forces and delay in humanity's readiness affects the timing of the Event. Hold the Vision without anxiously waiting. As we give up egoic power and control and trust the wisdom of our own *I Am Presence*, we will be cued to make the right choices. **Our responsibility is to be in a state of high vibrational readiness.**

Joining with like-minded persons also empowers us. Seeding the churches with this vision and the new revelations of Jeshua, the

Chapter 55: Heaven On Earth, A New Humanity

Oneness movement, the Divine Feminine, The Way of the Heart and Embodiment of new ways of being can reach greater numbers of people. Meditation is a beginning, and reconnecting to the earth and each other from the heart will manifest the promised Heaven on Earth. Hold the Vision.

CHAPTER 56

FINDING YOUR PURPOSE

Ascension Purpose/ Our Purpose

First it is necessary to accept the idea we all had a purpose in incarnating at this time. We have a highly personal purpose in releasing karma. To fulfill the purpose of Ascension, we need to release everything that hinders us from moving forward. Humanity's purpose is to awaken to the truth of who we are—One with Source.

Your Purpose

Awakening to your life's purpose is a major part of your Ascension process. Everyone is affected by the Ascension energies. Knowing your purpose can help you harness the energies. Waking up to who we are is the inner work of the 4th dimension. The Oneness movement includes both the 4th and 5th dimension, as the inner manifests the outer expression of Oneness. All systems—society, government, religion, medicine, economy, education and agriculture are all based on the *belief in separation* from our God Self, each other, and nature. You may very well be a system changer, drawn to one of the systems.

Many are alarmed by the poisoning of the planet, the bloodshed, power and control resistance present in every system as the energy of change is upon us. This is motivating protests and conflict, as well as deception, to keep the profits going. Tibetan immolations to suicides of third-world farmers under GMO domination, and record numbers of suicides of soldiers reveals the desperation of many whose lives are trapped by forces of power and control.

Most of us have been conditioned to see *purpose* as merely to make money or just to survive physically. Using our gifts isn't valued if it doesn't make money. Happiness is sought through money, and fails to satisfy. "To make money" invites the question, "What for?" Then our purpose can unfold and call up the desire of the heart.

"Why did you incarnate?" may seem like an impossible question. It is not one the ego can answer. Yet it is one of those questions that can prompt an inner exploration. What gives satisfaction is to feel the passion of purpose. This usually involves using our gifts to make a contribution. Easing the pain on the planet in some way provides a satisfaction that money can't buy.

"Be the change that you wish to see in the world." —Mahatma Gandhi

Simply to **be** the change we want to see in the world can involve intense inner work. Many have made significant contributions without doing this work—yet they have missed their ultimate purpose of knowing themselves. And, they may have sabotaged their contribution through an addiction of some kind, such as in an eating disorder, alcoholism, or sexual exploitation. The compulsive nature of addiction temporarily eases the pain of not knowing who you are, the pain of separation.

In my son's case, overcoming his alcoholism became his purpose in the service of taking care of his partner, Sue. Self-healing is an important part of fulfilling our purpose, and may in itself become our purpose. Here the twelve steps of AA can become the map to recovery. With my son, it was daily prayer to Jesus to handle the cravings. He lived his core purpose to be love, without judgment. To be love in whatever we do is our ultimate purpose.

Accepting and using our intuitive nature becomes a practice, which magnetizes our guidance. It is always a higher vibration that allows creativity. Knowledge of our vibrations is helpful to our creative process. We can monitor our thoughts and feelings with the *Feeling Frequency Guide*. We need the energy of Passion to fulfill our purpose.

Chapter 56: Finding Your Purpose

Without passion we have no juice to stay focused or to carry out our Heart's Desire.

The Four Keys can be applied to both finding and carrying out your purpose. What is your **Heart's Desire**? Clarify and create a vision. Your life up to now can give you cues and clues. **Intention**, the 2nd Key, focuses on use of your attention and energy to envision your purpose accomplished, and to take inspired action. **Allowing** invites process, and the unexpected. It trusts the Universe to provide the *how*. **Surrender** lets the higher Self be in charge of the outcome.

As I pondered my Purpose, I received the following from Jeshua:

Excerpts from Jeshua 5-19-11

…You are becoming aware of your own feelings of separation and fear of not being accepted. Indeed the ego can sabotage and facilitate what you fear! Let the TaBIA take care of the ego.

What gives you a niche is your emergence from fundamentalism to embrace your divinity in your crone years. This is especially important to the church-going population. Yes, you may feel more judgment from this crowd—stay in non-judgment. There are many who are waking up and are ready for a 'new' message, and you are being primed to make it. Yes, you will have a partner in this when you simply stay in the flow of your purpose. Like Peace Pilgrim, keep your message simple—Love is your identity and God is love.

Only the belief in separation needs to be released. Purification and Embodiment is your mission. The Vision is the Unity of all beings through the Heart's Desire for Oneness. Apply the Four Keys to this desire. The Oneness comes with Heart Awakening, the claiming of the I Am in the Spiritual Heart.

Self-forgiveness is the need of most people sitting in church pews, who feel regret over choices made. Projection through blame and judgment, the false personality identification with the ego and the body, is a major issue. Relief from pain motivates change. Begin here. Allow the queendom within, the wisdom of the awakened heart, to be expressed.

I am with you always, Jeshua

Our Soul's Purpose Resulted in our Choice to Be Here Now

Some thoughts follow from a friend, Linda Masterson, who does readings based on Astrology. She has this to say about souls, titled, *Souls on the Move:*

"Souls are multidimensional, existing not only in multiple dimensions, but also in diverse locales and timeframes. While the local personality has access to the soul's full expanse, previous to our current age, few personalities have attained multi-dimensional awareness. The soul has a biological interface, seated in the physical heart, along with an extensive multidimensional, multi-dynamic, network of meridians, supporting the function of twelve bodies: physical, mental, emotional, etheric, astral, light soul…" And she mentioned five other bodies, unfamiliar to us, given to her by her master teacher from the non-physical world.

Linda describes the beauty and power of the soul. It "vibrates in the realms of knowing. These frequencies are characterized by peace, harmony, joy and universal tranquility." In these vibrations, we can access our soul's purpose, again with the Four Keys.

"Souls have no need of beliefs," Linda tells us. "All beliefs are inherently flawed, as they arose from a soil of uncertainty at best, and terror at worst, in attempts to protect the illusory self." Beliefs are of the personality and those who control and manipulate personalities. Since souls deal with inner knowing, they have "no need for traditions, and are by nature unique, sovereign, and untamable." This aptly describes the "new children" who have more of their DNA activated. They know who they are.

Commitment to knowing and aligning with our soul and our soul's purpose is a major part of our spiritual process of God realization. My intention to *Know Thyself* has quickened my Observer Self.

Chapter 56: Finding Your Purpose

Our Deepest Fear

"We can easily forgive a child who is afraid of the dark. The real tragedy of life is when men are afraid of the light." —Plato

"Death is not the biggest fear we have; our biggest fear is taking the risk to be alive… and express what we really are."—Miguel don Ruiz, author of *The Four Agreements*

"Our deepest fear is not that we are inadequate. Our deepest fear is that we are powerful beyond measure. It is our light, not our darkness that most frightens us. We ask ourselves, 'Who am I to be brilliant, gorgeous, talented, fabulous?' Actually who are you not to be? You are a child of God. Your playing small doesn't serve the world. There is nothing enlightened about shrinking so that other people won't feel insecure around you. We were born to make manifest the glory of God that is within us. It's not just in some of us, it's in everyone. And when we let our light shine, we unconsciously give other people permission to do the same. As we are liberated from our fear, our presence automatically liberates others."—Marianne Williamson

Your DNA; Cues to Your Higher Purpose

Gene Keys: *Unblocking the Higher Purpose Hidden in your DNA,* by Richard Rudd, gives us another resource for self-awareness and discovery. "Regardless of outer circumstances, every single human being has something beautiful hidden inside them. The sole purpose of the Gene Keys is to bring that beauty forth—to unveil your *incandescence,* the eternal spark of genius that sets you apart from everyone else." He goes on to say that the DNA, the coiled code that has made us who we are today, has been shaped by our attitude toward life! Every feeling, thought, word and action we make has been encoded in every cell of our body. This affirms the tenants of the Law of Attraction and the importance of monitoring our thoughts and feelings, not in a fearful way but from the Observer Self that can notice and correct. He reminds us, "You alone are the architect of your evolution."

Everything Scattered Will Be Gathered

The 64 Gene Keys, a universal codebook based on the I Ching, is a map for exploring the transformation of consciousness needed now. The I Ching or "Book of Changes" is an ancient Chinese divination manual and book of wisdom. In *Gene Keys*, Rudd offers us an opportunity to unlock our higher purpose. We each have a part to play in the transition of the old world into the New Earth and period of peace we are promised. The 534 pages (the paperback version) is truly an inspired work from his guides in the nonphysical world. You can feel the resonance when your pattern is described, offering both the gift and the shadow. Thus it offers a vibrational leap in consciousness.

Though I felt resonance with all the Gene Keys I have encountered so far in the group, the 12th Gene Key (involving the throat chakra) shed more light on my shadow, characteristic energy, and spiritual gift. My thyroid, the physiology involved in this Gene Key, became cancerous and was removed. It reflects the purpose I am undertaking of Purification, discernment, and expression of my truth as a woman with cellular memories of suppressed expression.

Transformation and death are the teachings of the thyroid system and reflect my journey and purpose. The task associated with this Gene Key is to fall in love with the Beloved, which is the I Am, our divine Essence. Purification is the process that allows this to happen. The death that is welcomed is the death of the illusion of separation. Oneness is then possible.

A Bodymind Reaction

With the completion of this book, I experienced the following:

During this final week of editing, I have felt considerable fatigue and had trouble breathing, not all due to the sleep apnea currently affecting me. A doctor's appointment didn't reveal any answers, other than a low-grade temperature and elevated blood pressure.

In doing my usual Intuitive Inquiry, I got that cellular memories are stirred up by this book project. Though I did TaBIA on it, I had no relief—until I received a flash that I had unfinished grieving from past lives affecting me. As soon as I felt that realization, my breath and voice normalized. The lesson is to allow the grief to come up.

In fulfilling our life's purpose, we may have physical reactions, stirred up by cellular memories. When we follow guidance, buried memories will come up for healing. We do not necessarily need the details. The desire and intention to release and forgive the experiences that caused our separation is sufficient.

CHAPTER 57

EMBODIMENT

A Breathing Practice Invites Spirit

Witnessing the differences in the birthing experience for those trained in the Lamaze method, and those without training, was an important lesson for me. A relaxed breathing practice to deal with pain or any stressful experience encourages a powerful habit of inviting spirit as a partner. "Breath is spirit," by definition. We co-operate with the body's agenda through conscious breathing.

Remember the breathing exercise suggested by Jeshua for I Am. Repeating "I Am"—inhaling with "I" and exhaling with "Am"—has proved to be an easy centering exercise to relieve scatteredness. One returns to the Now moment and aligns with cues from the heart. It also brings our masculine and feminine into balance. It affirms my identity when I forget who I am. It is the easiest spiritual practice I know, and amazingly helpful. The "I Am" breathing practice also helps me go to sleep.

Breath

Breath reminds us of Spirit, the life force within us, when we are mindful of it, as in meditation. Breath awareness in any endeavor can remind us of the *I Am Presence* within us. Breath is our connection to all life. Let it remind you of your oneness through our heart connection.

Conscious breathing is instructive to our response to the contractions of Mother Earth in her birthing process of a New Earth. When pre-occupied with past or future, we can take three conscious breaths to bring us into the *now*. Saying the affirmation while tapping the I Am point on the thymus, as in *I am one with Source, I Am that I Am,* can help to ground us in the present, as well as in your *I Am Presence*! Another exercise is to inhale, using words "love in," and exhale "fear out."

A Body Scan Exercise

Take three conscious breaths. Focus on feeling your body from within. Notice the flow of air through your nose and out through your nose, and then in through the nose and out through your mouth. Switch to in, through mouth, and out, through mouth; then, in through mouth, and out through nose.

Feel the aliveness of every part of your body from the hairs on your head to your toes. Breathe into these parts, giving thanks for their vitality. There is power in three, so three breaths with gratitude for each part of your body will be sufficient. If there is a part that is in pain, you can ask that part what it needs.

Breaking Addictive Habits

With practice, you can learn to interject three conscious breaths before any knee-jerk reaction, allowing Awareness. Take three breaths before you open the refrigerator to satisfy an emotional compulsion to eat to relieve stress. You may be able to ward off a craving or a compulsion simply by taking three conscious breaths and saying to yourself, "I don't need this. What I do need is to take a walk," for example. Build a list of alternatives to indulging in any addictive habit. Even if you do indulge, simply notice the arguments and justifications of the addictive voice and continue to return to conscious breathing. Catch and release.

The "I Am" breathing practice reminding you of your God Self also empowers you.

A Free Gift

"Being aware of your breathing takes attention away from thinking and creates space," Eckhart Tolle says. He also suggests that frequent moments of conscious breathing for a year can be more transformative than spending time in various special spiritual courses, and it is free.

Like the old adage, "count to three...," before speaking or acting from anger, take three conscious breaths. It allows the voice of Peace to be heard. Anger too, is an addiction for many. Recognize anger as a demand to have things the way we want them, i.e., to feel *in control*. Creating space allows us to use the intense energy of anger in a more positive way rather than in an impulsive lashing out.

Focus on the breath is the preparation for most meditation and *prayer without ceasing*. Conscious breathing brings us into the awareness of being. Be particularly conscious of the breath of acknowledgement and the breath of release in the TaBIA process.

Breath is Embodied Spirit

Conscious breathing recognizes our spirit essence and invokes the *I Am Presence* into the present moment. It is the invitation to the wisdom of the heart, our intuition, to respond to whatever the present moment calls for.

It reminds me to relax my muscles as I sit in the dentist's chair, walk on stage, or encounter an angry dog. I can banish any fear thoughts, replacing them with love and gratitude. It is said an animal can pick up the energy in our thoughts coming from our bodymind and will respond accordingly. So it is with an audience.

A conscious inhale of our Love spirit and exhale of ego fear can move us into our *I Am Presence*. It is a cue to enter the chamber of the Beloved in our Spiritual heart. Any number of spiritual exercises can make use of this simple process. It is an Intentional way to shift a negative feeling state as soon as we notice it. Our ANTs, or Automatic Negative Thoughts, will be recognized quickly and released. Asking to see a hurtful situation differently is always a heart-opening process calling for a Love response.

CHAPTER 58

THE WAY OF MASTERY

Discovery of a Universal Experience

In a March, 2013, email, I read an invitation to an experiential course. Craig Hamilton, a protégé of Ken Wilber, after a communal 15-year experiment, has created an Internet program for Emergence, "The Evolutionary Impulse." As I read through the eight modules, I realized how it paralleled my awakening experience on Kauai. I feel affirmed of the value of my experience and the urgency to articulate my discoveries for those who are identified with Christianity and ready to experience their Essence. In most Christian churches, we hear the words that we are created in the "image of God" but it is seldom embraced as our true divine Essence.

When I heard an enticing offer to join Miguel don Ruiz in his "Way of Mastery" course, I remembered that I had been privileged to experience the reading of Jeshua's ***The Way of Mastery*** channeled by Jon Mark Hammer with my spiritual family over the past several years. Since Jeshua's Way of Mastery course entails three books, a total of 35 lessons, I wondered about a briefer version for a wider audience.

We have a perfect Master Teacher in Jesus who can directly communicate with each student committed to his Way of Mastery. The Holy Spirit is the "Evolutionary Impulse" described by Craig Hamilton. The Holy Spirit is your inner teacher and coach. Spirituality invites the evolutionary process of inner experience, in contrast to creeds and doctrines of church authorities. When the distortions of Jesus are corrected, many more people can experience the power of Jesus as a Way Shower for embracing our Divine Essence and becoming the evolved human, embodied love essence, necessary for Heaven on Earth.

The Way of Mastery, According to Jeshua

Given in a transmission on 3-2-13, these words came through as a request to put forth a concise *Way of Mastery* for those already into his teachings such as those in the Christian church, the alienated, or those seeking a non-patriarchal spiritual path:

You have just heard Miguel don Ruiz describe his Way of Mastery course, and recognized that you have already read through my Way of Mastery Course in your Way of the Heart group. I am now asking you to share it in a briefer format with a wider audience. You do not need to go through the manuals again with your bodymind as I can dictate it to you. Simpler, is it not? This is the whole point. When your Heart's Desire is to live the Way of Mastery, it will be revealed to you from within you!

The WAY OF MASTERY includes three ways, each a book: The Way of the Heart, The Way of Transformation and The Way of Knowing.

So we begin with The Way of the Heart. Now I will personalize it for you, or whomever undertakes this journey. The Master Teacher is in your Spiritual heart.

You have opened up your Emotional heart and cleared the way through forgiveness. In your case, I gave you the 'Tap and Breathe I Am' process for you to use and share. You asked and received a very specific release process to help one move from the issues in the head to the wisdom of the heart. Affirming your identity is an important part of this process along with the high vibrations of gratitude. I may give something else to another, according to their needs.

The important thing to remember is to be willing to recognize and clear the obstacles despite the ego's resistance. Judgment and guilt do not serve you. Simply notice, and desire to be free above all else. Know you are not alone as the Master Teacher is within you, ready to respond when

Chapter 58: The Way Of Mastery

you are ready. Recognize all resistance as fear and Love yourself in any and all dramas you have created. You are powerful beyond measure. Now you can redirect that power with the help of your Master Teacher. Some of you have yet to recognize that power, the power of your words, your thoughts, and your actions. You fail to act because you think and believe 'it won't matter anyway' because you believe 'I don't matter!'

Throughout the three Ways of Mastery, I use the Four Keys to the Queendom within. In response to the Patriarchy 2000 years ago, I said, "The Kingdom of God is within you." Now you can allow the feminine energy to be expressed and valued as I teach you the Four Keys to the Queendom within you. Heart's Desire, Intention, Allowing and Surrender are the Four Keys!

When your <u>Heart's Desire</u> is for Mastery, you have begun using the Four Keys. The Way of the Heart requires practice as the default setting has been the mind. You ask the Holy Spirit, the I Am Presence, for its perspective **whenever** you feel less than peaceful in your thoughts about anything or anybody. This is the work of <u>Intention</u>, the 2nd Key to the Queendom within.

Intention requires vigilance to recognize the self-deception of the ego. The energy of self-deception can be activated by any reminder of something you don't want to look at. Here is a word of caution—the fear of magnetizing the negative can cause those with the highest intentions to ignore the 'elephant in the living room,' something glaringly obvious, though unwanted.

Denial of the problem does not make it go away. You can hold the belief of your perfection as a divine expression of the One and still identify a block to be released. These blocks have all been the work of identification with the ego, your false personality. It is a process. It may be instant for some and gradual for others. Let there be no judgment.

As you practice the Way of the Heart, Transformation naturally takes place. It comes more quickly in the process of <u>Allowing</u>, the 3rd Key. Transformation refers to manifestation of the quiet inner work of the Way of the Heart. The way you experience your world will change.

The way others experience you will shift. Old habitual ways don't work anymore. Allowing new behaviors to replace old patterns and habits is your focus here.

New desires emerge. Values have changed. Support through joining with others who affirm rather than resist your changes will happen. Clarity of your Purpose and inspired actions take place, almost without effort.

Your main goal is to listen for direction first. The ego likes to engage the mind to plan. Controlling what happens next is a big issue for the ego. 'Letting the Heart be the master, the mind becomes a useful servant,' a lesson given in the Way of the Heart, can be quickly forgotten at this point. Many a venture has failed for this reason. Giving up control is a major issue on the planet now and dictators are killing their own people over it.

The <u>Way of Transformation</u> is often precipitated by an external crises or realization that something has to change. It involves a willingness to do what it takes to become free of patterns and behaviors that keep one from experiencing peace.

The outer evidence of Transformation lies in Being. Doing flows from Being. Sometimes doing takes over and prevents the quiet needed for Being. A spiritual practice is especially important to one who is engaged in active doing and responding to those in need of their services. As you listen within, practicing 'prayer without ceasing,' guidance will point to the solution.

<u>Surrender,</u> the 4th Key, is a gradual process already undertaken in your identification with the I Am Presence, your Higher Self. No longer do you look to the world for your identification. Its glitter has no appeal. The blocks to Love's Presence become much more subtle. Your vigilance in rooting them out has become a habit. Challenges can come anytime, in physical, mental, emotional or spiritual form. They can be relationship challenges. Acceptance of severance from your physical family can be grieved. Because you have trusted the orchestration of your life to your Master Teacher within, you will receive the comfort your heart desires.

Chapter 58: The Way Of Mastery

Ruiz was accepted by his family and they joined him in carrying out his purpose. In your case, and many others in your Spiritual family, you have been cut off. No one way is the right way. Allowing Love to lead will bring the highest good to all. As Passion for your Purpose takes your focus and energy, you hold your loved ones in a chamber of love and acceptance for the paths they have chosen. Keep your vibrations high in gratitude for your mission and for the spiritual family you have attracted. Peace is your constant goal. Love includes your Self and Joy expresses your liberation.

Part III of the Way of Mastery is <u>The Way of Knowing</u>. This inner knowing has nothing to do with "knowledge." The Four Keys to the Queendom within has brought you to a level of Surrender where the ego is more subtle as you fully embrace the rule of your I Am Presence. This place of trust in your own knowing is higher than any external authority. This trust will be challenged. The more you trust and act on this knowing, the greater your confidence. This is true Allowance of your I Am Presence to be in charge. A deep relaxation occurs. You no longer need to figure anything out. Playfulness is a natural expression as you have become 'as a child' in all its innocence and freedom.

Knowing you are playing in a play on earth's stage, and part of you is with your non-physical family watching the play, you can comfortably ad lib, and change the script. Yes, and you can laugh at yourself. Then 'the world will end in laughter.'

The Way of Mastery can totally transform religion. As people are taught to meditate and trust the wisdom of love over fear and embrace their own divinity, it weakens the ego-controlled system built on the *belief in separation*. As more people put their *I Am Presence* in charge of their lives, all systems have to change.

Release processes, such as TaBIA, aid allowing and celebrating change. Then change comes more easily. Forgiveness is all about letting go our resentments, and trusting the orchestration of our lives to our higher Self when we have surrendered the ego. Gratitude is the practice we need to keep up our vibrations. It is through gratitude that we receive more of what we want.

Surrender is a process of our blindfold coming off and seeing as God sees. The Vision of the One Self is beyond our comprehension and will unfold according to our readiness. We have unseen helpers at every turn. Let yourself know this and experience unspeakable bliss.

CHAPTER 59

THE WORLD WILL END IN LAUGHTER

I awoke from an awful dream at 5 AM on January 2, 2007. I can still remember it. On my premises, on stairs near a doorway from the basement, a woman fell and got a nasty cut on her leg. Her friend demanded some supplies; antiseptic, bandages, tape, etc. That began my anxious and desperate journey through medicine cabinets to find the right remedy to fix her. My surroundings appeared to be a huge barn where my children, grandchildren, and others were moving about, and there was crap (literally) in places all over the floor. "Let's clean this up," I said. "Don't touch it!" No one paid any heed. It was picked up and tasted by the young. I was appalled. Conscious of time passing, I continued to look for medical supplies, while the woman waited. I tried to avoid the shit and couldn't keep others from it or clean it up fast enough. Some of it began to look like playdoh and it was everywhere.

Getting a fix to the injured woman in time to do any good was a lost cause. I felt desperate, disgusted and powerless, just before I awakened with great relief from this dream. Jeshua's interpretation follows:

Jeshua 5-12-11

Indeed it is the world you are living in. It is but a dream and it serves no good to focus on the problems. They are endless. Clean up one and another appears like automatic popups in your computer bodymind. [I began to laugh.]

Everything Scattered Will Be Gathered

Only laughter at the absurdity of efforts to focus on the chaos of the dream is appropriate, when all you have to do is to wake up. You cannot fix the dream in your consciousness. To <u>awaken</u> to the One Self is the only solution. From our awakened consciousness, truly inspired acts of compassion have power to awaken those we touch.

The Tap and Breathe I Am process is about correcting perception. Owning and hearing the feelings is a present-moment awareness. Releasing the feeling energy to Source is the process of allowing the issue to become playdoh for use in creating. The ego cannot create. It only reacts. Allow the 'perceived pain' of life to become the playdoh for your co-creation with Source.

Love is letting go of fear. The Golden Buddha appears as you crack and undo the fear-based ego, the camouflage of the Buddha. The Source behind the Buddha mind is the Heart. The Heart of the Buddha is the Christ energy we are calling in to heal the planet. It is the unconditional love that is being awakened in the hearts of the many expressions of the One energy we call God.

The Buddha Mind and Jesus the Christ are one, and will bring East and West together. They are not separate. Indeed Kauai is a meeting place for East and West to connect as One.

Desire to embody the Christ energy. Commit to an **Intention** you hold in common. This involves will, and focus to hold the Vision. Trust the process of **Allowing** the 'how' to be orchestrated by Source. SURRENDER resistance to the I Am Presence within you.

Our words to you for birthing the New Earth is to **hold the vision** and **trust the process**. Forget not **gratitude** and remember the **truth** is true always.

I Am with you in All Ways of Love, Joy, and Peace, Jeshua.

TaBIA Seriousness, for Humor

Norman Cousins laughed himself well. He left the hospital with a dire prognosis and holed up in seclusion to watch funny movies, and recovered to write about it.

Chapter 59: The World Will End In Laughter

Laughter as a vibration of Love neutralizes fear and anger. It is primarily laughing at ourselves, even as we see seriousness demonstrated in fundamentalism. Fear of hell has not worked to help people embrace the truth about themselves. Awakening from the dream of fear and ignorance and releasing our judgments shifts us into gratitude and love vibrations. We are not separate from Source, our I Am within.

As we realize our oneness with Source and look at the script we chose, we can laugh.

Discerning the purpose of our current incarnation is a process calling for intuitive questioning. Accurate answers come forth when we surrender our thoughts in contemplative silence. Even though blindfolded, we could experience melting the illusion of fear with love, and embrace our path of learning through hard knocks.

When Everything Scattered has been Gathered

Realizing our Essence through the mill of experience, we create our chalice. The scattered pieces we have gathered have become a work of art. As we look at each piece with love and courage and ask for the highest perception, we see where it fits into our chalice. Tears become the clarifying, the polishing of each piece into peace.

The chalice is a symbol of the feminine. It holds and integrates the pieces of our life with heart energy. It is a chalice of compassion as we embrace the wounded and distorted masculine. We nourish the masculine energy to carry out our purpose, letting Spirit direct each step. The feminine and masculine energies become One in the embrace of a common purpose.

Many spirits, with great interest, observe us. Our lives are like Sunday football on TV. Some envy us. Others find much to laugh at with compassion, noting we are veiled. All want to help and be called upon. Experiencing the earth play is a privilege; don't waste it.

HEART AWAKENING CIRCLES

Jeshua 10-26-13 on Heart-Awakening Circles

Heart Awakening Circles can assist in the mass heart-awakening of humanity. Heart-awakening was my purpose 2000 years ago. It is on you I trust, to help fulfill the mission begun by Mary Magdalene and me. It is time to undo the 'belief in separation' that dominates 3rd dimension consciousness.

Each of you have your own gifts and opportunities to share. Heart Awakening circles would be based on fundamental teachings of who you are and my Presence as your I Am Presence within you. They are one and the same when we let go of personality and bodymind identification.

These Heart Awakening circles are core to the Ascension process and they include Purification of the Emotional heart through forgiveness and embodiment tools such as TaBIA. These circles are meant to be sharing circles, where feelings are expressed and awarenesses shared from individual observations, and from listening to the Holy Spirit in their Spiritual heart. Some may choose to form Heart Awakening groups in a neighborhood or business or other organization. Support of each other is very important in a time like this to help address the fear and isolation people feel.

Ascension in consciousness is the true meaning of my return. It is for each of you to recognize the Christ in yourself. It is the ego's identification with the body that put 'Jesus coming back in the clouds to take up believers to heaven' in your scriptures. This idea of Ascension is false. It may be disappointing to many to discover that there is no outside rescuer. The Love energy of the group can provide the comfort needed.

Using the Four Keys in a group will help to bring minds together to serve a shared Intention. These Four Keys to the Queendom within serves to correct the distorted masculine

Principle and bring the Feminine principle into balance. Introducing Heart Awakening circles in the context of the Four Keys will give them the substance that has made the 12 Steps so successful for addicts. I will certainly assist you in this formation.

I am with you always in all ways, Jeshua

Contempletive Prayer Groups

One can begin a group in their neighborhood. This can be easily combined with a contemplative prayer practice, which could come first. If there is an openness to communicating directly with the Voice for Love, the *I Am Presence*, ask group members to share. The energies are changing and one will be surprised when the "least of these" comes forth with Jeshua's words. Reflection and discussion can follow.

You are invited to initiate a Heart Awakening group, which can be a supportive spiritual family for you. Using the Four Keys will help you manifest it. There is abundant inspirational material on Ascension now. Pray for discernment. Observe group process, confidentiality, no judgment or advice, safety for expressing feelings, and time allowance for everyone to share. The Heart Awakening focus can naturally lead to fifth dimensional Oneness, our vision for Heaven on Earth.

These groups assist in heart awakening. A book on heart awakening can accelerate the process. Working with what is accepted is a place to start. Indeed, Mari Perron's book, *A Course of Love*, received from Jesus and published in 2014, has come to my attention. It is for those ready to embrace a new way of being, by living from the heart.

A Course Of Love

This has been described as a sequel to ACIM. The three books are available in one volume of 677 pages. It is more readable and is

Chapter 59: The World Will End In Laughter

directed towards the heart rather than the mind. It is less complicated and more accessible than ACIM. Mari Perron received the words after considerable study of ACIM and her joining two other women in a search for answers to the meaning of their life experiences.

In her union with the inner voice, words came that were not her words. She notes that "thinking" put her back into a separated state. Her willingness and acceptance of her assignment, plus the bliss of union, kept her on task, which she described as easy and effortless. Being interrupted by the tasks of functioning in her human roles in the energy of separation consciousness became a painful, unbelievable experience of contrast.

"This is a course for the heart. The birthplace of the new." The process of awakening bypasses the mind. No efforting is required. Accepting our One Self and the I Am Presence within is the focus of this course. Jesus takes us from the egoic image of our self to the experience of the Christ, our Self. We are called to a new way of being, seeing, and perceiving.

Establishing our identity as One with the Source within us is the primary focus of this course.

Separation never really occurred. Moving into the density of form, blindfolded, created the illusion. "Now a new degree of union is occurring to allow for a new type of experience." We are called to demonstrate a new visual pattern of "spirit resurrected in form" through relationship. You demonstrate by showing your feelings, unique from "your interaction with the Christ consciousness within you."

The *Course of Love* tells us, "It is time to be a channel for the awareness of union with God that exists in every living being."

ADDITIONAL TRANSMISSIONS FROM ASCENSION MASTER JESHUA

Many messages come to us throughout our lives from Jesus or Jeshua via the Holy Spirit and we are not fully aware of their origin. They come as promptings of the heart—an *a-ha*, an idea, or prompting of a higher vibration, a vision of what could be— any could be a prompt from our God Self.

Until I desired to connect specifically to Jeshua's directives for my life, I didn't record them. After I received the TaBIA process, a gift I asked for, I received cues to go to the computer after getting a *yes* to "Do you have a message for me?" The typed messages began in 2006. I typed out what I heard in my mind, usually during the wee hours of the night. Even some ego doubts that have re-surfaced found answers in re-reading these early transmissions. I will share a few excerpts here:

Jeshua 1-6-07

Now we begin. Lo, I am with you always in all ways. I will give you cues of my intent. Yes, I have a style of speaking for you to recognize. I come in Peace and Love. As you allow yourself to feel Peace and Love, you resonate with my energy. You may not feel the Joy when the body is in resistance. The ego means well when it gets protective around your sleep time.

You move into fear when you wonder or worry how all can be accomplished in your goals. Use the TaBIA process on your tendency to complicate tasks and confuse yourself, another form of fear. Do the TaBIA release of this or any limited pattern for three days.

Develop a balance of writing, clearing and client focus…Focus on sharing the TaBIA process… Using the Four Keys will bring through what the reader can grock, as you say.

Feeling overwhelmed, or the feeling of stuckness can be tapped on. Ask me for a shift in perception.

Yes, you are being given understanding about the importance of allowing feelings to be felt and the misuse of ACIM to deny negative feelings. The TaBIA process allows that and provides instant release. Feelings are a guidance system and expose cell memories that need to be healed. To embody Christ does not do away with feelings. They are merely pointers to what you need to let go of, when they are painful and cause separation.

Pain in the body as well, is calling for attention. It is helpful to ask the body, while being careful not to jump to conclusions. Not every sensation is pointing to an error in thinking! The body knows what it needs. Yes, the power that made the body is in the body, and dis-ease is the result of blocked flow. The body is very forgiving of poor health habits, for a time. Over-concern about what one puts in the body is not helpful.

The mind's focus on wholeness and peaceful feelings allow the body to heal itself. The Voice for Love can inform the mind when some action will serve the bodymind's optimum functioning. Whether it is cancer or heart disease, denial of feelings is a blockage of energy or chi. Dumping feelings, as in projected anger, is actually a cover for lack of self-responsibility. Owning the feeling and asking what it is really about is helpful in uncovering judgments and changing perception. When the intensity is felt and released through the TaBIA process, it brings back clarity and a response can be chosen, rather than simply reacting. Forgiving the data, indeed clears and creates space for a heart connection.

We are complete for now. Take your rest. J.

Jeshua's use of "Father" in Reference to God

Now we begin. …my use of "father" in referring to God is to symbolize the intimacy and relationship with the one who seeded my creation. The father loves what he creates and represents first cause. Without the seed there would be no manifestation. Indeed the mother is equally important, as without her, there would be no growth or emergence. Matter is the mother and she is also Spirit—Shekina, equal to the father. Neither the divine Father or Mother are beings, but energies of giving and receiving which are one, yet will produce male and female forms which are merely symbolic of the giving and receiving relationship. Both energies are present in each form.

Indeed the Patriarchy has denied its nurturing or feeling energy as it turned its seeding or creative energy into a need to control. With incarnation into form, fear came in with the experience of the physical senses and the veiling of spirit identity. Identification with the body then produced a sense of vulnerability and a sense of separate beings. The belief in separation came about when a power recognized in the phenomenon of weather, nature and the fragility of life, beyond human control, was named God.

*Dualism of spirit and matter led to dualism or separation in general— you and me, dark and light, good and bad, male and female. Feelings, the energy in relationships, emerges from the heart—its desire to love and be loved. Yet, the perceptions in the mind, a masculine energy in all human forms, will distort the feelings when reason is in control. Ego, the Voice of fear, generally controls the mind until one's Spirit identity is acknowledged. Reason tends to deny feelings. The emotional heart, portal to the higher frequency of love, becomes closed. The higher wisdom of the spiritual heart is denied. That is why I said, 'Let the **heart** be the master and the mind becomes a very useful servant.'*

The Patriarchal age is coming to an end. The Patriarchal ego's need to control is evident in the extreme violence, deception, and push for external power now being unleashed. America is not exempt, as human rights are being taken away. The voice of fear seems to be dominating, and is intentionally fostered by those in power.

The Voice of love is being heard by many. The energy of the One Self is being sought by open hearts. The centering prayer groups are an example of this going within to hear the inner Voice of the heart. Higher consciousness is a natural result.

The voice of the One Self is being heard by many though listening to known spirits. I represent many, including the Magdalene energy. The human mind feels safest with a known spirit. There is no personality here. The energy of Love is one. Buddha, Krishna and I are one. True Religion, in its many forms, are all expressions of divine Love, the One Self, that embraces all. That is why the Yin energy of the heart needs to come forth in every being. Only here is unity possible on planet earth.

Your recognition of feeling separate is a cue for releasing. It is a practice that anyone can do. It is really a feeling of separation from the One Self or the effect of that belief. Each soul expresses differently. If your expression is different and doesn't immediately resonate, it is not a cause for feeling rejection or un-acceptance. This is a pattern for TaBIA. Ask for an opportunity to share the process and set a date. Speak with confidence in offering this gift. Not everyone will take to it. You have enough benefits to report that something of value will be received. I am always here to inspire your presentation to touch the heart. Only allow it. Jeshua

Healing a Pattern of Several Lifetimes
The Martha Wound, Jeshua 1-8-12

Now we begin. The process you just went through unveiled a core issue you have carried through many lifetimes. Allow the grief to come up. It is an issue, which has blocked the sharing of your work. This issue is why I gave you the TaBIA process; that you might value yourself.

It is your <u>perception</u> that my rebuke was of your value. It is not only your perception, but also those who read and expound on the Martha Mary story. It is quite incorrect. You simply played a part in illustrating priorities and choices in the earth drama. Your work in that lifetime was of great value to me, and many others. Indeed you listened to me with great regard, and therefore were deeply wounded by my rebuke. Indeed, forgive me.

Your perception has attracted scripts to support it. Beginning with this lifetime, rejection at birth by your father of your gender is an example of the Patriarchal denial of women's value. This denial also resulted in the omission of my relationships with women. It was a denial that many of my teachers were women. All this you are now becoming aware of through channeled books, mostly by women. The Patriarchy greatly distorted the truth about my life and works. You are of great value in the undoing of this distortion.

Allow the grief your perception has caused. You played a role that helps others see the importance of shifting perceptions, identifying beliefs and the feelings they cause, and identifying with Source. Indeed your work is the TaBIA process, which is everyone's work.

Self-Inquiry is an important part of the TaBIA process. As you ask, your intuition kicks in. Let the heart do the asking. The ego cannot discern the right questions. Focusing on the heart brings you intuitive questions, which pop up in your daily life as you 'pray without ceasing.' This kind of prayer is simply listening to the Voice for love in every moment. It is that voice Mary listened to. The ego feels very responsible with many shoulds and interprets its value as carrying out the perceived expectations of other egos. Sound familiar?

When one does not love one's self, one is vulnerable to the ego's interpretation of everything. Loving oneself is not based on merit. It is the knowing that 'I Am that, I Am.' This is knowing you are One with Source. The 'belief in separation' is the main block to this knowing. The TaBIA process addresses that. This process belongs to everyone as it describes in a nutshell the shift in Perception that is necessary to ascend.

This is your message. You are simply a messenger. Claim it for yourself by removing the blocks to Love's Presence. You have perceived 'Love's Presence' in your son, despite his drinking problem. This is the necessary intention to shift the energy on the planet to Oneness. Remember your own Intention is a worthy one when it comes from the heart. What are known as Resolutions at the beginning of a new year would be more successful if the Four Key process were used. Yes, you have material for many messages on this.

You do not have to charge a high price to value your work. Money, as an indicator of value, is coming to an end. Results of one's work are not criteria of value. Being true to the Desire of the heart for abundance by using Intention, Allowance and Surrender will generate work of value. Then you are authentic and true to yourself.

So the teaching is this. Forgive everything that occurs. Ask for a shift in perception first and it will be easier to forgive. Many are carrying perceptions from past lifetimes, which blocks the expression of their divinity. As hearts open to the love they are, they become open to the knowledge of past lifetimes and wounds. They can then relate the effect of that wound. We are pau. I Am with you always in all ways. Jeshua

Unfinished Past-Life Relationship Issues
Judas, alias "Al" Jeshua 3-16-12

Now we begin. Your awareness that you have had a persistent image of comfort, namely lying with a man, goes back to your relationship with Judas. You have interpreted that throughout your lifetimes as a need for sex, or as a need for comfort or security. Indeed it is an image of your last lay with Judas, where he had unspoken thoughts of suicide. He was unable to perform and held you in a prolonged hug of farewell. You had completely accepted him and sensed his sorrow and regret. You attempted to comfort him, knowing I had asked him to do what he did.

That image was also persistent because of your guilt that you were unable to keep him from taking his own life. Coming together now is an opportunity for completion and a different outcome. Yes, there are other women, duplications of Martha; some who have resolved this and some who have not. Women in general tend to carry guilt over not being able to resolve a man's emotional turmoil, as emotional comfort has been their domain. It is often done through offering sex.

Explain that your last time with him in that lifetime left some unfinished business for both of you. Your potential for being his teacher

is possible because of his interest in my teachings. It can also awaken repressed or blocked memories. Yes you can give him anything relating to

<u>A Course in Miracles</u> or <u>Way of the Heart</u>. Even some photo-copied pages can be helpful, as you have much of that.

The important thing now is completion of unfinished business in your past lives. The more you clear, the more unlimited you become in any endeavor. This you have already done with several men you have had past lives with. This will continue until you know you are complete. You have asked, and we have responded. You no longer need be surprised at the experiences you are having—all in divine order. You are indeed working off any karma stemming from your relationships with men.

When you are in a mode of receptivity, you will be given the information you need. Once you exercise your willingness with a suggested action step, all manner of positive change will occur.

You have some dedicated prioritizing to do. Your life is full and rich and letting go some of the good things will feel like a loss to you. You don't have to do it perfectly. Create the Intentions you need to support your vision. Hold a Vision that includes these Intentions along with releasing your resistance and blocks through TaBIA, then simply Allow. Allow my love to fill you, embrace you and empower you. Your Abundance will include helpers to do the tasks you don't need to do. .

In the process, you are Surrendering to the One Self you are. This is the ongoing goal of Ascension as you become Ageless, Awake, Aware and At One.

I Am with you always, in all ways, Jeshua.

A Current Experience of Fundamentalism and Jeshua's Response

I attended a 7th Day Adventist special service following a mishap with my car and a rescue from a member of that church. A friend also invited me to attend. Indeed, the special speaker gave an urgent and emotional plea to get right with God to avoid hell and be together in heaven. Bibles were promoted as the *only* Word of God. Jeshua had this to say:

Everything Scattered Will Be Gathered

Jeshua, 6-16-2012, 5 AM

Now we begin. Indeed you have heard a very convincing presentation by a 7th Day Adventist. The power of belief is the power of the mind, which is foundational to the Adventists. Selecting the Sabbath references as core to their faith and commitment to Saturday worship is one answer to 'why the many denominations?' So 'a Universal theology is impossible, but a universal experience is not only possible but necessary.' That universal experience is the experience of an open heart, one which welcomes the I Am Presence in another as the same I Am Presence in oneself. In spite of their dogma, the love was present.

This is the key to overcoming the 'belief in separation.' It is connecting from the heart. Indeed you did experience many loving people, but knew that your thoughts or theology would not be accepted. This is not your mission field. Notice your ego wants the mind connection to feel safe. There is a place for the expression of your thoughts. First finish our book, 'Everything scattered…' and the book will be picked up by the persons ready to shift to listening to their hearts.

Your need for expression can be in the form of a response in appreciation for their loving welcome, the clarity and conviction in sharing their beliefs, and their focus on health. Heart awakening and acceptance of the many expressions of the One Self is your focus. The Way of the Heart replaces the way of the mind, which still is the domain of the ego. Outward expressions and spiritual practices will differ in form. Preferences need not cause division when the focus is on the inner states of Peace, Love, Joy, Gratitude, Compassion and Forgiveness. Forgiveness is a bridge, a purification, which allows the experience of these qualities.

Focus on outward forms is Patriarchal. Your mission is to focus on the feminine, the recognition of the fulfillment of the law through Heart awakening and Purification. Sharing one's process, or living in process is to be valued over form. The Patriarchal Bible is not needed to prove anything. The I Am Presence is the authority. It is the still small voice accessed by the Four Keys to the Queendom within. Sometimes it takes a major disruption of form to get one's attention. Your present beliefs have come out of the experiences processed on the inner level aided by others who support the feminine way of process.

Articulating the shift of moving from head to heart, that is, what is needed to embrace heaven on earth, is the focus of your writing and speaking. Identifying the Patriarchal, which strengthens the ego, is the value of attending some of these meetings. The mind wants to lead. This is so strong that it usually takes some external event to awaken the heart and the acceptance of its guidance.

The one anchor that can help in this transition in the churches is the acceptance of continued revelation and my corrections of the Patriarchal theology. I do not want to be worshipped, but the shift out of the Patriarchy needs the recognition of my corrective teaching. The Ascension is Mary Magdalene and Jeshua's project.

Form is useful as a discipline. A writing schedule you can commit to is very important at this time. Our thoughts are blending. This may be confusing to you. It is actually a positive sign of becoming one mind, which is my intention for many who choose to listen. Actually the worship of me by the Patriarchy has made me a bitter idol for many. This is the correction I see you making in the writing and speaking you will be doing. I Am as you are, as One, J.

Jeshua, 6-19-12, 1 AM (following an evening at the 7th Day Adventist Church hearing about hell)

Now we begin. De ja vu. Awakening memories of your father's preaching, not much has changed except in style of presentation. The same feelings have been evoked of fear and separation and self-doubt, as "in me dwelleth no good thing." Indeed, some of the feeling response of that period in your life came up for healing. If you thought or interpreted otherwise you would be condemned to hell. What you have learned since, through experience with me, I might add, would be suspect. That minister would not have the capacity to understand this. Experiencing oneness with the energy of fundamentalism would be impossible. I appreciate your memory of my statement, "A Universal theology is impossible, but a universal experience is not only possible, but necessary." You had that experience at the side of the road with Celeste. (She was the church member who stopped to help me).

Your experience of tonight's message brought up memories of your father's preaching when you had no ability to censor or doubt his interpretation. Tonight's experience brought up that energy for healing and release from your bodymind computer. Don't confuse your experience of love at the roadside with the damaging energy of fundamentalism. You are not the only one hurt by it. Indeed it is a literalistic, rationalistic approach to the scripture and an elevation of the Bible to an inerrant object of worship. Much suffering has resulted from distorted interpretations as well as the omission of key gospels which elevated the role of women in my life and the oneness with creator source. I was made a bitter idol, which has caused separation between East and West. The Eastern religions perceived me most accurately as a wisdom teacher, unacceptable in that time.

Do not doubt your path and experience. You have persisted in your process of self-healing, and have come to a place of peace and accurate awareness of my message. Do not doubt your learnings. Forgiveness is the key, the bridge to oneness. You discovered me anew through <u>A Course in Miracles,</u> after you had learned to trust your guidance through Process via the 12 steps in Al-Anon. It was an introduction to the feminine way. Without a trust in Process, the Ten Commandments become a source of guilt and judgment. This was the Patriarchal approach to use guilt to control. The belief in the power of fear by many clergy displaced the power of love to effect change.

In spite of the distortions in their message, the emphasis on my love has generated a loving congregation. Their experience of love has softened the literal and limiting interpretations of scripture. The anger and self-rejection by your father is an energy you absorbed. TaBIA this.

In your review of your process of emerging from fundamentalism, you will see the value of process, the feminine way of the heart. This your father shared in his channeled message to you when he attributed his heart problems to his denial of his feelings.

Jeshua further elaborated on what I could share to help undo the patriarchal message taken in by so many.

You can say, 'We are at the end of an age, 5000 years of Patriarchy. Focus on the wisdom of the heart where the I Am Presence dwells is a necessary shift from a separate God out there. The belief in separation is behind all the misery of suffering. We are not our bodies, but expressions in form of the One Self. All are eternal Spirit.'

'Yes, we can choose to separate and experience the absence of Love. The ego is the Satan energy of fear, which attached itself to form when souls incarnated. There is much to be revealed which you cannot understand right now. The ego dominates the mind until one has learned to listen to the I Am Presence, the Holy Spirit in the heart. This seed of Source has always been there. The belief in separation in the mind has hindered the growth and expression of this seed. When we speak of surrender, it is to surrender to Love's Presence, which is your true Self. Therein is your Oneness with Source and each other.' Yes, this information is in the books banned from the Bible.

Don't limit yourself to the Bible. The Word of God can simply be the prompts from the Voice for Love within each person. The gathering of seekers to worship Creator Source/God is to experience oneness, encourage one another, and express one's gifts. Especially now, your focus is on new ways to live together in Peace on planet earth. Regular gatherings provide the opportunity. Learn to identify <u>resonance</u>, the language of the heart.

You are blessed. Live in the higher vibrations of Love, Light, Peace, Joy and Gratitude.

I am with you always in all ways, Jeshua

Angelic Affirmation
Archangel Michael 5-31-13

Indeed your thought of me was a cue of my Presence and readiness to speak through you. There is no time. Indeed we are present in great force to you now. Few have any sense of this. Your willingness to hear gives us joy.

The 'Everything Scattered…' book is important and you are nearing completion. The energies are magnified. Transitions are quickening. Many are awakening to who they are. Fundamentalism is loosening its hold. The boxes are crumbling. Allow your voice to be heard. Clarify your message and know that there are many more ready to hear.

I am one who heralds or commands attention in the midst of so much preoccupation with troubles and details. It is this energy I would have you claim in the calling of attention to what you offer. You have received many messages from Jeshua, and some from your nonphysical family because you have acknowledged your spirit reality. Ask and you will receive. Tell your groups that we want to speak to them. Each will attract their individual guides.

Some will channel directly. Others, through asking and Intention with Allowing and Surrender can call in their guides. Doing this has given you courage to take on the responsibility of your grandson, a very significant task, trusting your guidance for strength and direction. It is a knowing that comes from the heart.

The many messages you have received does make you a messenger. Know I am with you when you have an audience to hear what you have to say. Let your voice be heard. Speak with authority. You know that you know.

The most important thing to emphasize now is to move from the head to the heart through the portal of feelings in the moment. Asking the I Am Presence for a different way of seeing whatever challenges one is facing allows receiving a new perspective. This raises the vibrations into the excitement of one's participation in the birthing process the whole planet is going through.

Emphasize that the TaBIA process is specifically designed to acknowledge what is in the head and move one into the heart. Tapping on the bodymind computer as instructed is an embodiment process, which can heal in all PEMS (Physical, Emotional, Mental, Spiritual) areas. Not everyone will need to do the tapping to embody their divine

Essence. Learning the TaBIA process can lead to an automatic shifting whenever a response is called for.

Learning to ask is the focus of your Inquiry process. 'Just ask!' Asking invites in the angels and guides. The 'right' questions are heart-based. Thus begins a dialogue with an unseen guide. Authentic answers give you peace. If contrived, you will not feel peaceful.

Do not take it personally if your offers aren't accepted. There are audiences ready and waiting. Again ask and an idea will pop into your mind as it did with your reading about Friendship House. Offer on a donation basis. We want all who can benefit to receive the tools, which can relieve a lot of stress and anxiety. Bring your book to completion, mentor your grandson, and be a midwife in the glorious birthing process of a New Earth.

—Archangel Michael

I have had many more transcribed messages over the past eight years. Many are very personal, referring to my reactions to a specific situation and/or persons. The point of these messages is to know we are not alone and can have a very intimate relationship with Master Teacher Jeshua and other guides from the nonphysical world.

When we are open to Purification and our Heart's Desire is for connection to Source, we have begun the process. Our Intention is declared through our commitment to a spiritual practice of *prayer without ceasing* (tuning in to our inner feeling process). We ask and then Allow answers to come in unexpected ways. Surrendering to the I Am that I Am within awakens us to our Oneness with All That Is.

BIBLIOGRAPHY

Michael Abrams, EVOLUTION ANGEL: An Emergency Physician's Lessons with Death and the Divine

P. M. H. Atwater, CHILDREN of the FIFTH WORLD: A Guide to the Coming Changes in Human Consciousness

Silvia Brown, LIFE ON THE OTHER SIDE: A Psychic's Tour of the Afterlife

Cynthia Bourgeault, The WISDOM WAY of KNOWING: Reclaiming an Ancient Tradition to Awaken the Heart

Delores Cannon, CONVOLUTED UNIVERSE

Alan Cohen, A DEEP BREATH OF LIFE: Daily Inspiration for Heart Centered Living

Alan Cohen, I HAD IT ALL THE TIME: When Self-Improvement gives Way to Ecstasy

Deepak Chopra, THE PATH to LOVE: Renewing the Power of Spirit in Your Life

Deepak Chopra, THE SPONTANEOUS FULLFILLMENT of DESIRE

Lee Coit, LISTENING: How to Increase Awareness of Your Inner Guide

David A. Cooper, SILENCE, SIMPLICITY and SOLITUDE: A Guide for Spirit and Retreat

Patricia Diane Cota-Robles, WHAT ON EARTH IS GOING ON?

Ceanne DeRohan (received by) RIGHT USE OF WILL

Al Diaz, CONFIRMATIONS: Self Impowerment and Blessings

Al Diaz, BEING: The Titus Concept

Everything Scattered Will Be Gathered

Wayne Dyer, The POWER of INTENTION learning to Cocreate Your World Your Way

Wayne Dyer, CHANGE YOUR THOUGHTS, CHANGE YOUR LIFE: Living the Wisdom of the Tao

Maureen Edwardson, YOUR MASGICAL EVOLUTIONARY CODE UNLEASHED The Science of INNER RESONANCE

Donald M. Epstein, THE 12 STAGES OF HEALING: A Network Approach to Wholeness

Peter O. Erbe, GOD I AM: From Tragic to Magic

Matthew Fox, MEDITATIONS WITH MEISTER ECKHART

Pierre Franckh, THE DNA FIELD and LAW of RESONANCE: Creating Reality through Conscious Thought

FOUNDATION FOR INNER PEACE: A COURSE IN MIRACLES ACIM, *Combined Volume: Text, Workbook for Students, Manual for Teachers (Jesus channeled by Helen Schucman, transcriber William Thetford, Professors of Medical Psychology at Columbia University* Supplements to A Course in Miracles: *Psychotherapy; Purpose, Process and Practice The Song of Prayer; Prayer, Forgiveness, Healing*

Mari Perron, A COURSE OF LOVE Three books in one volume self-published with Take Heart Publications. Copyright 2014 by The Center for A Course of Love, a non-profit corporation.

Shakti Gawain, LIVING IN THE LIGHT:A Guide to Personal and Planetary Transformation

Mary Gerard, THE MENTOR WITHIN: Let your SELF be seen

Glenda Green, LOVE WITHOUT END: Jesus Speaks

Jon Marc Hammer, THE JESHUA LETTERS: A Journey of Awakening

Jon Marc Hammer, THE WAY OF THE SERVANT: Living the Light of Christ

Louise L. Hay, LOVE YORSELF, HEAL YOUR LIFE WORKBOOK

Bibliography

Claire Heartsong, ANNA, GRANDMOTHER OF JESUS and ANNA, THE VOICE OF THE MAGDALENES *sequel, co-created with* Catherine Ann Clemett—*Channeled voices of Jesus' family members, ministry of male/female oneness.*

Esther and Jerry Hicks, THE AMAZING POWER OF DELIBERATE INTENT: Living the Art of Allowing (The Teachings of Abraham)

Siobhan Houston, INVOKING MARY MAGDALENE: Acessing the Wisdom of the Divine Feminine

Barbara Marx Hubbard, EMERGENCE: The Shift from Ego to Essence

Karel & Caroline van Huffelen, THE BELOVED ONE: The Magdalene Mystery

Gerald G. Jampolsky, LOVE IS LETTING GO OF FEAR

Thomas Keating, OPEN MIND, OPEN HEART The Contempletive Dimension of the Gospel

Tom Kenyon & Virginia Essene, THE HATHOR MATERIAL: Messages from an Ascended Civilization

Ken Keyes, Jr., HANDBOOK TO HIGHER CONSCIOUSNESS

Pamela Kribbe, THE JESHUA CHANNELINGS: Christ Consciousness in a New Era

Bruce Lipton, The BIOLOGY of BELIEF: Releasing the Power of Consciousness, Matter, and Miracles

Jo Ann Lordahl, THE END OF MOTHERHOOD: New Identities, New Lives

Tricia McCannon, RETURN OF THE DIVINE SOPHIA: Healing the Earth through the Lost Wisdom Teachings of JESUS, ISIS and MARY MAGDALENE

Drunvalo Melchizedek, LIVING IN THE HEART

Inette Miller, GRANDMOTHERS WHISPER: Voices, Timeless Wisdom

Dan Millman, EVERYDAY ENLIGHTENMENT: The Twelve Gateways to Personal Growth

Sara Paddison, THE HIDDEN POWER OF THE HEART: Achieving Balance and Fulfillment in a Stressful World

PEACE PILGRIM: Her Life and Work in Her Own Words

Rasha, ONENESS

Lisa Raphael, O-BECOMING, A Trilogy, A Dialogue with the Brotherhood of Light

Pat Rodegast & Judith Stanton, EMMANUEL'S BOOK II: The Choice for Love

Richard Rohr, THE NAKED NOW

Sanaya Roman, PERSONAL POWER THROUGH AWARENESS

Sanaya Roman, LIVING WITH JOY: Keys to Personal Power and Transformation

Petra Rose, A JOURNEY OF PS AND CUES TO INNER PEACE AND POWER: The Embodiment of Our Divine Essence

Marshall B. Rosenberg, NONVIOLENT COMMUNICATION: A Language of Life

Anne Wilson Schaef, LIVING IN PROCESS: Basic Truths for Living the Path of the Soul

Mona Lisa Schulz, AWAKENING INTUITION: Using Your Mind-Body Network for Insight and Healing

Robert Schwartz, COURAGEOUS SOULS: Do We Plan Our Life Challenges Before Birth?

John Selby, SEVEN MASTERS, ONE PATH: Meditation Secrets from the World's Greatest Teachers

Ariana Sheran: Numerous unpublished and self-published books on Ascension, In progress: Channelings from Elvis, Egypt and Jeshua. Cloverleaf Connection, 138 Sturgeon Drive, Saskatoon, SK Canada S7K 4B3

Marsha Sinetar, THE MENTOR'S SPIRIT: Life Lessons on Leadership and the Art of Encouragement
ORDINARY PEOPLE as MONKS and MYSTICS: Lifestyles for Self-discovery
DO WHAT YOU LOVE, the MONEY WILL FOLLOW

Bibliography

Marsha Sinetar, TO BUILD the LIFE YOU WANT, CREATE the WORK YOU LOVE:

The Spiritual Dimension of Entrepreneuring

Lola Starr, Karmic Flashbacks: Memoir of a Psychic Healer

James T. Twyman, The ART OF SPIRITUAL PEACE-MAKING: Secret Teachings from Jeshua ben Joseph

Doreen Virtue, THE LIGHTWORKER'S WAY: Awakening Your Spiritual Power to Know and Heal

Kenneth Wapnick, FORGIVENESS and JESUS: The Meeting Place of "A Course in Miracles" and Christianity

Peggy Watson, HOLDING THE RESONANCE FOR THE NEW EARTH

Marianne Williamson, ILLUMINATA: A Return to Prayer
   A RETURN TO LOVE
   A WOMAN'S WORTH

To Contact Petra Rose
Tel: 808-332-0504
Email: coachpetra@hawaii.rr.com

ABOUT THE AUTHOR

Born Ruth Petra Oas, "Petra Rose" became Ruth Akre when she began her 32-year marriage. Divorced, she took her mother's maiden name Sundheim, and Petra as her first name and uses her mother's first name as part of her pen name. The pen name Petra Rose represents the profound healing she has experienced with both parents, Peter and Rose.

Though trained in multiple careers—nursing, MSW hypnotherapist, OMC Ordained Ministerial Counselor, CPC Certified Professional Coach, it is her life experience in patriarchy, gender rejection at birth by a minister father, six brothers, and Lutheran church environment that qualifies her to write this book after a lifetime with un-diagnosed Attention Deficit Disorder.

Focused on change and self-healing through Inner Healing work and Living in Process, her divorce from a minister became her first transformation. Her move to Kauai, and introduction to her spirit family through channeling, began her second transformation. The Way of the Heart Spiritual family introduced her to Jeshua and his messages detailing a correction of the churches distortions. Intuitive Inquiry revealed her past life with Jesus as one of 12 Magdalenes in partnership to the twelve disciples, many who also are reincarnated in this lifetime.

Encountering past life partners on Kauai allowed karmic completions. Using the self-healing Ascension tools given to her, she is experiencing an ongoing fourth transformation, experiencing the divine feminine. Besides writing, she is committed to sharing these tools along with sharing the true message of Jesus.

Previously published by Author:
A JOURNEY OF PS AND CUES TO
INNER PEACE AND POWER:
The Embodiment of Our Divine Essence, copyright 2010

www.ingramcontent.com/pod-product-compliance
Lightning Source LLC
Chambersburg PA
CBHW070549100426
42744CB00006B/247